The College History Series

STATE UNIVERSITY OF NEW YORK AT FARMINGDALE

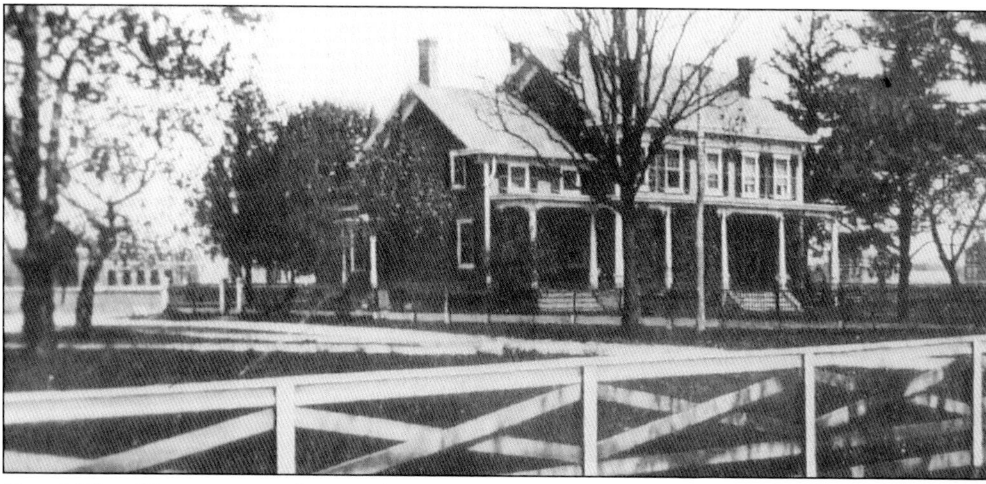

The old Mott House, pictured in 1916, was the home of the family that owned part of the original farm where the school was later built. The pine trees surrounding the house were decorated at Christmas time and could be seen from a great distance. When the school was first opened to students in March 1916, Mott House was used as a women's dormitory because the regular dormitories were not yet completed. The building at the right in the distance is the Director's Cottage (Residence), built in 1914. The building at the left is Hooper Hall, completed in 1917.

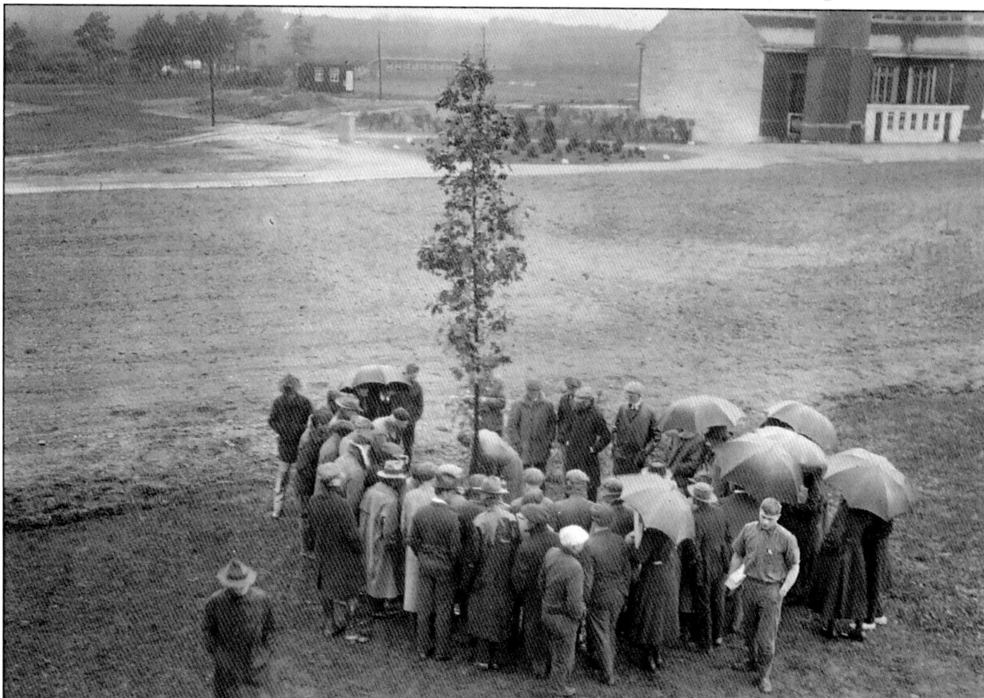

This June 1921 photograph shows the planting of the World War I Memorial Oak on campus. Every state and every allied nation sent soil to be used in the tree planting and to commemorate the bond that kept the Allies fighting together. At the ceremony were Jesse Merritt, the secretary of Nassau County Historical Society, and Henry W. Hicks, the donor of the tree. Pres. Warren G. Harding sent a letter of support, expressing the significance of the event. To the right in the background is the power plant, now Conklin Hall.

The College History Series

STATE UNIVERSITY OF NEW YORK AT FARMINGDALE

FRANK J. CAVAIOLI, PH.D.

ARCADIA
PUBLISHING

ISBN 978-0-7385-0484-1

Published by Arcadia Publishing
Charleston, South Carolina

Printed in the United States of America

Library of Congress Catalog Card Number: 00106514

For all general information contact Arcadia Publishing at:
Telephone 843-853-2070
Fax 843-853-0044
E-mail sales@arcadiapublishing.com
For customer service and orders:
Toll-Free 1-888-313-2665

Visit us on the Internet at www.arcadiapublishing.com

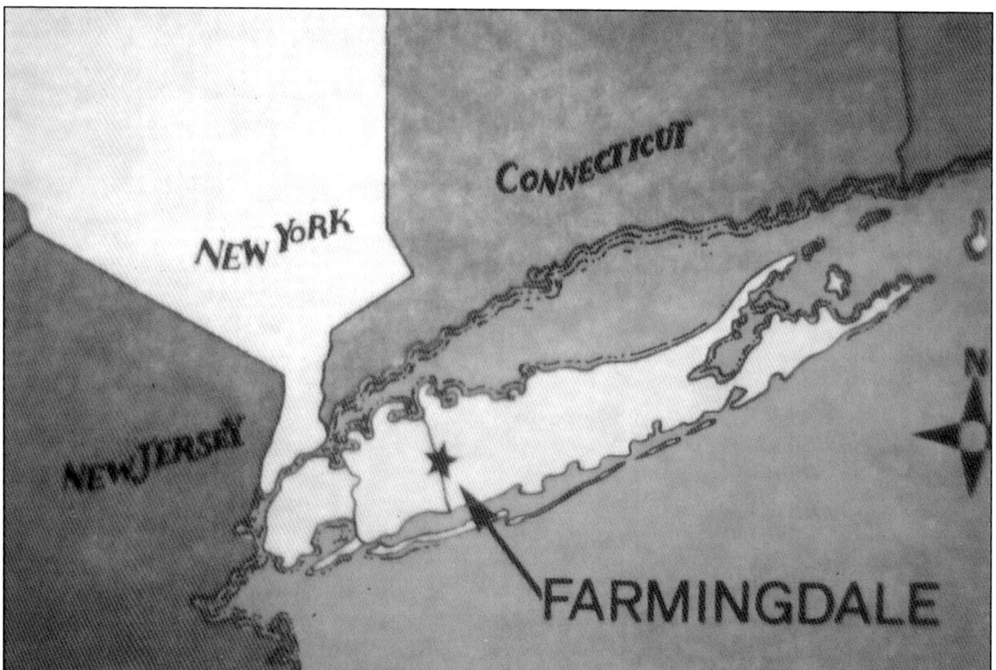

This map shows the tristate area served by Farmingdale. The location of the campus is on the border between Nassau County and Suffolk County, Long Island. Note the regional areas that are accessible to the school, which is centrally situated and only 32 miles from the center of Manhattan and convenient to Brooklyn and Queens Counties by way of the Long Island Railroad (LIRR). The Farmingdale branch of the LIRR is only 1.5 miles from the campus.

CONTENTS

INTRODUCTION

The State University of New York (SUNY) at Farmingdale is the oldest public college on Long Island, having been founded in April 1912. Its more than 50,000 graduates have distinguished themselves in agricultural and technical education, which in turn has been enriched by the humanities and social sciences. The college now offers more than 40 academic programs that include baccalaureate and associate degrees, one-year certificates, liberal arts and sciences, health sciences and human services, engineering technologies, and business. Located on 380 beautiful acres on the Nassau-Suffolk border in the heart of Long Island, SUNY Farmingdale is one of the 64 colleges and universities in the State University of New York system and has a current enrollment of 6,000 residential and commuting students. During its history, SUNY Farmingdale has mirrored the growth of Long Island from rural-agrarian to suburban-postindustrial in the development of the region's high-tech and service economy.

The college has had different names in its history: the New York State School of Agriculture on Long Island; the New York Institute of Applied Agriculture; the Long Island Agricultural and Technical Institute; SUNY Agricultural and Technical Institute; SUNY Agricultural and Technical College; SUNY at Farmingdale; SUNY College of Technology at Farmingdale; and back again to SUNY at Farmingdale.

State Assemblyman John Lupton of Mattituck introduced a bill providing for the creation of an agricultural school in 1909. It passed in both houses of the legislature, but was vetoed by Governor Dix, who nevertheless signed another bill into law authorizing a committee to develop an educational plan in agricultural schools. The committee's work led to considerable interest and information for the need of such a school.

At this juncture stepped in a New Englander who was determined to build a school on Long Island that would train young boys and girls in agriculture and that would develop land to grow fruits and vegetables in the profitable New York City market. Franklin W. Hooper was born in New Hampshire, graduated from Harvard, and accepted a professorship at Adelphi College in Brooklyn. In 1889, he became director of the Brooklyn Academy of Arts and Sciences. Around 1908, Hooper became aware of the need for an agricultural school and worked indefatigably to establish one. Suffolk County's Sen. George Lincoln Thompson introduced legislation providing for the establishment of the school. The bill was cosponsored with Assemblyman Harte. Governor Dix signed the Thompson-Harte Bill into law on April 15, 1912, thus creating the New York State School of Agriculture on Long Island. Other community leaders who had lobbied for the school were John M. Lupton, Frederick Cox, Hal Fullerton, James Cooley, and C.H. Howell. The original mission of the school was to "furnish training in agricultural science." Because of scientific and social advances, the agricultural curriculum at Farmingdale ended in 1987. Three years later, the institution became a full-fledged four-year college that trains students in high-technology occupations. Two-year programs continued to offer the associate degree.

In 1913, the state legislature provided $90,000 for the purchase of land in Farmingdale; it appropriated additional funds for two educational buildings, a dormitory for men, power plant, gas plant, water supply system, dining room furniture and fixtures, and a cottage for the director. In 1914, Ward Hall (Old Dormitory I) was built. Two years later, 60 students were enrolled in a regular four-year course when the school opened on March 1, 1916, although the buildings were not yet completed. The requirement for enrollment was an eighth-grade education. The first graduation exercises were held on April 4, 1919. On May 26, 1920, the second commencement exercises were held in the newly completed barn. Twenty-two men and one woman graduated. Theodore Roosevelt Jr., delivered the commencement address. The bookstore, built in 1922, was originally a gymnasium and auditorium.

In 1917, when the United States entered WWI, 170 acres of agricultural land were under cultivation, and the students managed farm animals, such as hogs and milk cows. In order to meet the wartime labor shortage, high school boys attended cadet camps on campus in the summers of 1917 and 1918. During this period, military routine and instruction were followed. Daily exercises took place, and students wore uniforms. In addition, the tradition of equal access began when 32 female students entered in the summer of 1916, and 75 more entered in the summer of 1917. The school was so popular at its inception that the catalog of October 1917, stated, "The New York State School of Agriculture on Long Island was visited by more people during the past year than visited any of the National Parks during the same period."

In 1923, Halsey B. Knapp, who was the director of the New York School of Agriculture at Cobleskill, was appointed to replace Director Albert A. Johnson. Through Knapp's leadership, Farmingdale emerged as a leading agricultural and technical institution. He motivated the faculty to develop innovative programs and urged them to give service to the community. He resigned in 1956. Knapp's salary in 1935 was $4,077.50, while an instructor's salary was $2,438. Of course, Knapp enjoyed free use of the Director's Cottage, among other benefits.

Knapp faced several challenges upon assuming his position in late 1923. He discovered a Ku Klux Klan cell composed of faculty and staff operating on campus. When Klan members ordered him to fire his Irish Catholic bookkeeper, he refused, effectively eliminating the Klan's power. He was also joined by local leaders in defeating Gov. Alfred E. Smith's attempt to turn over the campus to the new state hospital being constructed at Creedmoor in Queens County. At the outset, it was clear that Knapp would exert strong leadership for the welfare of the school. He also maintained strong control over campus affairs. He was assisted by such dedicated faculty and administrators as Fordyce C. Deitz, Harvey Gray, Norman H. Foote, D. Hart Horton, Archie A. Stone, Carl Wedell, Locke James, Horton Amidon, Robert McLaughlin, David Allee, A.J. Holub, C.D. Thomson, A.M. Halleck, and Robert Davidson.

Dr. Michael Abbatiello—who graduated from the ornamental horticulture program in 1946 and was hired by Knapp as a technical assistant—described Knapp as a strong and fair administrator. He remembered the colored memos that faculty received from the director; if an instructor received a "pink" memo, it meant the instructor had done something wrong, and a "blue" note signified the instructor was being praised for good work.

The growth of the school assumed an important role in the Long Island region. Total enrollment in 1924 was 79. It grew to 201 in 1931; 359 in 1939; and 495 in 1941. During the academic year of 1944–1945, enrollment reached 800. As World War II ended, the school prepared for a significant educational transition.

In 1946, the mission of the college was expanded to include technical education under the leadership of David W. Allee. A temporary campus was rented in the village of Farmingdale at 520 Conklin Street where the old Nazareth Trade School was housed, and this off-campus facility remained until 1953, when Lupton Hall was opened on the main campus to house technical education. Faculty members who contributed to the school's success at this time were Raynor Wallace, Ann Senyk, Al Perry, Viggio Hansen, James Irwin, George Drennan, Carl Judd, William Haydu, Bert Willenbrock, Ray Bowman, Dan Waite, Jack Coogan, Al Hraba, Walter Truex, C.D. Thomson, and Ed Roberts.

The concept of technical education, as conceived by Allee, was based on a curriculum of an integrated sequence of courses of subject matter, including related shop and laboratory experimental work. It differed from vocational trade education by its sophisticated level and nature of content and instruction. The curriculum continuity distinguished it from the lecture technique and self-study pattern. It emphasized the practical application of the emerging engineering sciences and technologies. Casimir C. Rakowski—who was hired in 1947 as an instructor and who rose to the rank of distinguished service professor in machine shop and mechanical design—considered Allee a pioneer who put together a unique group of faculty members who could do what they said they would do. Veterans of WWII comprised the main student body in the early years. The graduates had little difficulty in securing employment.

During the 1930s, two of the campus's most stately buildings were erected in the Georgian style of architecture. Knapp Hall was built at a cost of $226,905, named in honor of the director, and dedicated October 30, 1937, during ceremonies attended by Gov. Herbert Lehman and 500 guests. In 1938, Thompson Hall was completed at a cost of $124,388. Thompson Hall was first used to house the director's office, main library, animal husbandry laboratories, and later to house the Food Tech Department, a dean's office, several academic departments, and classrooms.

The SUNY Agricultural and Technical Institute at Farmingdale, as it was then called, continued to broaden its mission in educating students and supporting the economy of Long Island. It trained farmers, nurserymen, and technicians. It developed products such as the Farmingdale grass seed, designed to fight the fungus that was attacking suburban lawns. In the 1940s, it prepared workers for the burgeoning defense industry.

The post-WWII housing crisis in the nation affected campus life when a mini-community emerged in the summer of 1946 with the construction of a veterans' housing development located between Knapp Hall and Thompson Hall, where Whitman Hall now stands. Campus Village, as it was called, offered 35 apartments for student-veterans and their families. Walter G. Becker and his wife lived here from 1951 to 1955, during which time two of their children were born. Becker was hired as a technical assistant by D. Hart Horton and went on to become a professor of agriculture. For $37 a month, the Beckers had two rooms and a bath, including all utilities. The 1948 yearbook, *The Islander*, described the Campus Village residents as "a wide range of family life, from newlyweds to old married folk of ten years. The present population consists of 35 families, which includes ten children. The birth rate is undoubtedly among the highest in the country." The Campus Village was torn down in 1956.

By 1972, when Charles W. Laffin was president, total enrollment had grown to more than 14,000. In that year, the SUNY Agricultural and Technical College at Farmingdale (now called a college) offered 34 two-year programs leading to degrees in Associate in Applied Science, Associate in Science, and Associate in Arts. The college boasted an arboretum, gardens, and a farm animal complex (with cows, chickens, and pigs, visited annually by more than 30,000 school children). But it also had computers, GAT link simulators, and a fleet of airplanes. It possessed the first Urban Center administered by an integral unit of SUNY.

It was under the leadership of Frank A. Cipriani, president from 1978 to 2000, that Farmingdale became a full-fledged four-year college, completing the transformation from an institution with livestock and dairy to one that educates students in high-technology occupations. He insisted that the college continue its emphasis on making the humanities and social sciences an important part of the total educational process—one that turned out productive citizens who were articulate as well as technologically sophisticated. The college also maintained its tradition of small classes under the guidance of a caring faculty.

At Cipriani's urging, the college established a collaborative venture with the Cold Spring Harbor Laboratory, a world-renowned research facility staffed by leading scientists, to construct a business incubator for biotechnology companies on the campus. This facility has pointed SUNY Farmingdale to the future. In a comprehensive and coordinated plan, New York State provided $22 million to finance the cost of incubators in biotechnology, software, and other technologies. The Biotechnology Park began construction in 1999 on 20 acres of campus land. It has provided research opportunities and jobs for faculty and students. This venture validated SUNY Farmingdale's mission change that began in 1993 in the development of degree programs in biotechnology and production and information technologies.

When the school was established, serving a largely agrarian community, Pres. Theodore Roosevelt, who lived 12 miles away in Oyster Bay, stated, "Among all valuable agricultural colleges of the nation, the institution at Farmingdale stands out, because it not only teaches farming, but to an extent equaled nowhere else, it creates farmers." However, the "call of the farm," a phrase taken from a verse published in the 1920 yearbook, is no longer heard on Long Island. The 70-year-old agricultural curriculum ended in 1987 because the move away from traditional agriculture reflected Long Island's changing livelihood and landscape. Today the college, as its rich and varied history has demonstrated, has grown to meet the needs of the Long Island Region and New York State through its emphasis on high technology. The State University of New York at Farmingdale is the only four-year college of technology on Long Island.

One

Farmingdale in the Early Years

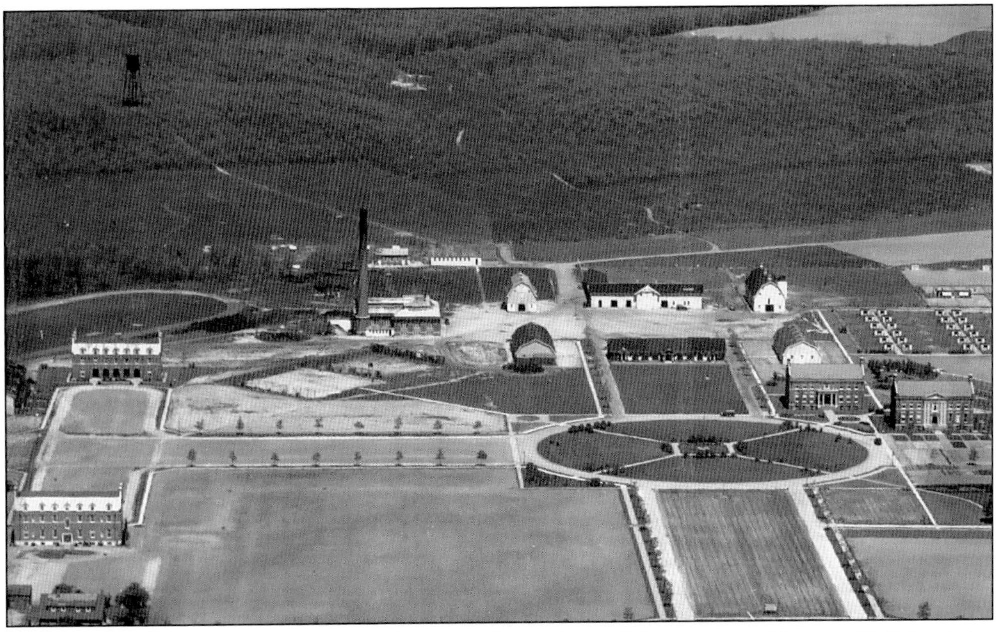

This 1924 aerial view highlights the basic configuration of the campus. Hooper Hall is at the lower left; Ward Hall, left, is near the track. Conklin Hall, with the smokestack, was the original power plant. The circle in the center has remained a fixture and orientation point to this day. At the right is Cutler Hall, and to its left is Hicks Hall, both off the circle. Continuing to the top of the photograph are the barnyard and poultry areas. This physical pattern has been maintained throughout the 20th century. Melville Road is at the bottom.

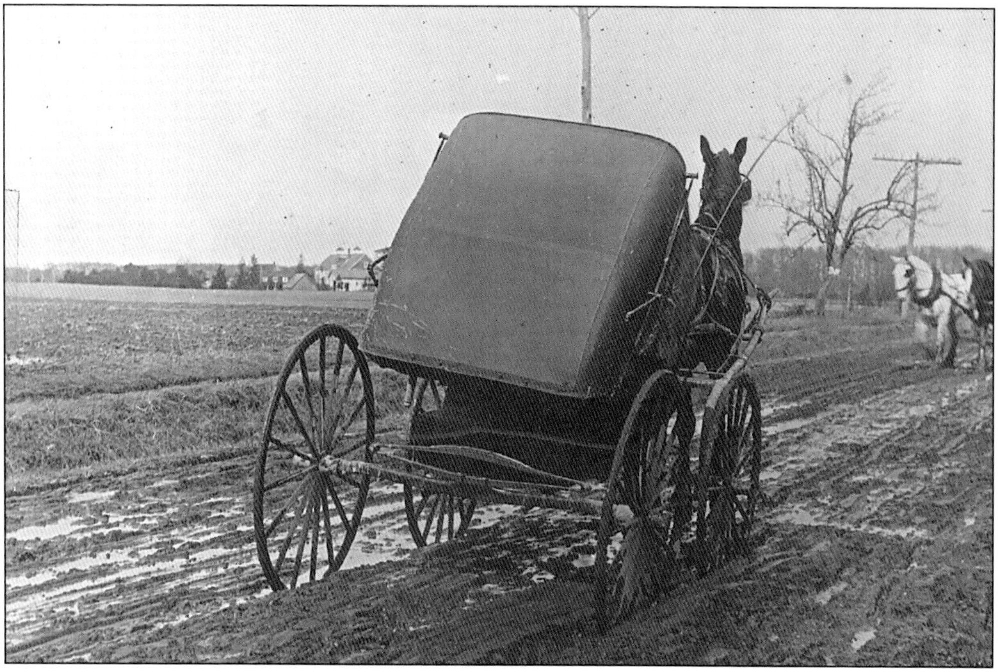

There can be no doubt that Long Island was a rural area in 1912. This is Melville Road on the south boundary of the campus unpaved and unmarked. The horse-drawn carriage is bogged down in the mud and struggling to get going. The poles in the background indicate that electrical power has penetrated Farmingdale.

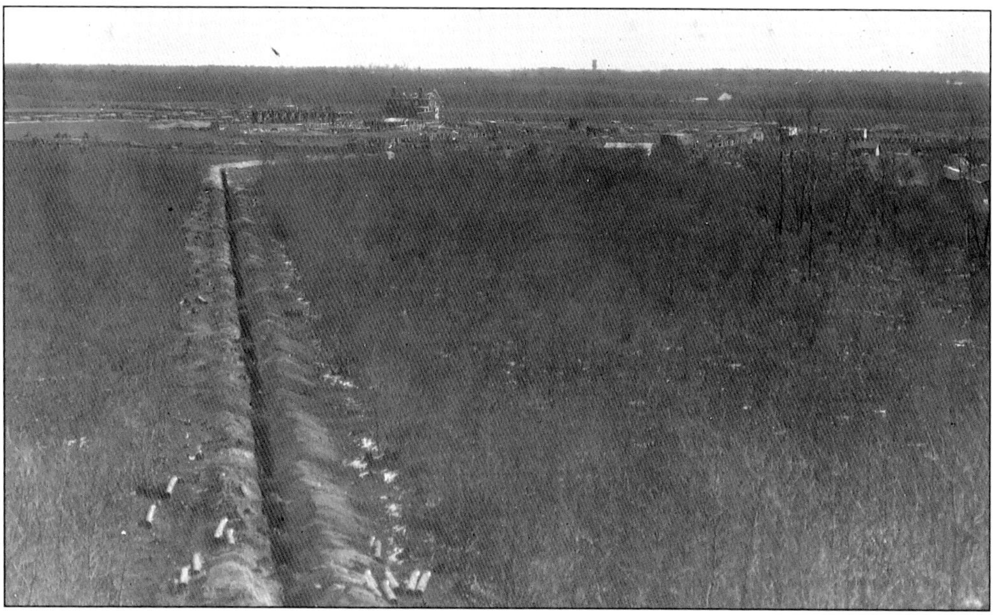

Many challenges arose during the early phase of construction. Temporary wells and temporary living quarters with kitchens and dining rooms had to be built to accommodate the workers. A network of deep trenches was laid out for the sewer system and heating system conduits, as this campus scene indicates. In the background, center, is the Director's Cottage in 1914, and to its left, barely visible, are Cutler Hall and Hicks Hall being constructed.

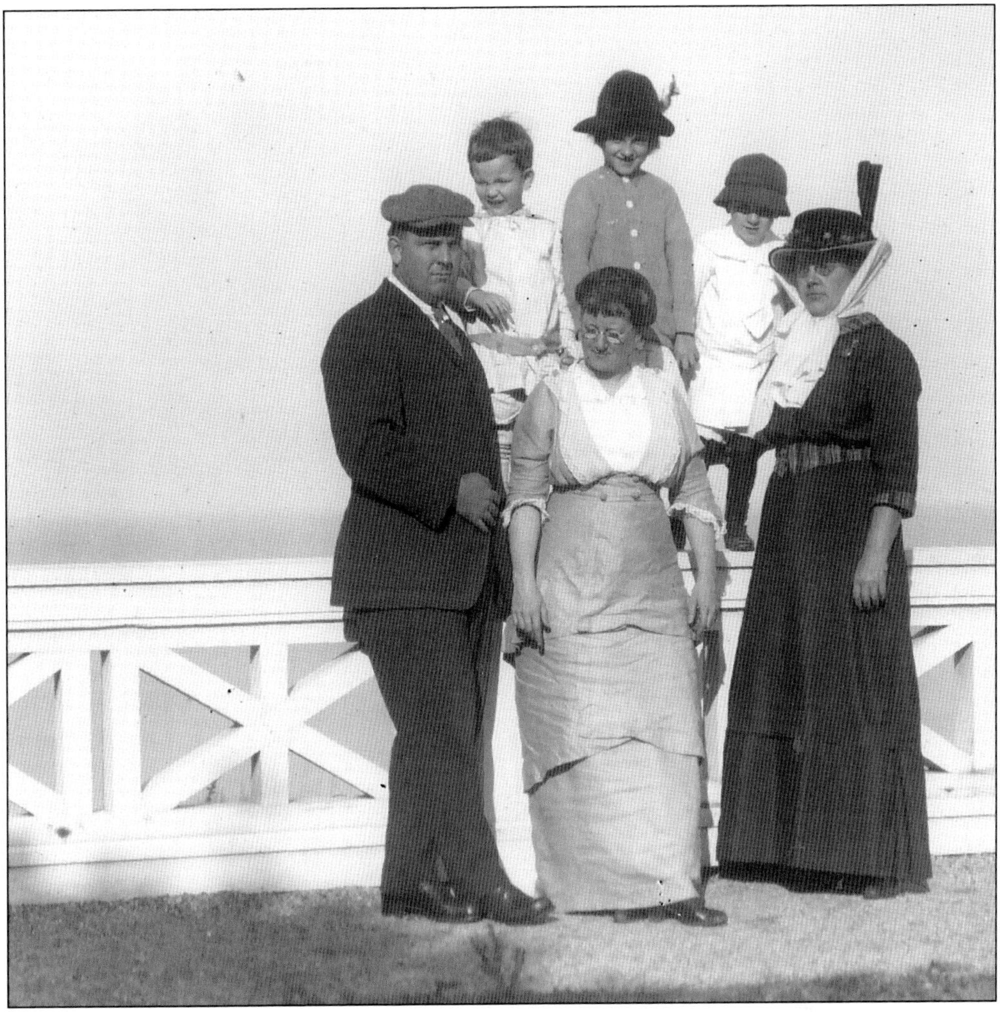

Albert A. Johnson, pictured here with his family, was chosen to be the first director of the school. He came from the Milwaukee County School of Agriculture in Wisconsin and was highly recommended to the committee that hired him. Johnson took up permanent residence at the school in early 1914. He worked closely with the New York State architect in laying out the plan of the campus and is mainly responsible for its physical configuration. Johnson remained director until 1923.

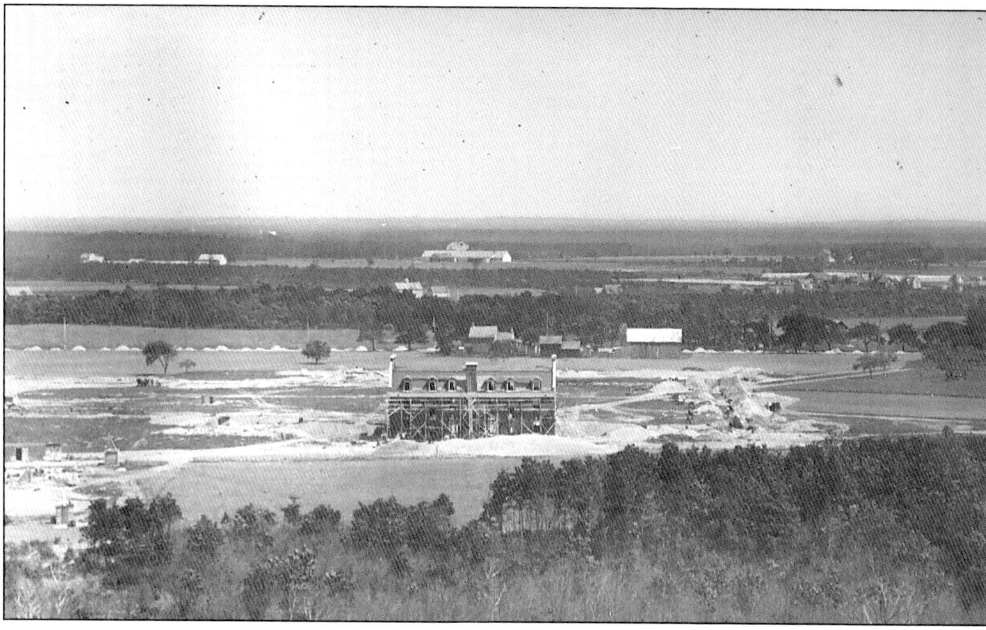

This impressive view of Ward Hall during its construction phase in 1914 provides a panorama of the school grounds in a bucolic setting. Ward Hall was originally used as a dormitory and later for laboratory and classroom space. Today it stands in the center of the campus surrounded by Whitman Hall, Hale Hall, and Gleeson Hall.

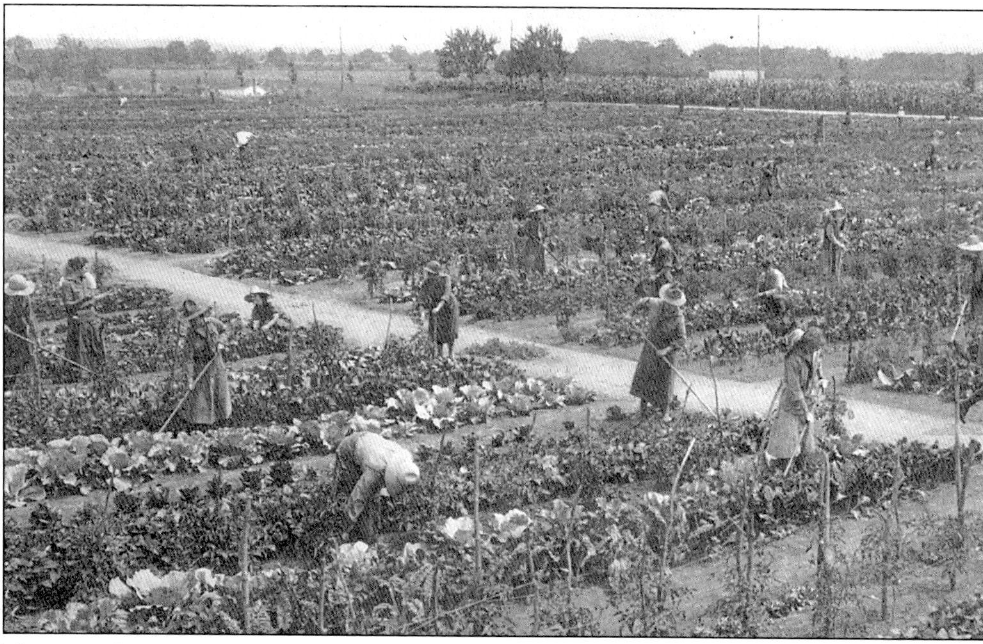

This view shows some of the individual student gardens with a class at work during a laboratory period. Note how lush the gardens are and that nearly all the students are women. This photograph is taken from the 1917 catalog of the New York State School of Agriculture on Long Island, as the institution was called then. It represents one of the very earliest documents of the period.

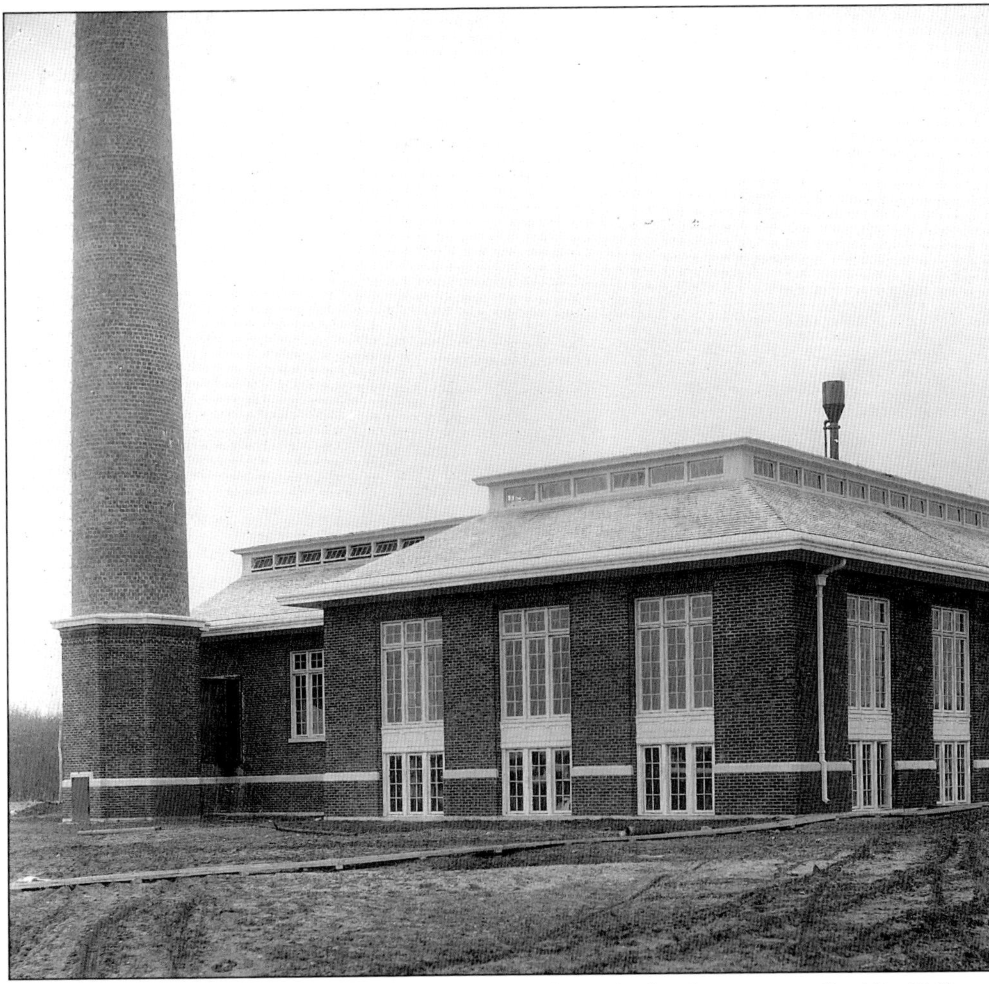

Today, Conklin Hall (without the smokestack) stands in the bookstore area. Conklin Hall was built at a cost of $190,000 in 1914. The smokestack, left, rose to a height of 165 feet and was constructed of radial brick. When the school opened in March 1916, temporary student sleeping quarters were arranged for use on the upper floor because the dormitories were not ready. The smokestack was eventually removed.

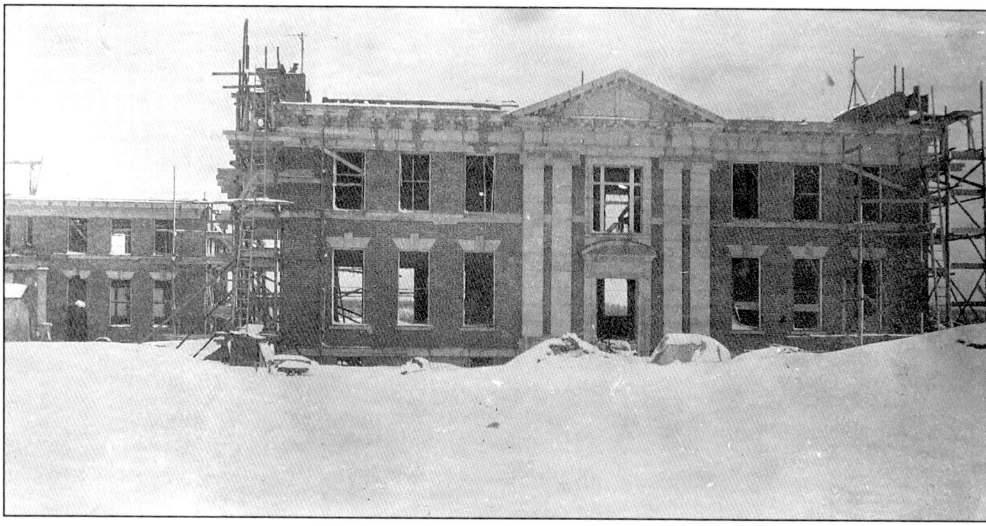

A large snowfall slowed the construction of the Horticulture Building, now called Hicks Hall, at left, and the Agronomy Building, now called Cutler Hall, at right. These brick buildings with columns were each built at a cost of $63,629. This photograph was taken on March 7, 1915. Today, these historic buildings are vacant and await significant funding for restoration.

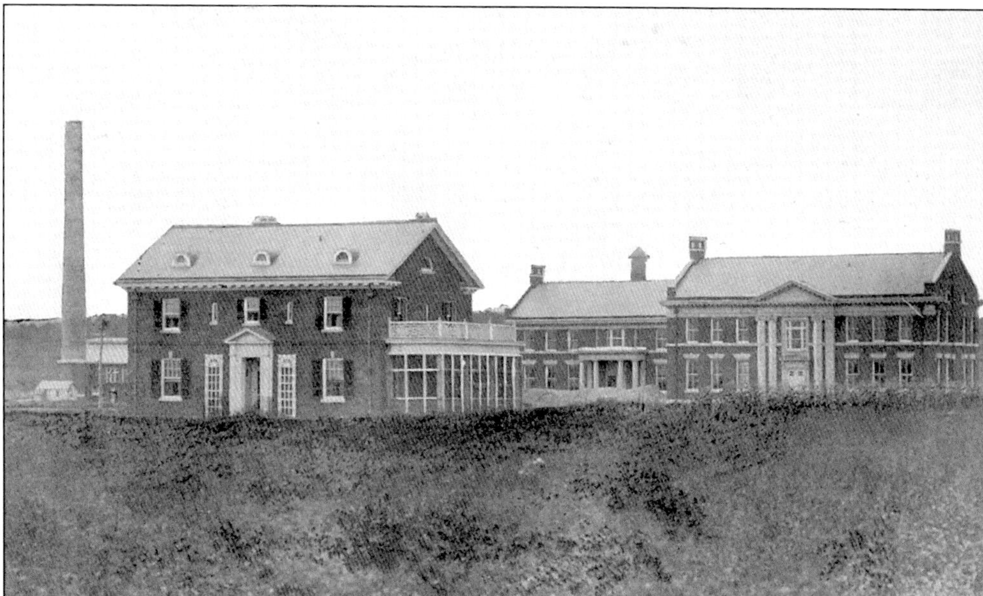

In the early years of the school, commercial postcards of campus images were produced for students to mail to friends and family. They were also sold at various Long Island locations to highlight local attractions. This 1920 postcard shows the main buildings on campus. Shown, from left to right, are Conklin Hall (partially hidden, with smokestack), the Director's Cottage, Hicks Hall, and Cutler Hall. At one time, the Director's Cottage was used as a conference center; today it houses the staff for resident housing.

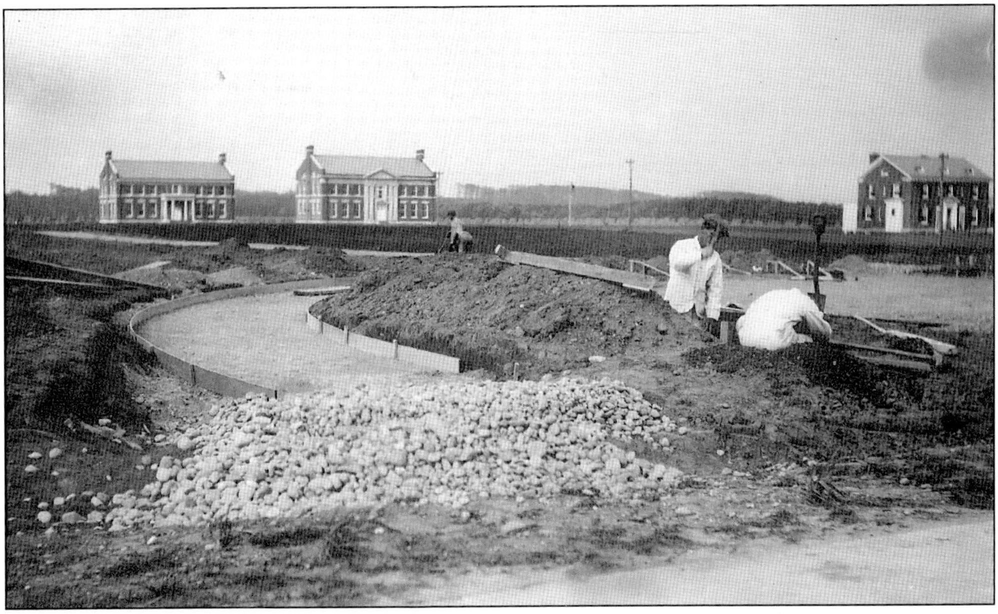

A view to the north reveals students laying a concrete slab as part of a hands-on project in 1918. It was part of the practical educational experience that students received at Farmingdale. Such a project also benefited the school. The buildings on the horizon are, from left to right, Hicks Hall, Cutler Hall, and the Director's Cottage.

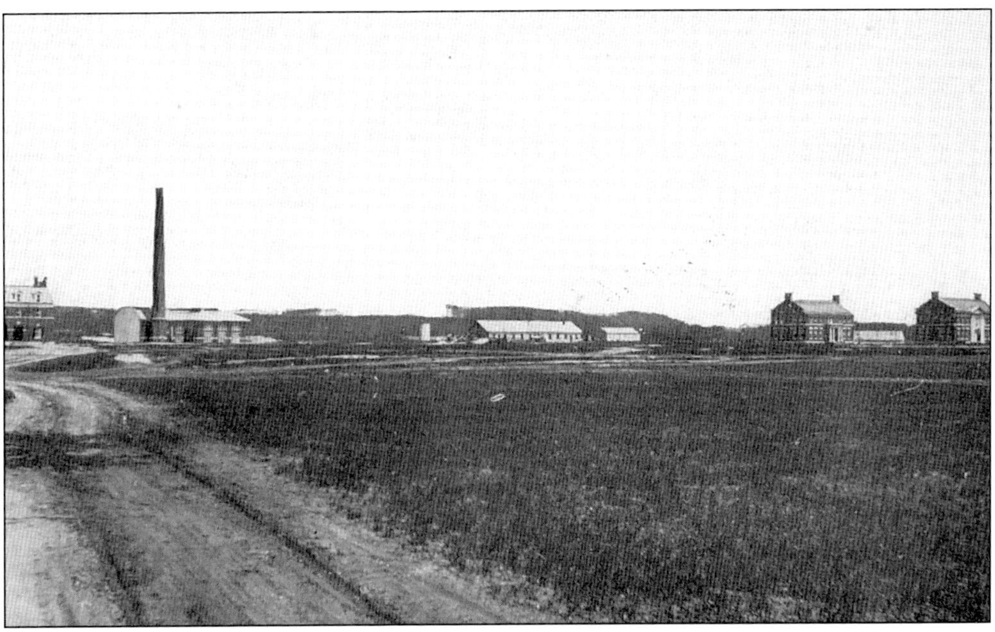

Another view from a 1920 postcard, this time much more comprehensive, shows most of the physical facilities of this period. Beyond the expanse of undeveloped land in the foreground are, from left to right, Ward Hall, Conklin Hall (with smokestack), a large dormitory, a barn, Hicks Hall, and Cutler Hall. Note that the road to the left is unpaved. Postcards helped to publicize the school and led to many inquiries. Today, Thompson Hall stands to the left of Hicks Hall.

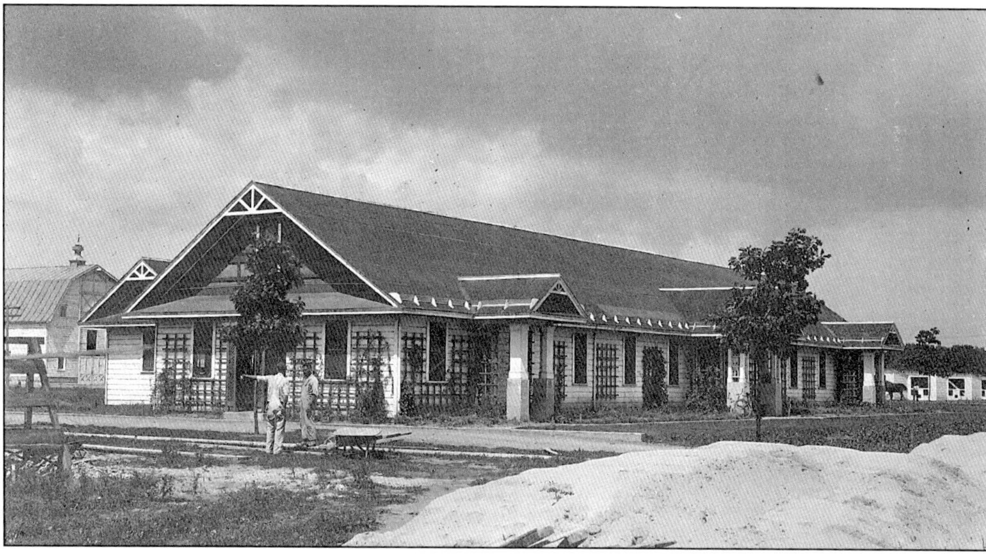

Old Dormitory II, in late 1916, was used for homemaking and a girls' dormitory. In later years, it was used for the Poultry Disease Research Laboratory and Dairy Test Laboratory until around 1950, when the building was taken down.

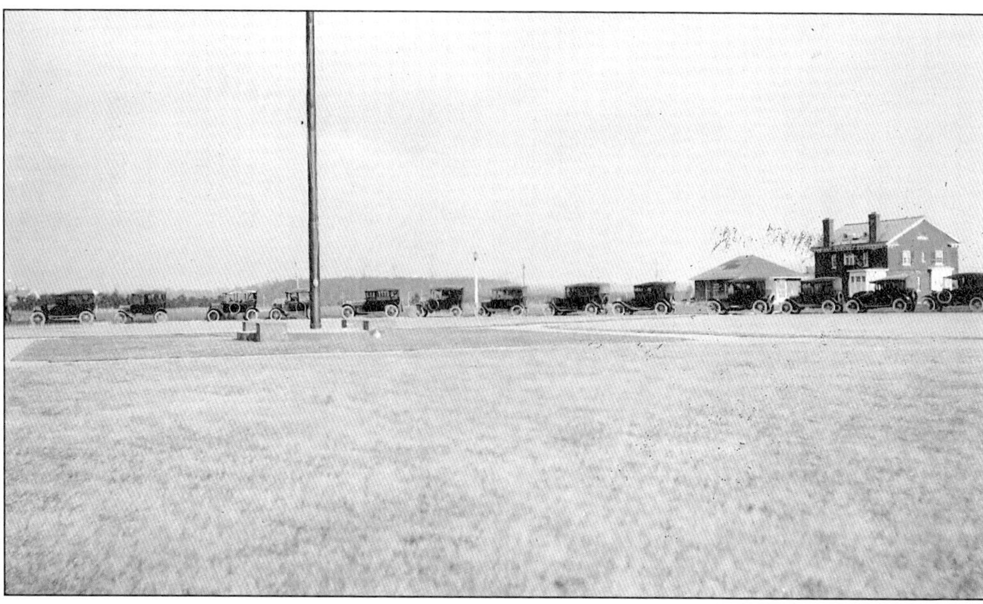

The Pickle Packers Association convened for a meeting at the school on January 29, 1919. In this view from across the circle, looking toward the Director's Cottage, cars are parked neatly along the circle by the flagpole. Hicks Hall and Cutler Hall are not in the picture. Since the campus was on the border of Nassau and Suffolk Counties, various associations found meeting here very convenient.

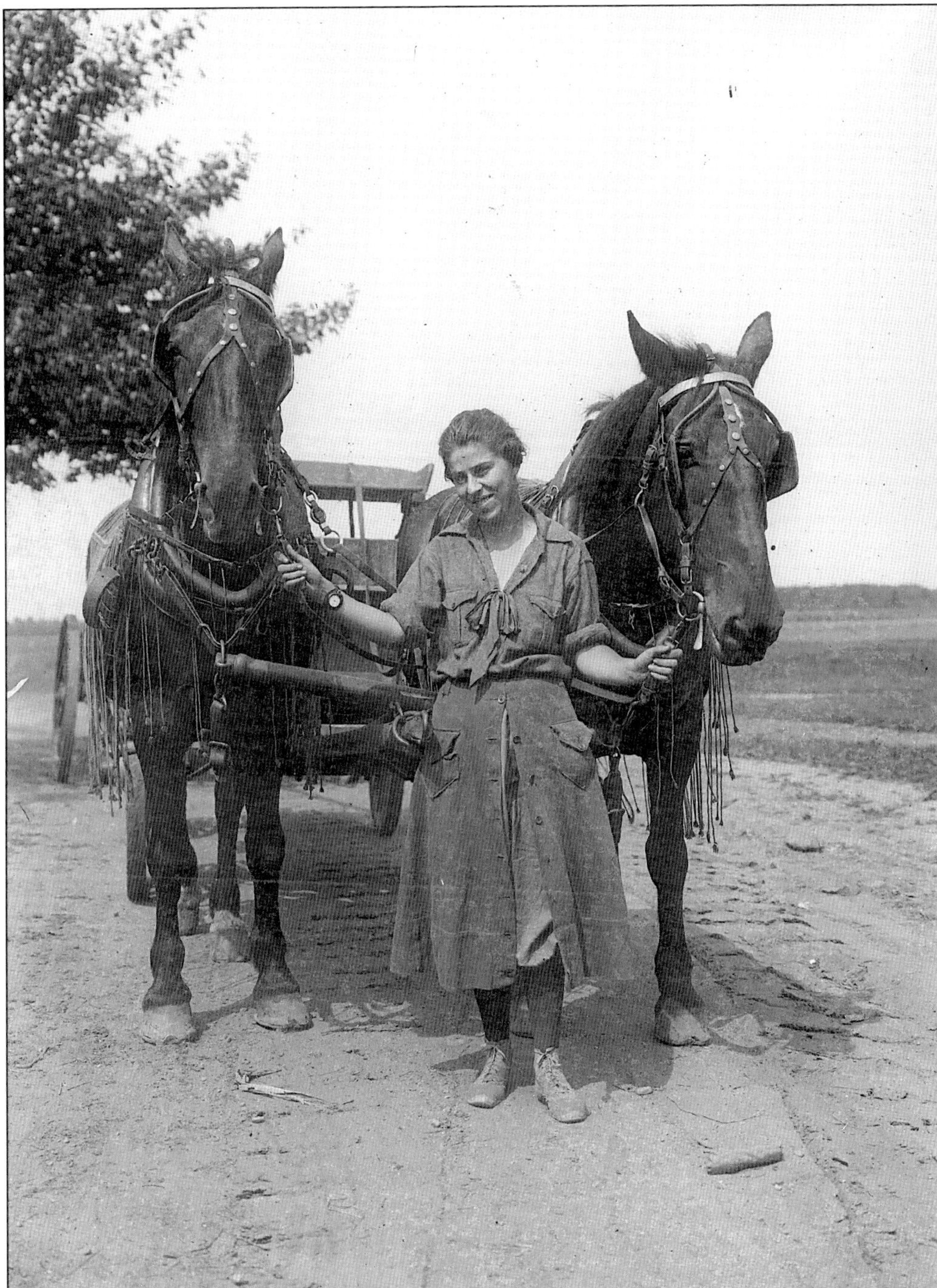

This student has just returned from the field in 1916 after a hard day's training in farming. The summer of this first year of operation, 32 women entered the New York State School of Agriculture on Long Island. In the summer of 1917, more than 75 women enrolled for special courses in agriculture. Thus began a tradition of providing equal access and equal treatment to all students.

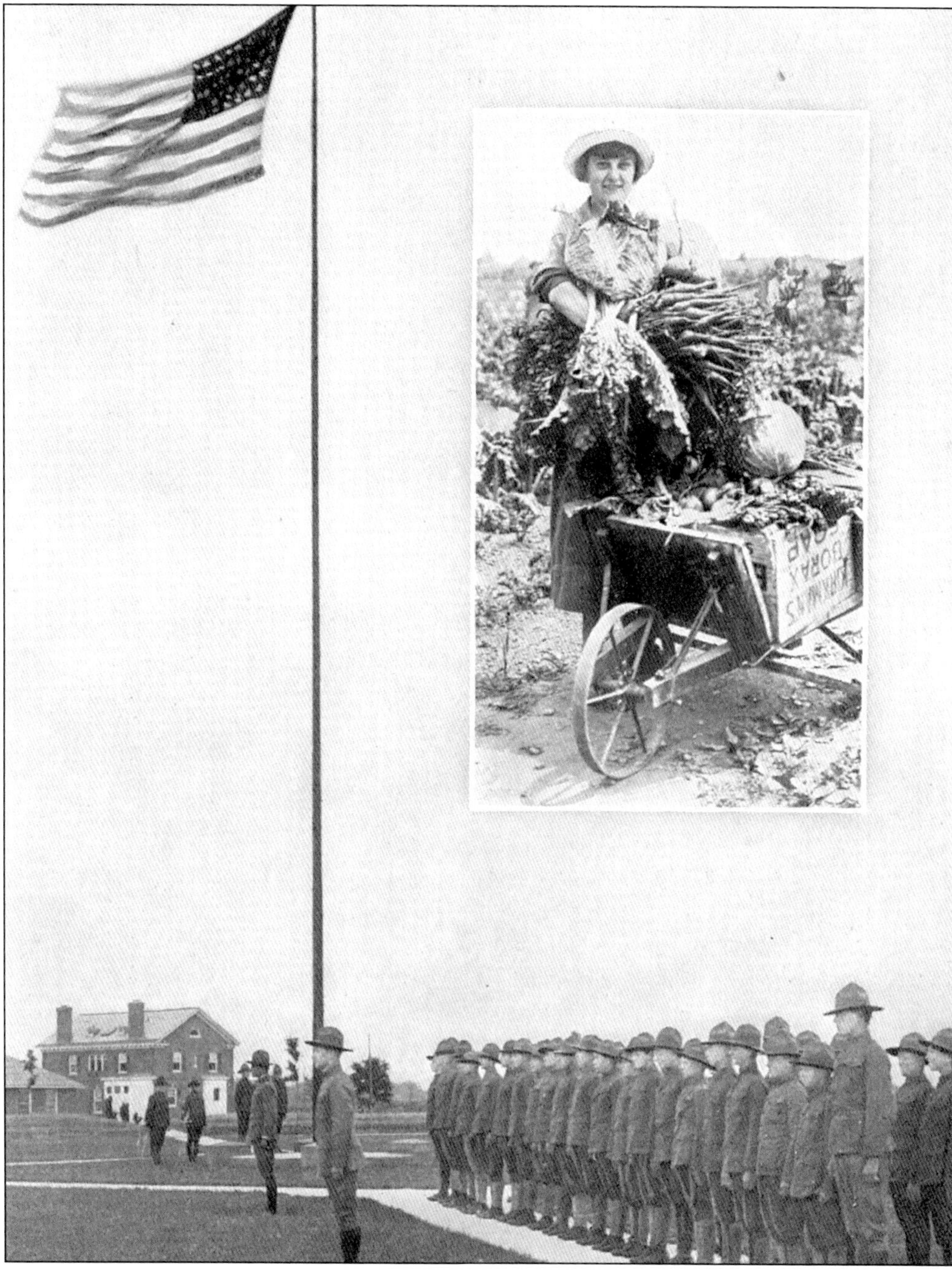

Students of Company A stand at attention during retreat as they train to be soldiers as well as farmers. Cadet camps were established at the school and functioned during the months of July, August, and part of September in the first several years. They helped to solve food and labor problems during the war years of 1917 and 1918. The Women's Land Army of New York City sent many women to Farmingdale for agricultural work and instruction. The Mott House and Dormitory II were filled with women during those years. Military routine, discipline, and instruction were important factors in the early educational system. The student cadets received military instruction and drill daily, except Saturday and Sunday.

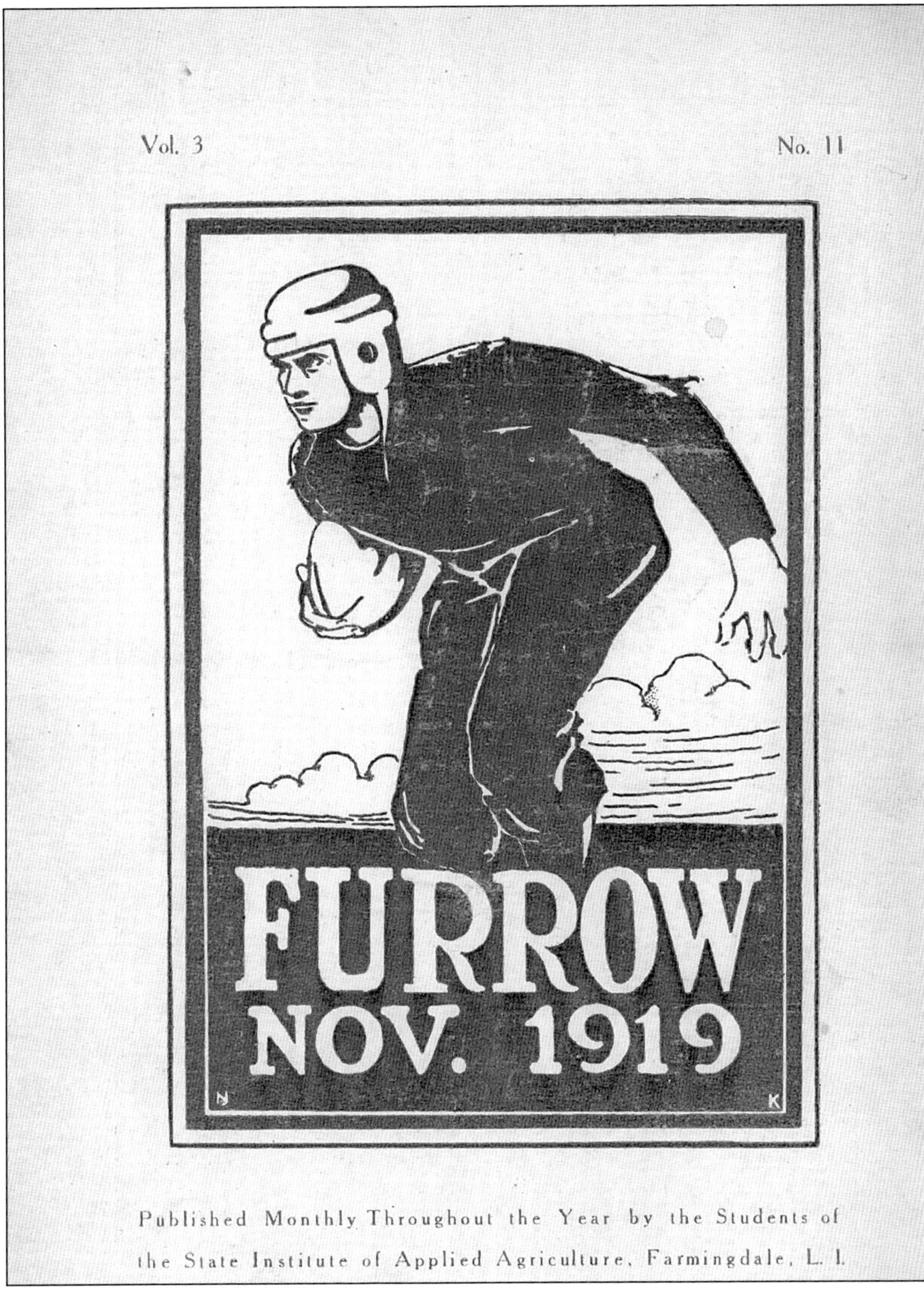

The *Furrow* was the name of the school's monthly magazine, edited and published by a board of editors selected from the student body. A faculty member served as advisor to the board. Not only did the *Furrow* disseminate news about campus life to students and faculty, but it also helped to bring the school before the public through its timely articles on agriculture and campus events.

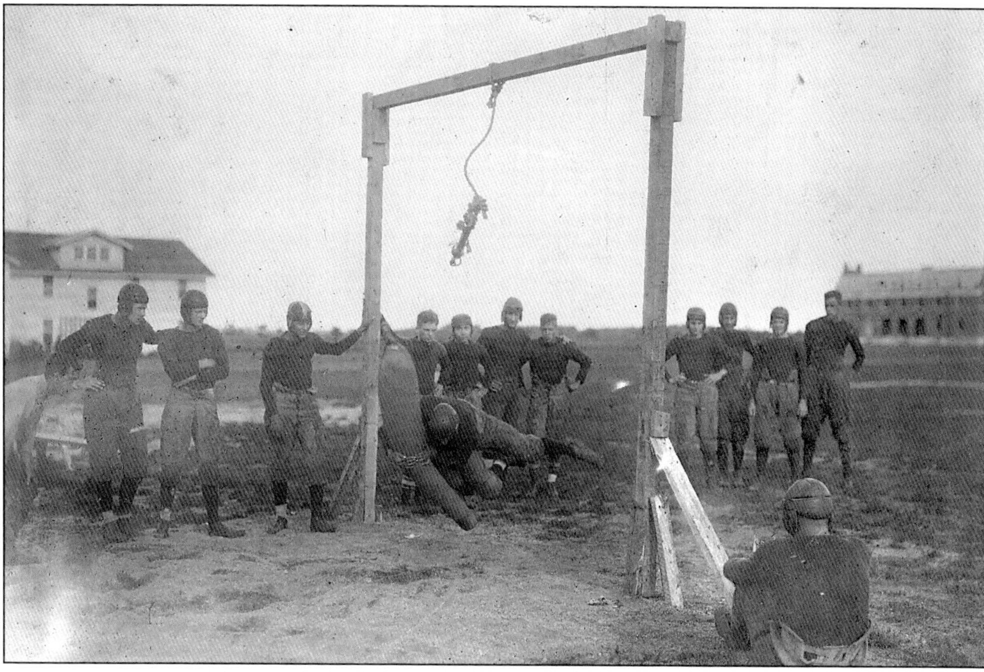

Athletics played a large part in student life, although no leagues or conferences existed. Baseball, football, basketball, and track teams were the first organized teams by 1920. They competed against high schools, colleges, club teams, and even the faculty. In fact, until the 1940s, most of their games were against high schools. A double tennis court was built in 1916 under the supervision of the Farm Mechanics Department. This photograph shows the 1920 football team at practice.

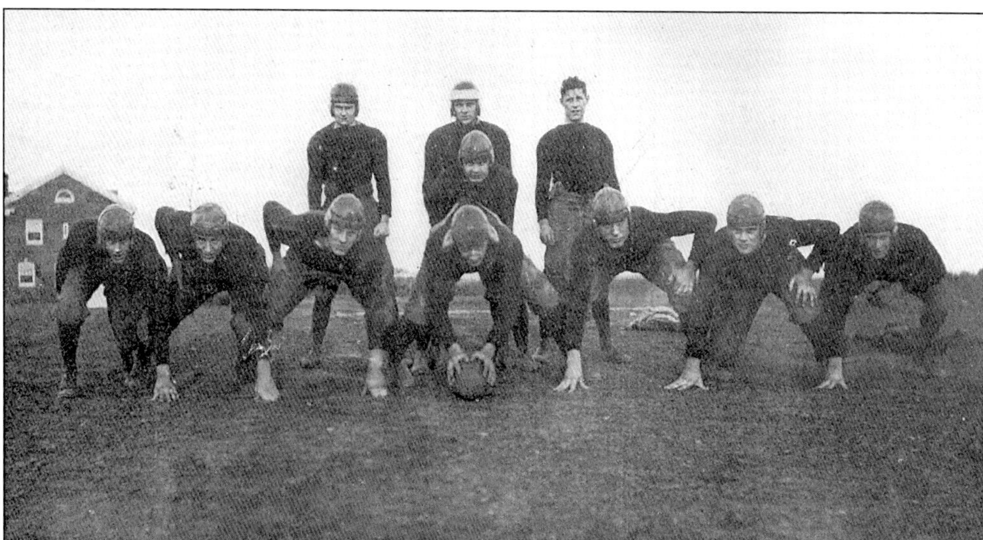

The 1919 school football team poses for a group picture. Shown, from left to right, are the following: (front row) Clark, Saar, Wilkinson, Ferguson, Falco, Moss, and Clark; (back row) Page, Winchester, and Nichols. O'Brien is the quarterback. The football team of 1916, small in number, finished the season with a 1–3 record. The baseball team of 1916 had a winning record of 9–2, including two victories over the faculty.

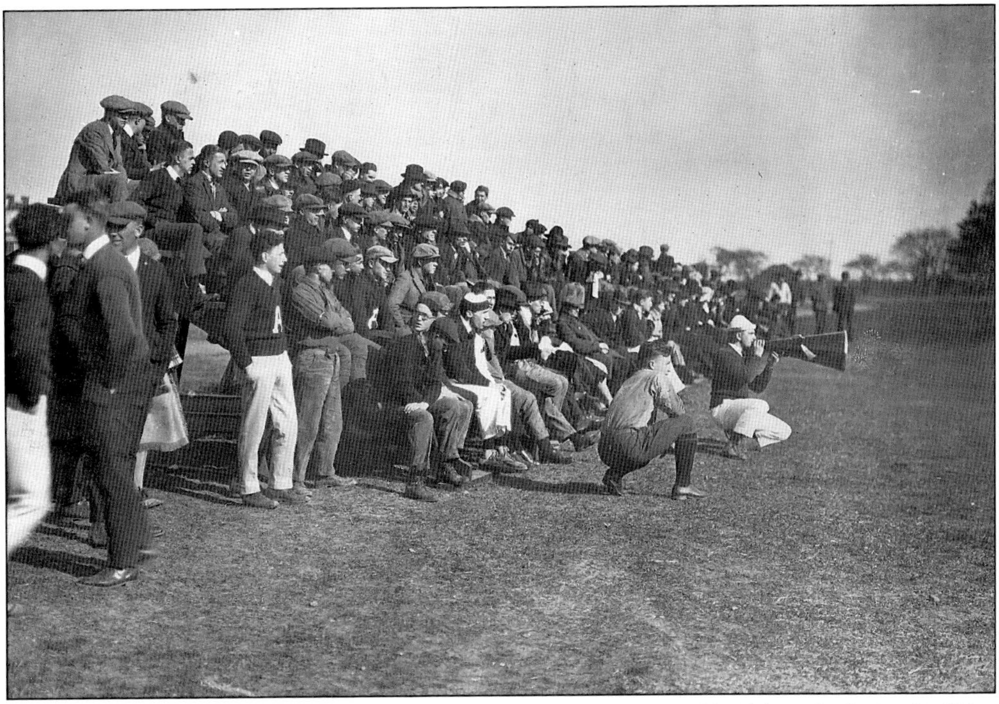

These male students are attending a baseball game on campus in 1923. Although playing facilities were somewhat primitive at the time, and organizationally there was no conference competition, school spirit was high. The letter A on the student's sweater at the left stood for "Aggies." The student kneeling at the right is using a megaphone to cheer the team on.

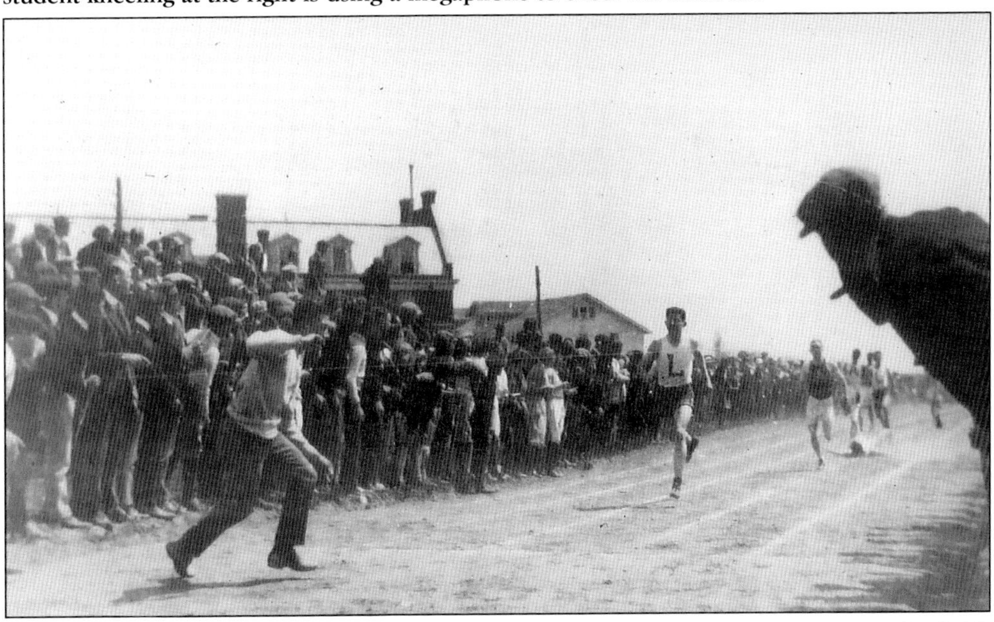

Ray Barbuti, Lawrence High School track and football star of Nassau County, races to the finish line to victory at the institute field in the spring of 1924. Barbuti won a scholarship to Syracuse University and excelled in these sports. He went on to win two gold medals in track events at the ninth Olympic Games held in Amsterdam, Netherlands, in 1928. Ward Hall is to the left.

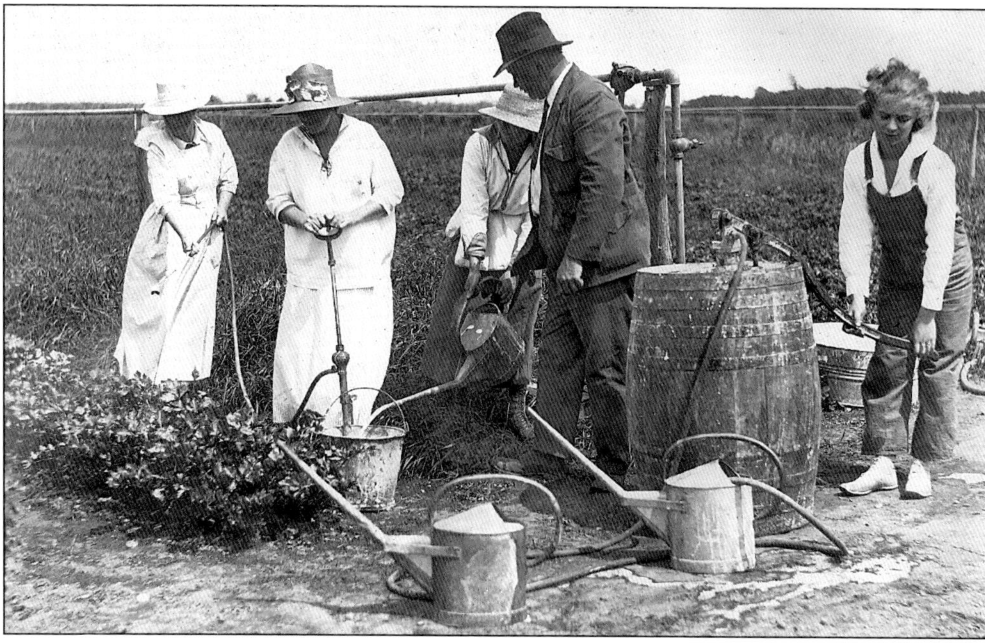

Beginning in 1919 and continuing to 1939, the school took on a new name: the New York State Institute of Applied Agriculture on Long Island. Apparently it was thought that the new title, especially using the word *applied,* was more appropriate. For example, this photograph affirms the school's philosophy as students apply the skills learned in the classroom. These students are practicing agricultural spraying techniques as they spray celery under the supervision of an instructor in 1921.

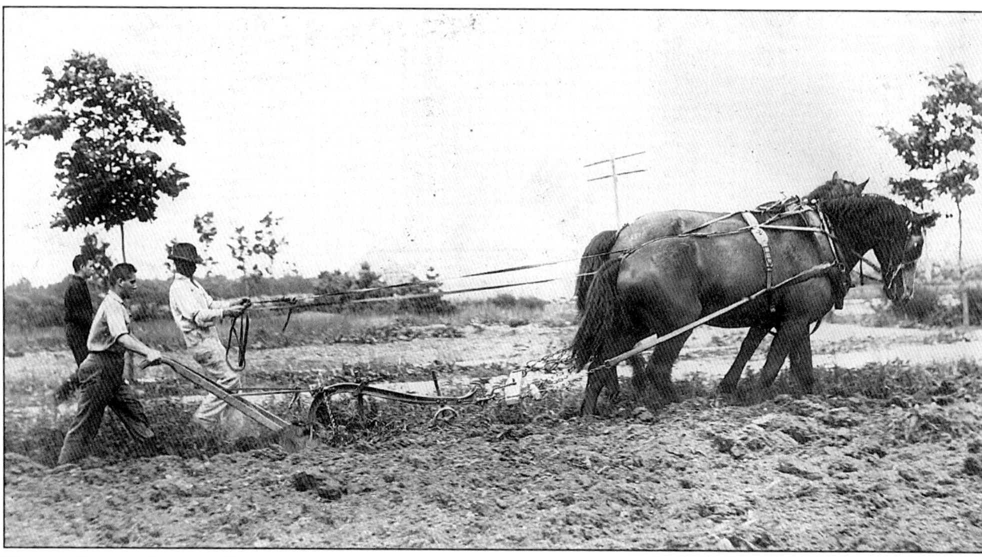

Every phase of agriculture was taught. Here, students are learning proper plowing techniques. Instead of the school hiring individuals to do the gardening and farming and to care for the livestock, students do this work as an essential part of their education. The work of the school continued without interruption throughout the year as the students followed the whole cycle of agricultural production. The school farm was the laboratory where the students learned by actual practice.

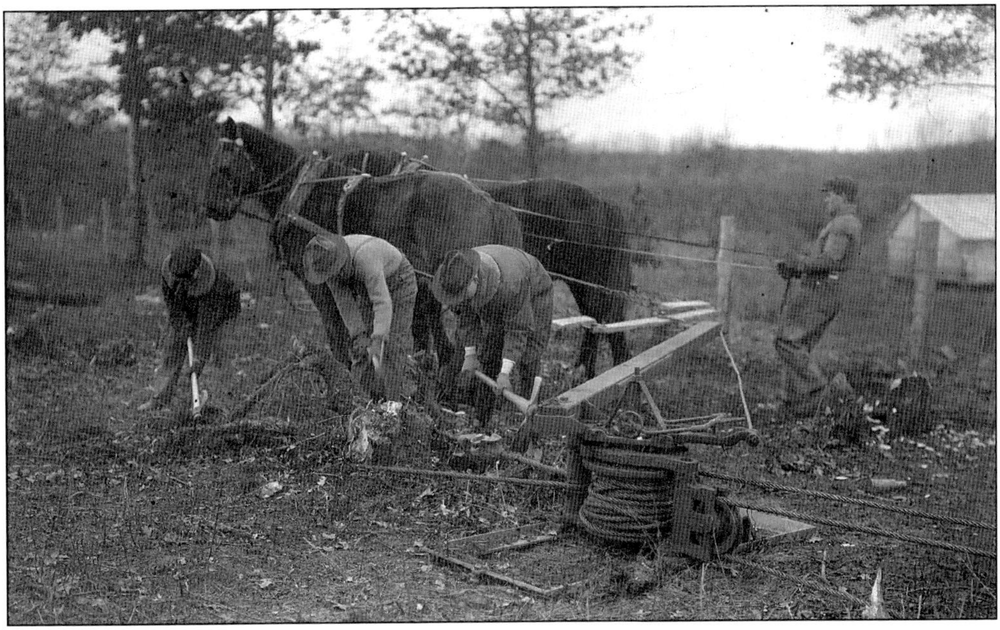

In January 1917, the school farm consisted of 333 acres. The campus was located in the center. The farm was conveniently divided into fields for instruction in the cultivation of all farm, garden, and orchard crops. Land had to be cleared. This photograph, taken on January 24, 1921, shows students clearing land for cultivation.

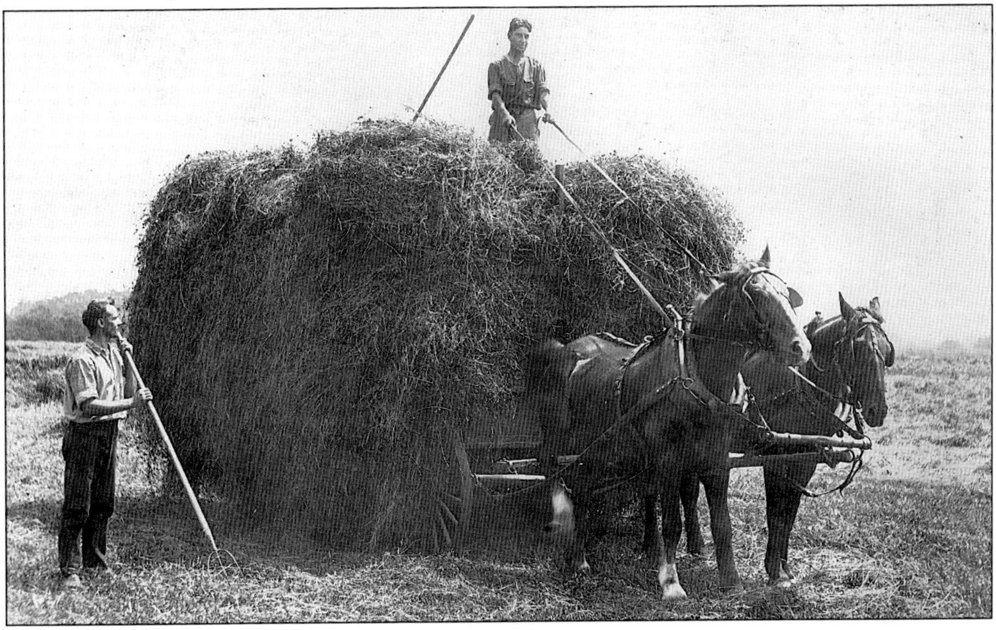

The school farm was not a commercial enterprise, since all the work was done by students who thereby acquired a proficiency that they could apply on their own farms after completing their studies. These students are gathering hay in 1921. The original object of the school was to provide agricultural training for boys and girls of New York City, and to promote agriculture in the counties of Nassau, Suffolk, Westchester, Dutchess, Rockland, and Putnam. The area was extended to the tristate region.

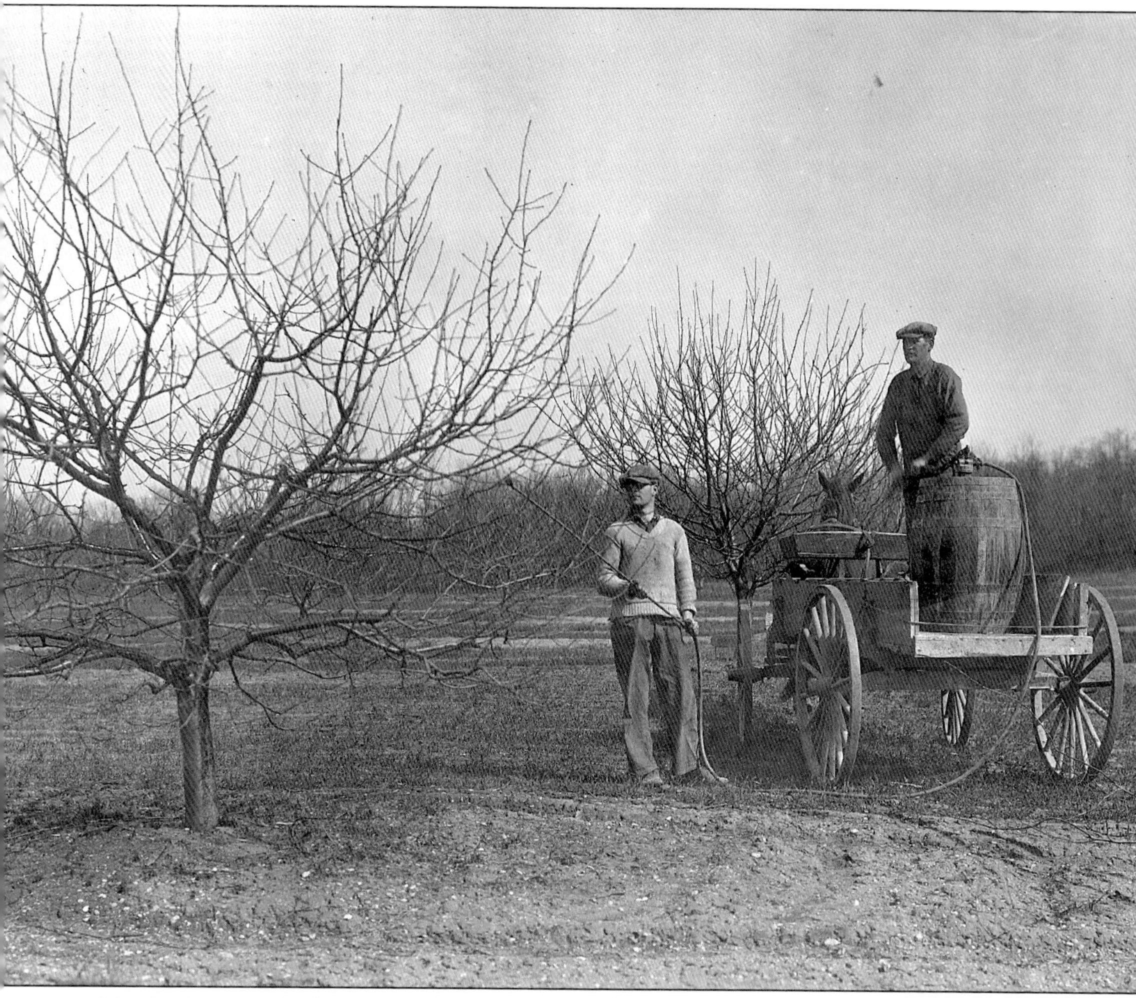

The institute orchards were quite extensive and required constant care. Here, students are spraying in the apple orchard with a hand-pump sprayer in 1926. Faculty members prided themselves on advanced methods of farming. The 1921–1922 catalog stated, "It is only the old, unscientific methods that have failed and never agriculture itself. Increase of production in all lines is the recognized source of prosperity, and agriculture and its products of no exception."

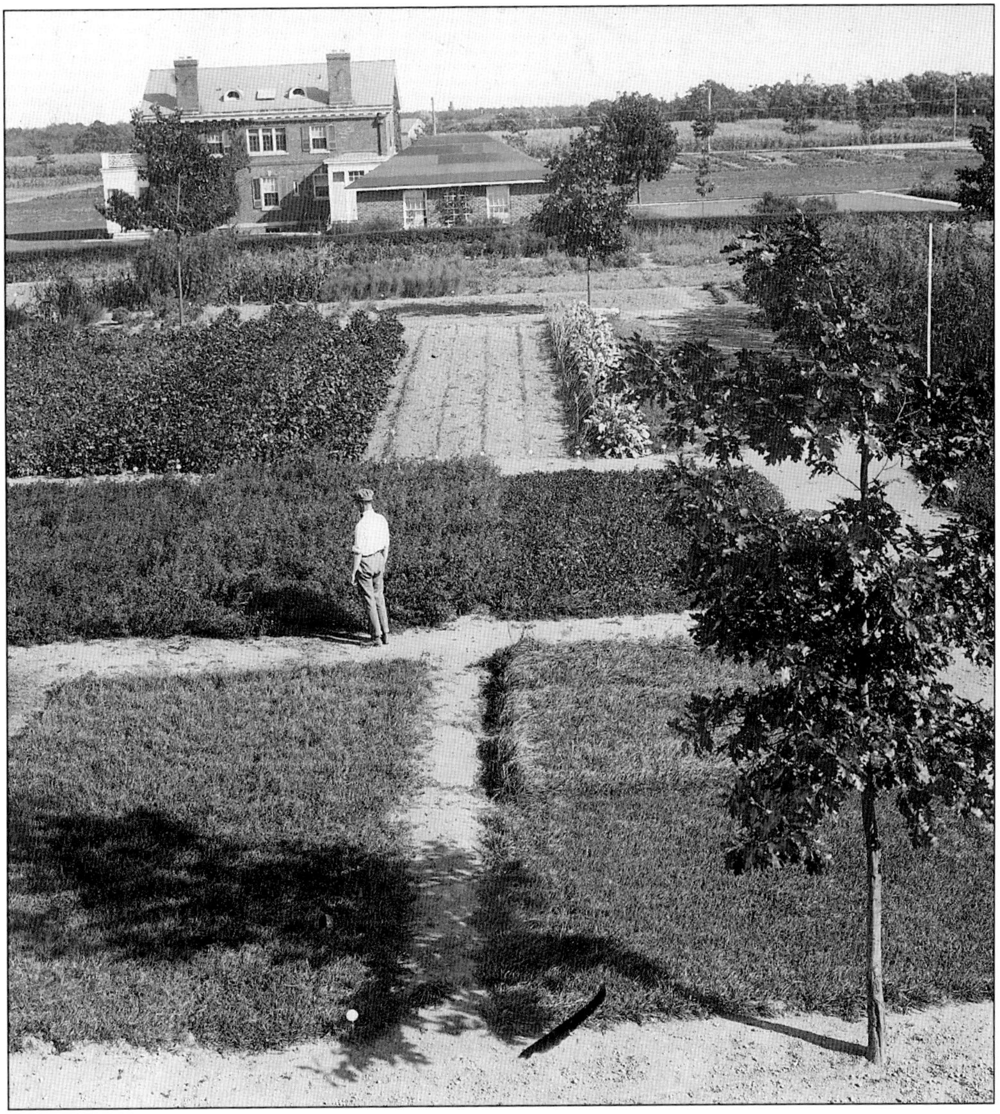

This in-depth campus view captures the turf demonstration on plots conceived and organized by students under the supervision of an instructor. These plots are part of an area that is now the lawn foyer to Suffolk Hall. The Director's Cottage is at the top left. The vista presents an agrarian campus as part of a rural Long Island.

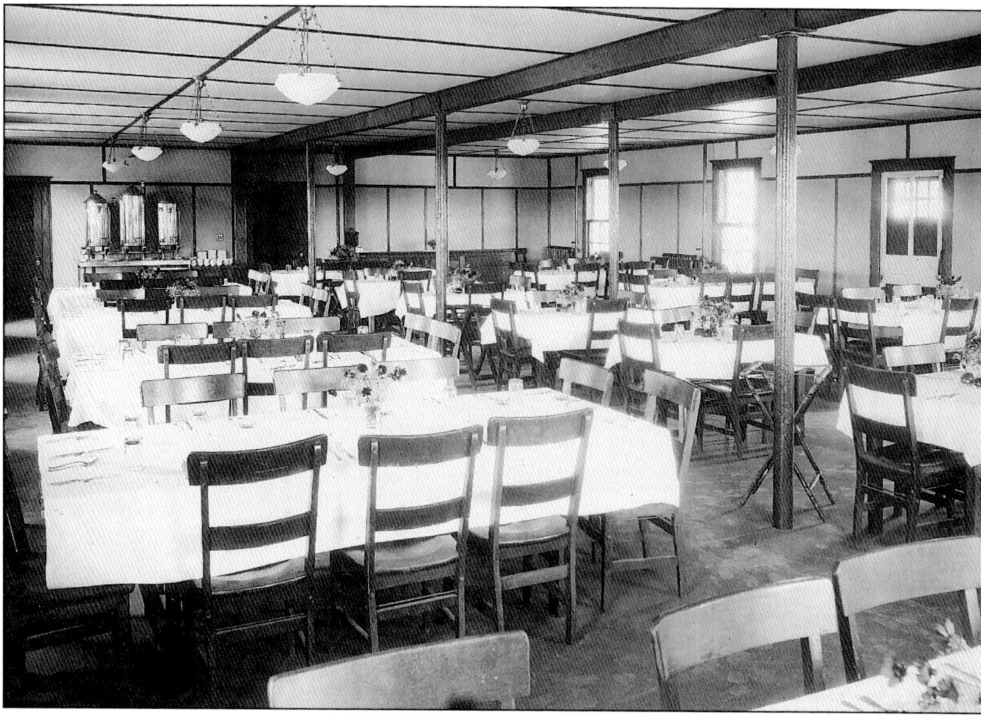

The dining hall in Old Dormitory III was central to the lives of the students. After a hard day's work in the classroom and the field, students replenished their energy here amid much fellowship. Old Dormitory III was used from 1919 until 1937, when Knapp Hall was opened. Note the flowers on the tables and the formal atmosphere of the room.

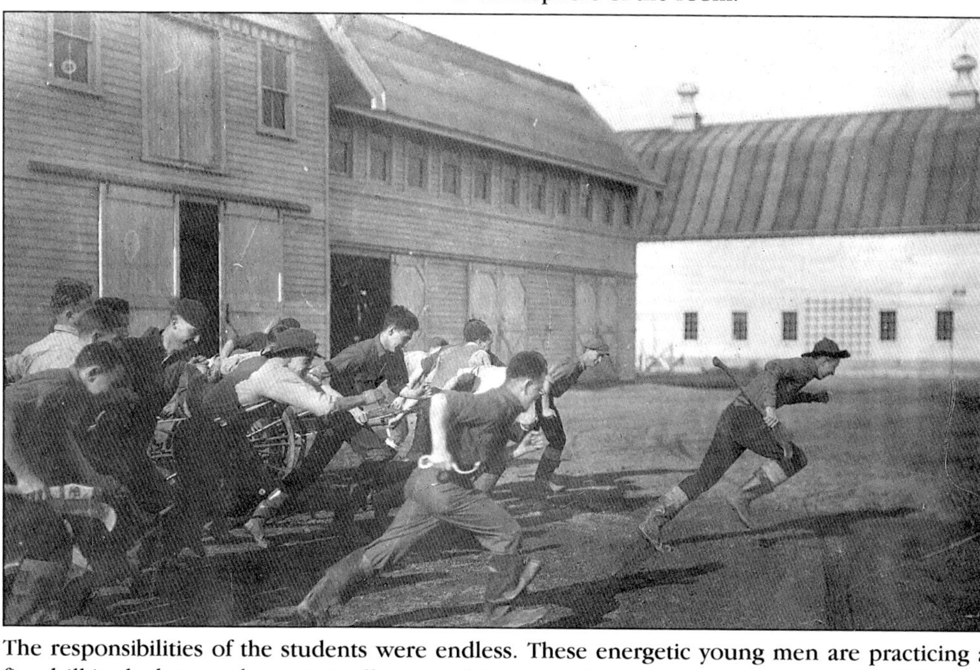

The responsibilities of the students were endless. These energetic young men are practicing a fire drill in the barnyard area. It is all a part of the total education process that produced leaders in society. They did not question the tasks that were assigned to them.

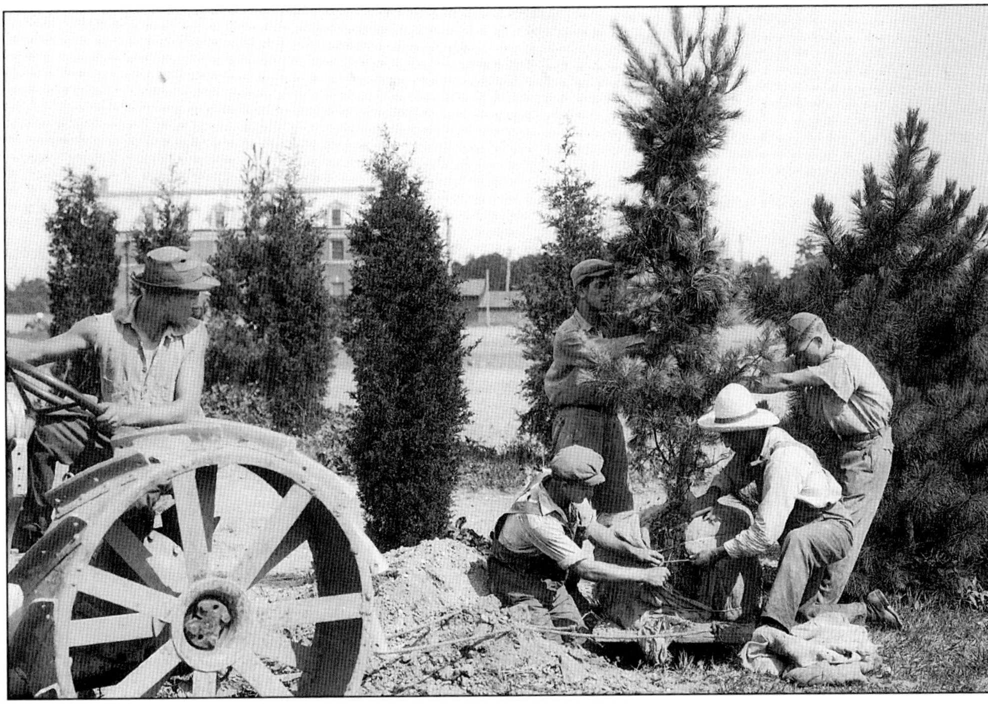

In another task, students are moving trees in a landscape redesignation project. They are serious and concentrating on completing the assignment successfully. Use of a tractor is also part of the project. Graduates were well prepared to engage in agricultural work for themselves or to manage farms for others.

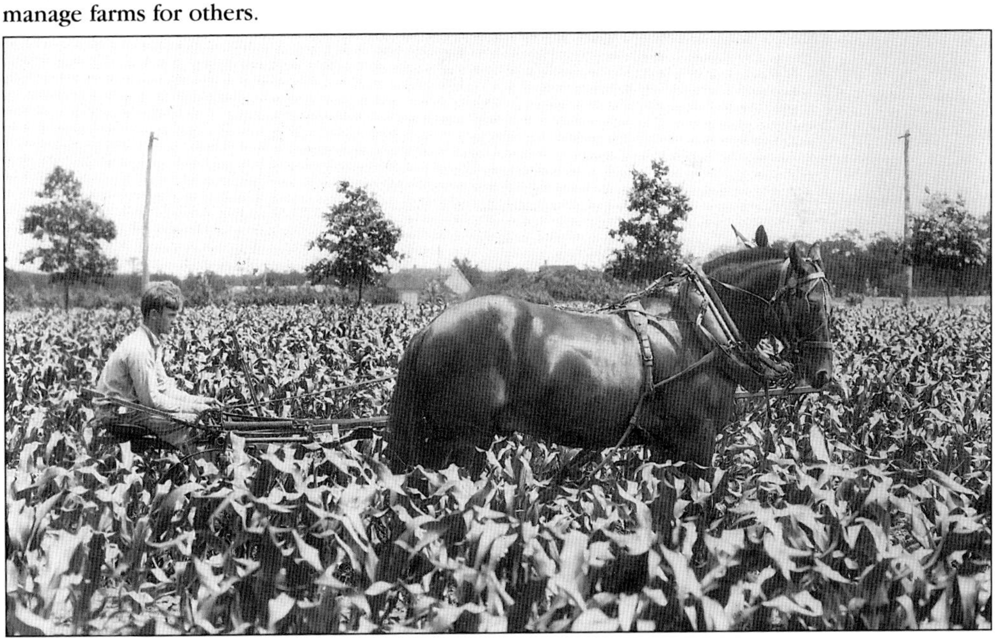

This student at the New York State Institute of Applied Agriculture on Long Island is cultivating a field of corn in the early 1920s. The institute maintained its own stable of horses to perform various farm functions. In fact, modern tractors existed side by side with horses, allowing students to be expert at both.

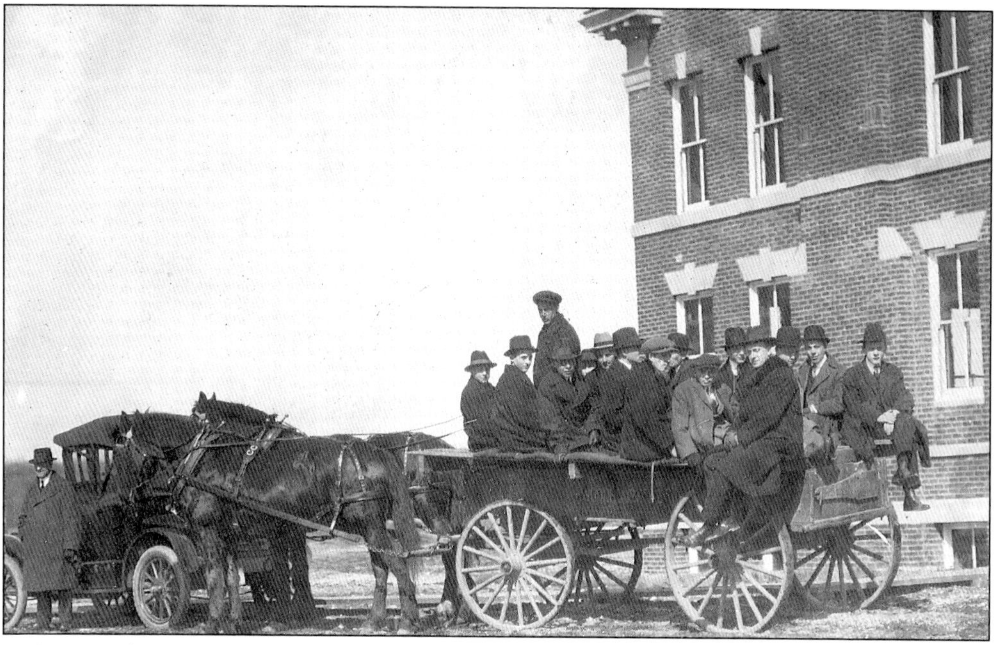

Early in its history, the school opened its doors to the community. Its leaders have proudly proclaimed the advantages of agricultural life and its relationship to civic duty and democratic principles in the true Jeffersonian spirit. Thus, conferences, open house programs, and demonstration exhibits have engaged the public. The group of visitors in this 1920 photograph is being transported around the campus to view various farm demonstrations.

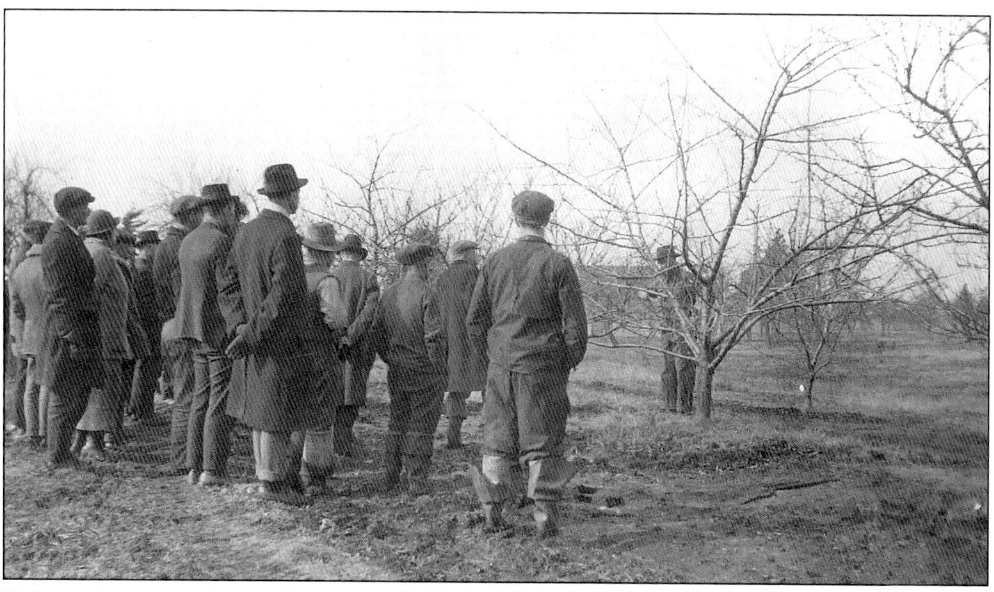

This visiting group is watching a student demonstration pruning fruit trees in the institute orchard in 1926 before the growing season. Such a successful demonstration often led to inquiries about the institute, awareness of its programs, and increased enrollments. Note how well dressed the visitors are for this agricultural outing.

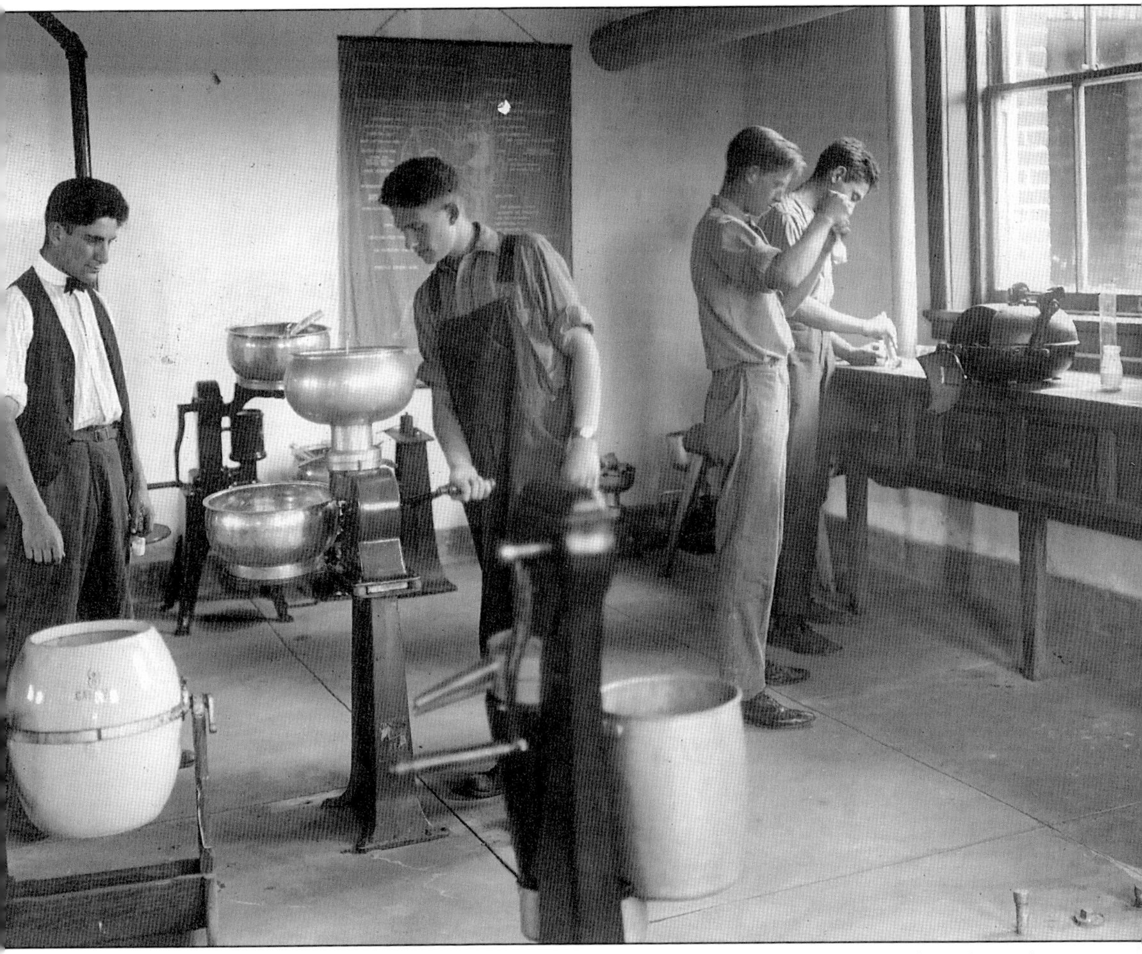

Theory and practice in education worked hand in hand; the one dovetailed into the other. This formula was pursued by the institute. The theory of improving the quality of milk combined with the practice of milk production is demonstrated by these students in the Old Dairy Laboratory in the Agronomy Building (Cutler Hall) in 1921.

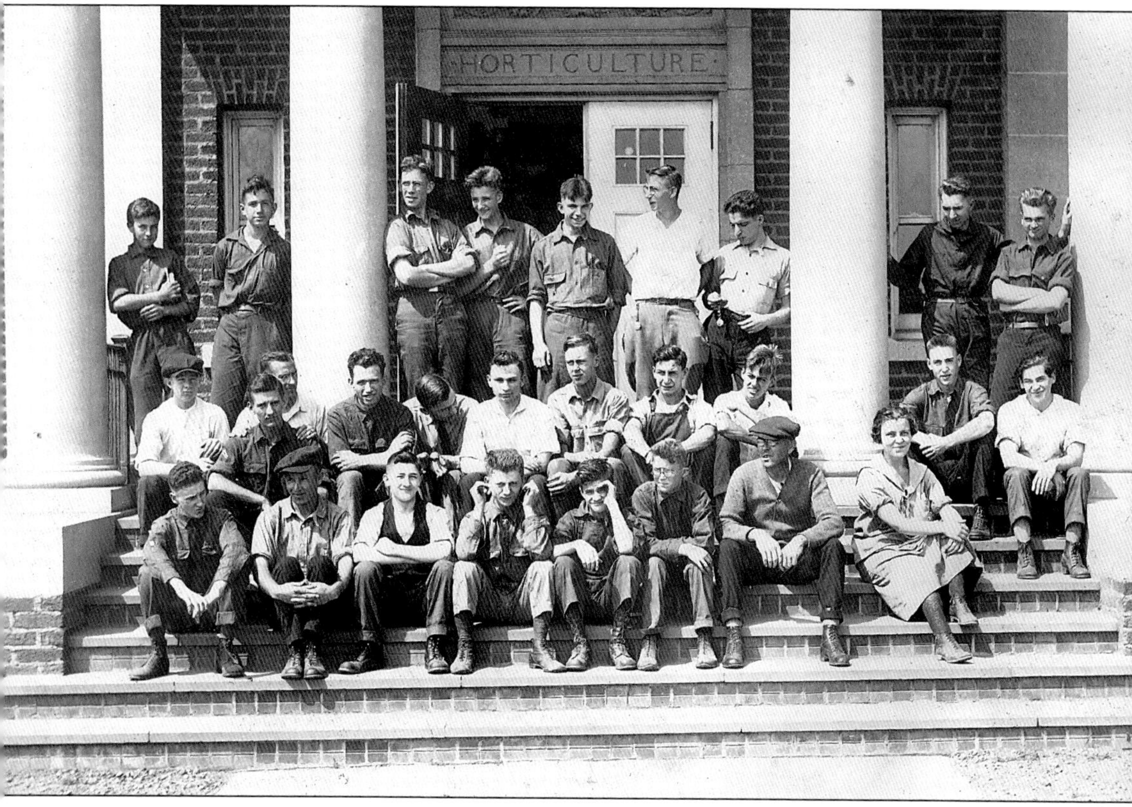

These students, posing together for the first time in front of the Horticulture Building (now Hicks Hall), have just entered the institute in 1921. They will become the Class of 1924 upon graduation, since the regular agricultural course of study at the time was for a three-year duration.

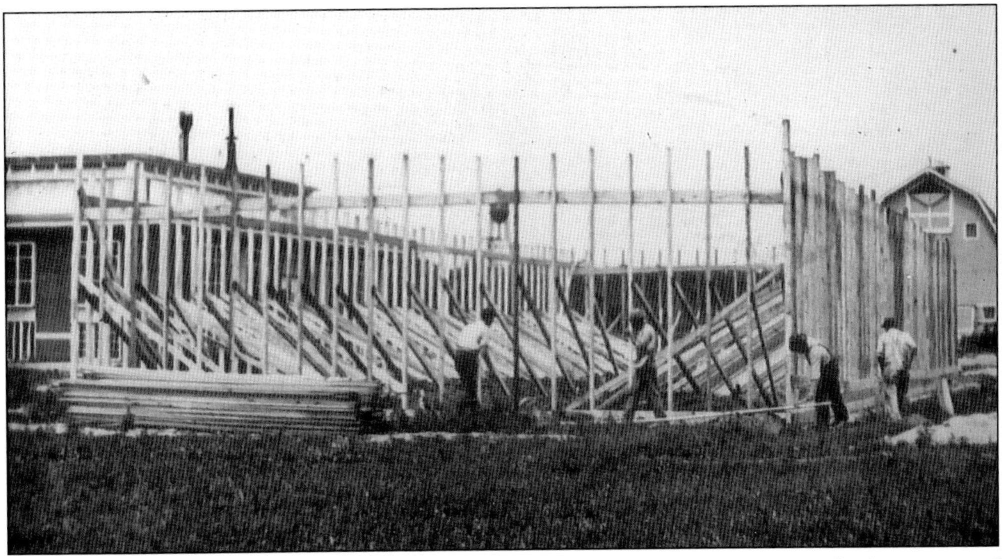

These workers are constructing the original gymnasium and locker room. It was built at a cost of $24,000 and completed in 1922. It had many uses over the years. It also served as an auditorium and conference center until 1953, when Allard Field House was erected. Gerald Allard was athletic director from 1929 to 1964. Since then, the building has been the campus bookstore. Conklin Hall is to the left rear, and the barn is to the right rear.

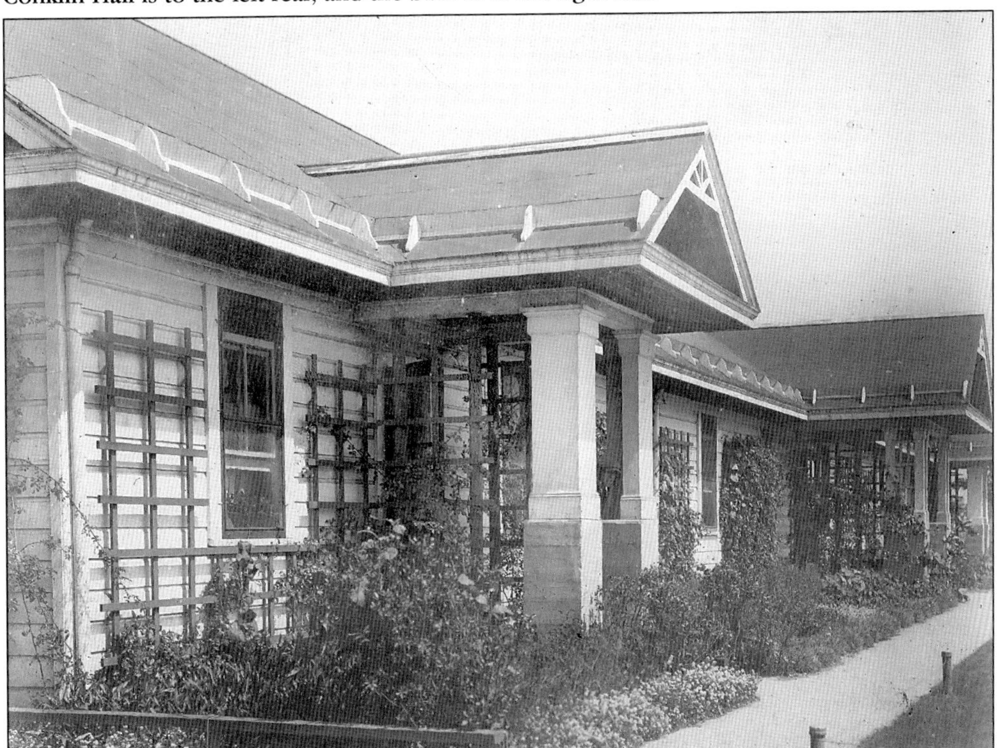

Old Dormitory II was built in 1919. It stood at the northern end of where Thompson Hall stands today. It also housed the Cornell Veterinary Laboratory, dairy testing lab, and an apartment for several resident clerical employees. The building was demolished in 1955.

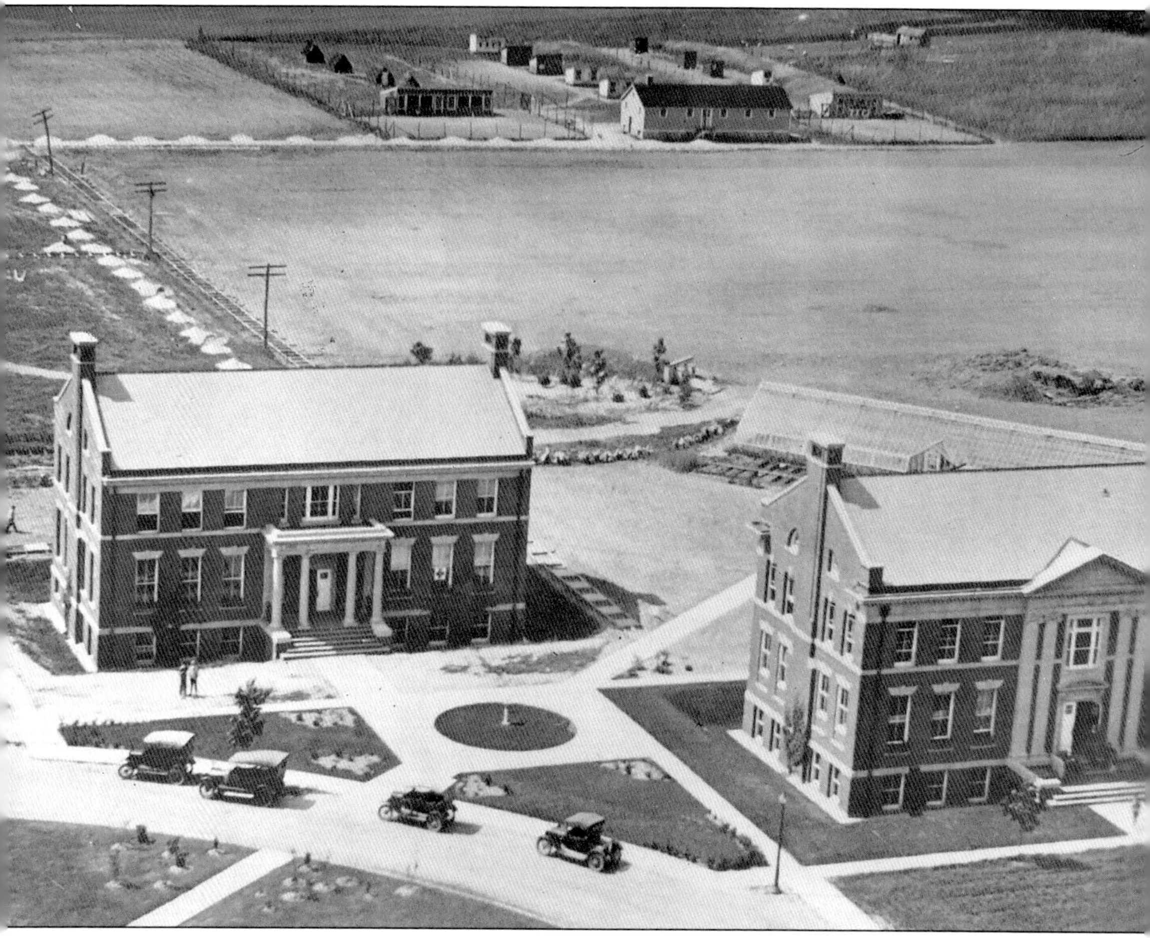

This 1920s aerial view shows the Horticulture Building (Hicks Hall), to the left, and the Agronomy Building (Cutler Hall), to the right. Cars are parked on the northern end of the circle. The greenhouse is to the right, behind the Agronomy Building. The buildings in the background comprise the Poultry Plant. The bare expanse of land behind the greenhouse, and to its right, is where the Ornamental Horticulture Teaching Gardens are today.

Two

Halsey B. Knapp Takes Charge

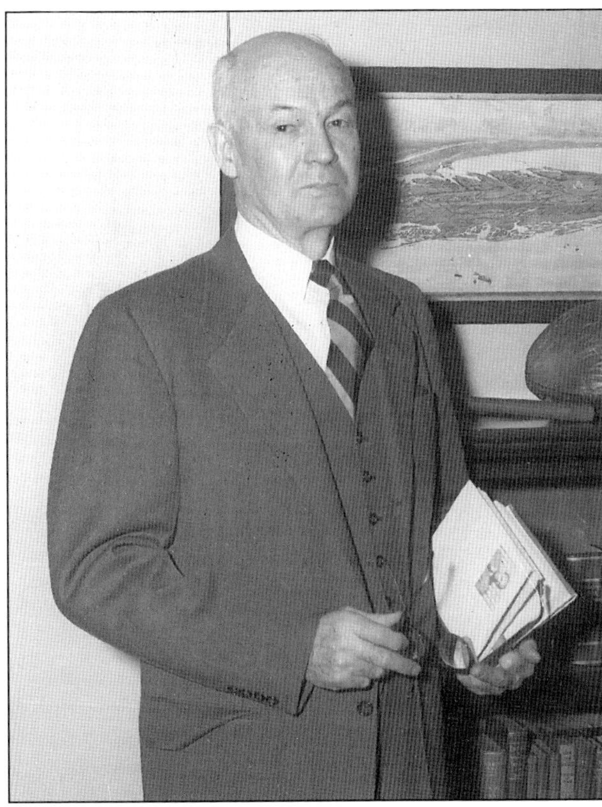

Halsey B. Knapp became director of the institute in 1923 and continued in this position until 1956, when he retired. He is shown in his office on the ground floor of the old administration building, Thompson Hall. During his long tenure in office, he worked to gain respect for the institute and to broaden its reach and influence on agricultural education. Before he arrived at his Long Island assignment, he was director of the New York State School of Agriculture at Cobleskill, where he achieved an outstanding record.

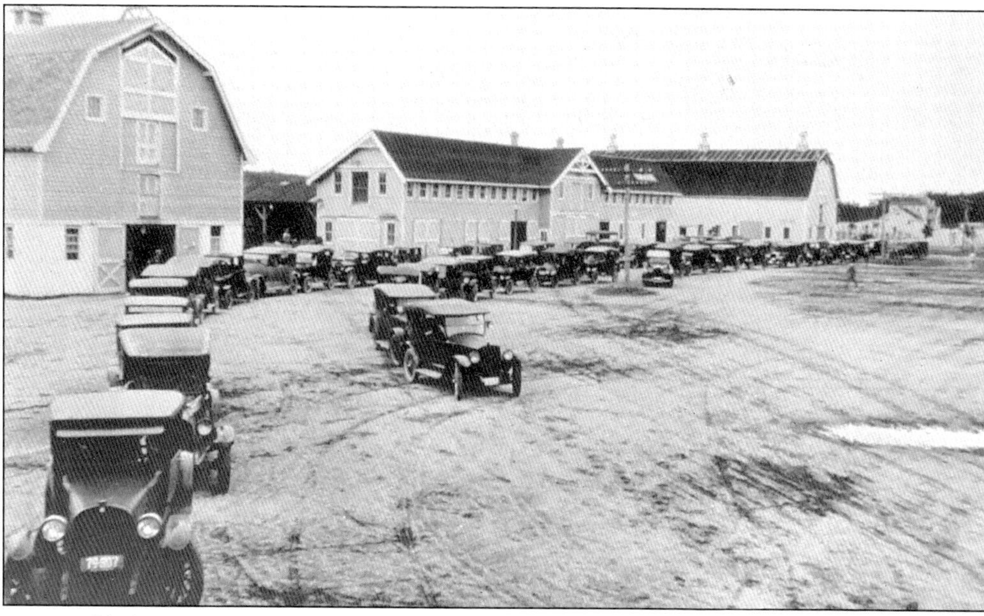

Knapp added new programs and expanded older ones. The first Country Life Program had been held in 1920 on campus. Its original name was the Farm and Home Equipment Show. The activity grew from a one-day affair to three days by 1926. This scene shows parked cars of visitors at the old farm complex barnyard area in the 1920s. The grounds are not paved, nor is the parking area sectioned off.

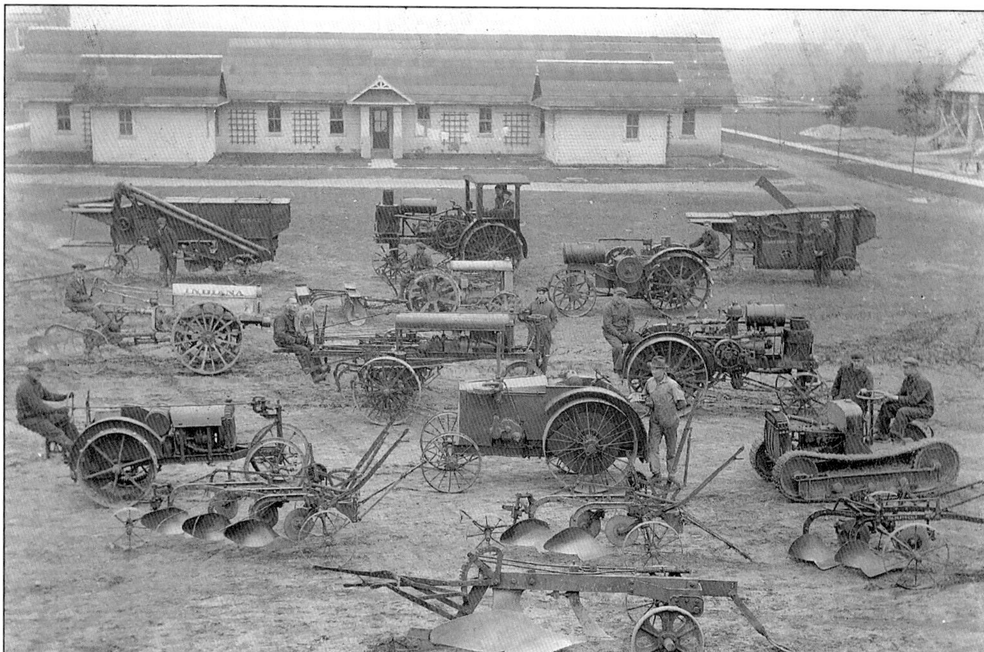

This display of tractors, reapers, and other equipment in front of the students' dormitory was part of a 1920s Country Life Program. Knapp firmly believed that modern machinery was essential in carrying out the mission of the institute. He insisted on having the faculty and students operate machinery and maintain it in good working condition.

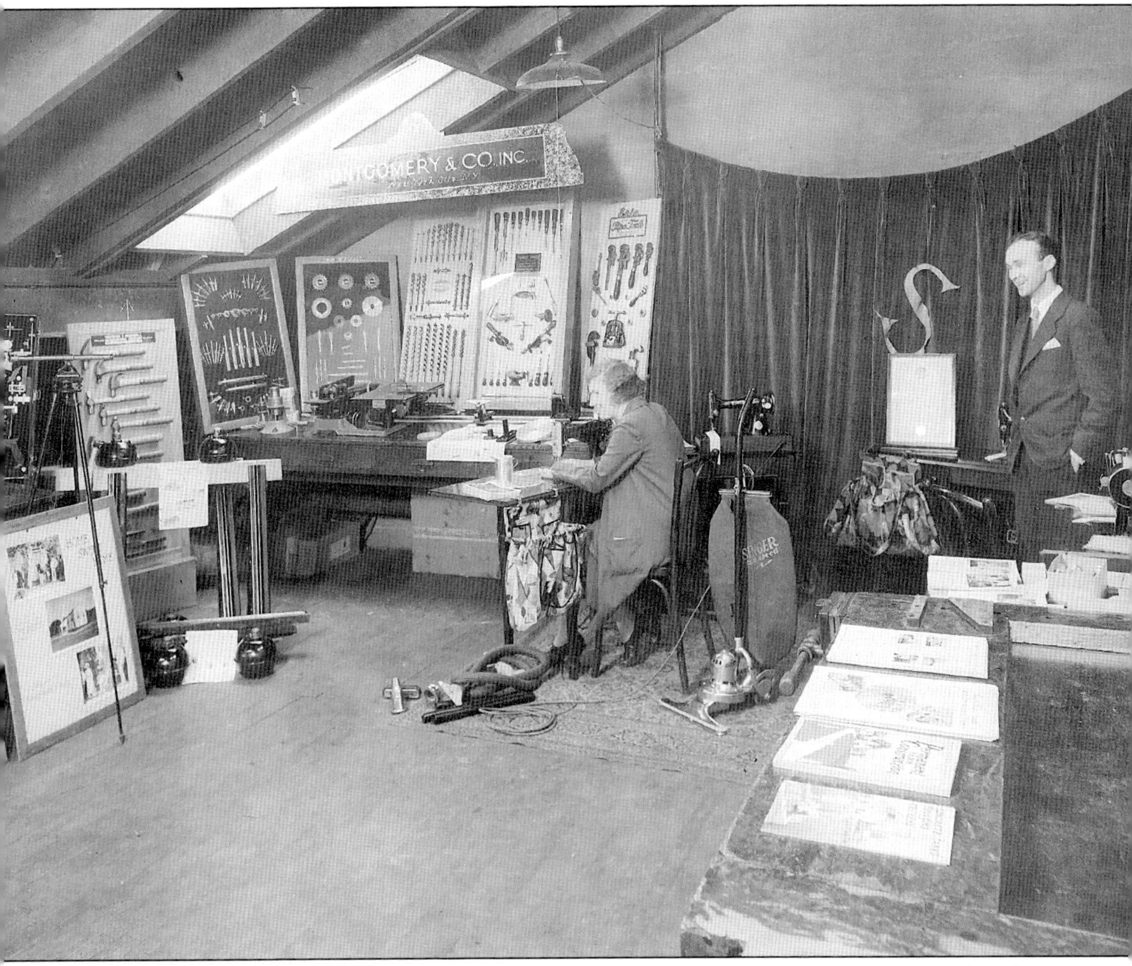

The Country Life Program was supported by the faculty and the community as the years went by. This Country Life exhibit was held in 1930 on the second floor of the Agricultural Equipment Building. Machine companies brought in their latest machinery for display on this occasion. Through these contacts, the institute was able to receive free use of valuable equipment and machinery from many private companies, thereby enhancing instructional programs up until WWII.

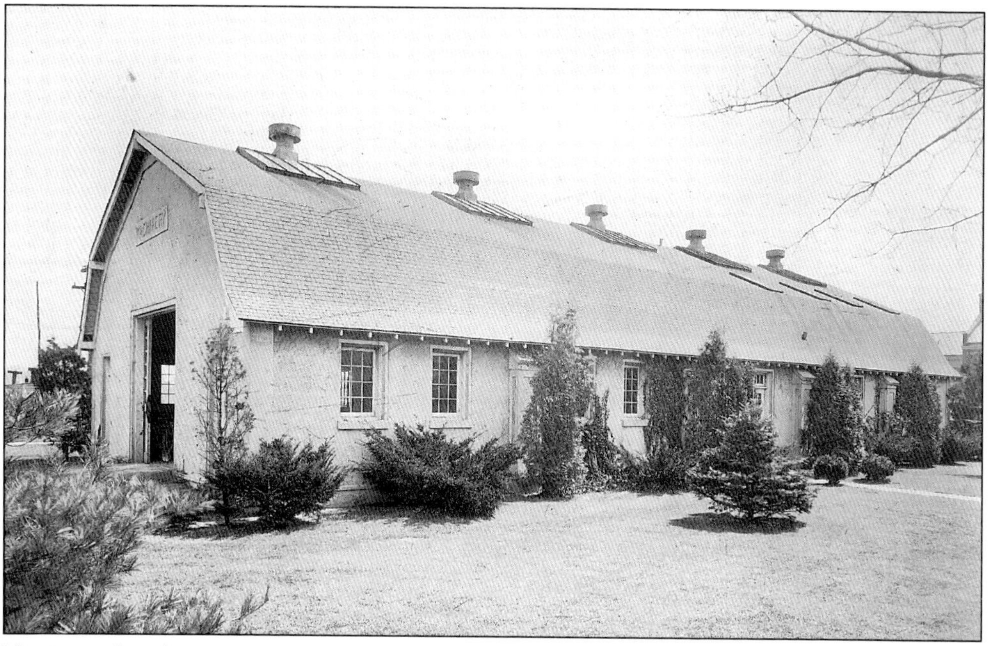

The Agricultural Equipment Building became one of the most functional of all campus facilities. It stands here with a sign reading, "Machinery" at the top left over the open doorway. It has served as a classroom, a laboratory, the site of Country Life Programs, and a storage center for equipment and machinery. It was converted in the 1980s into the Mini Mall and is used today by students, staff, and faculty for a quick beverage, a snack, or relaxation. There are also several offices in the right side of the building.

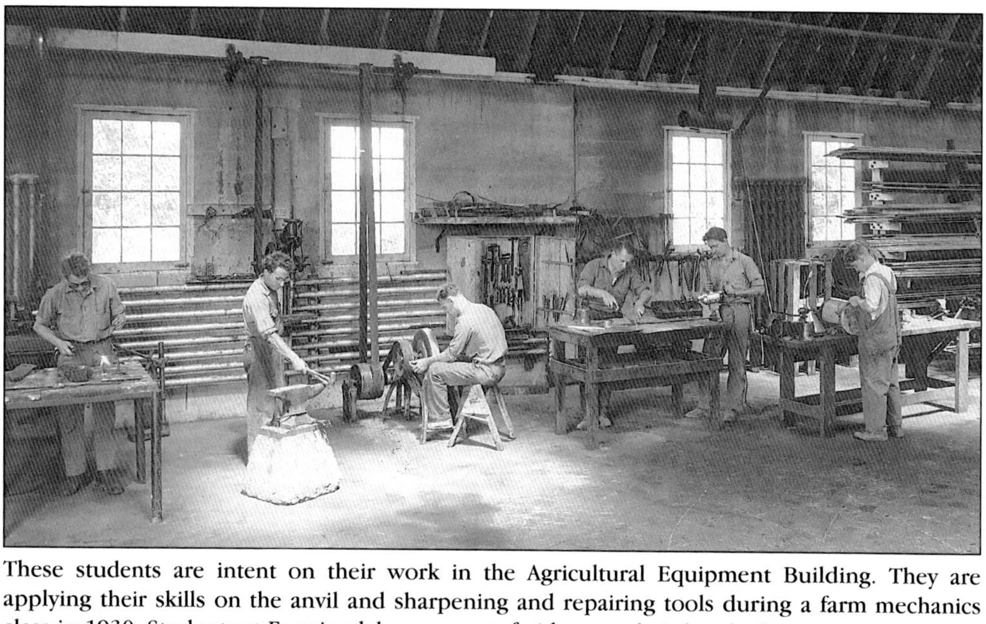

These students are intent on their work in the Agricultural Equipment Building. They are applying their skills on the anvil and sharpening and repairing tools during a farm mechanics class in 1930. Students at Farmingdale were not afraid to get their hands dirty.

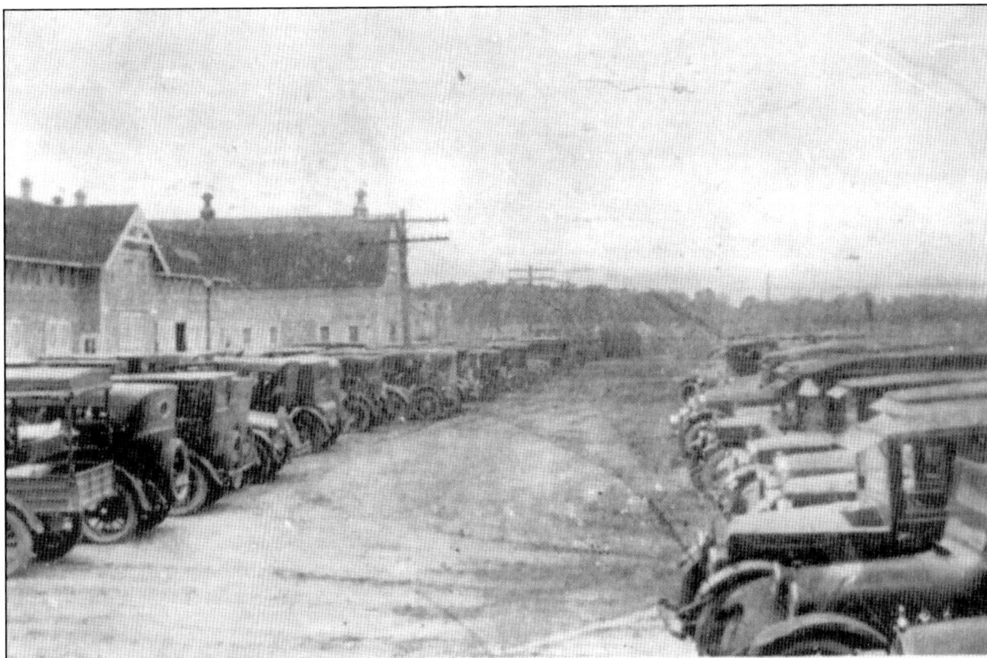

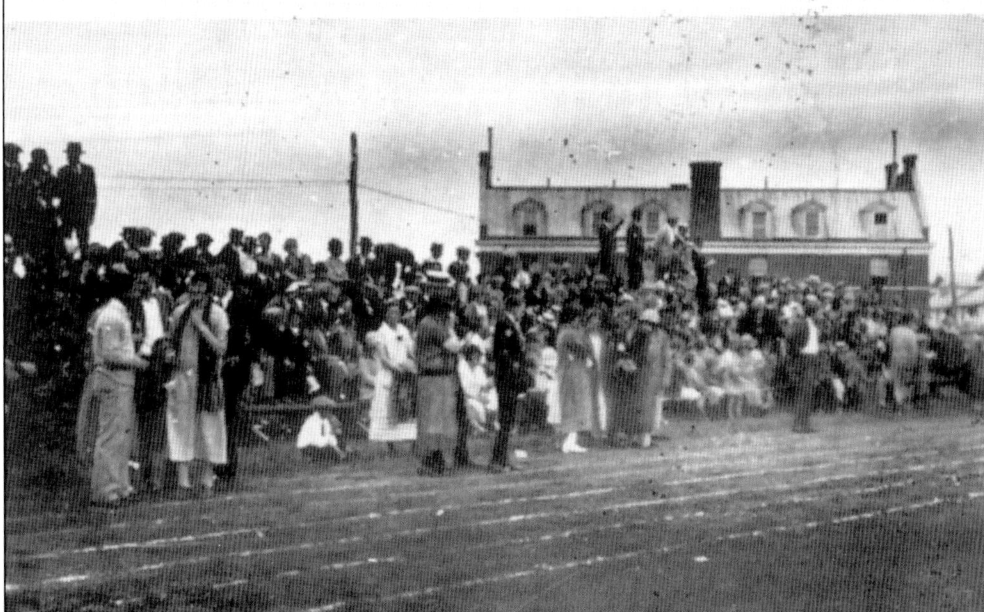

The top photograph is an affirmation of the popularity of the Country Life Program on the Farmingdale campus around 1930. Visitors' cars are parked tightly together in the barnyard area in the front of the horse barn, garage, and dairy barn. The bottom photograph shows a large crowd at the old athletic field during a track meet in the early 1920s. In the background is Ward Hall, which then served as a dormitory. The spectators are well dressed with suits, dresses, and hats, quite a difference in style from what people wear at today's sporting events.

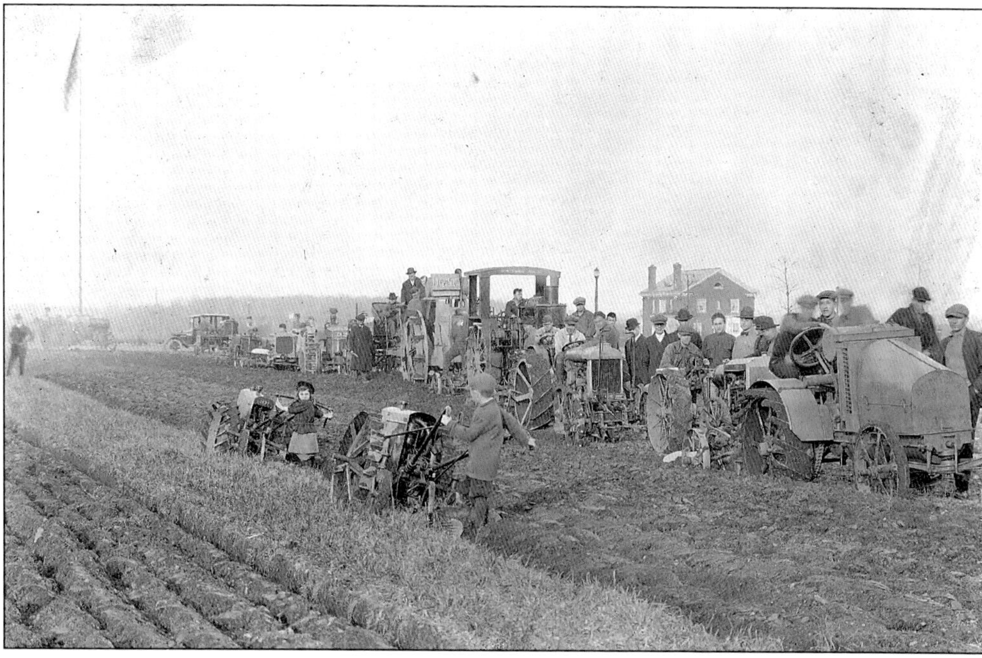

This tractor and machinery demonstration during the Country Life Program in the 1920s was held at the right of the flagpole, off the circle area. The Director's Cottage is to the right rear. Such a rural appearance no longer exists, since this part of the campus is fully developed. Even the children in the foreground are enjoying themselves, while the adults are examining the machinery.

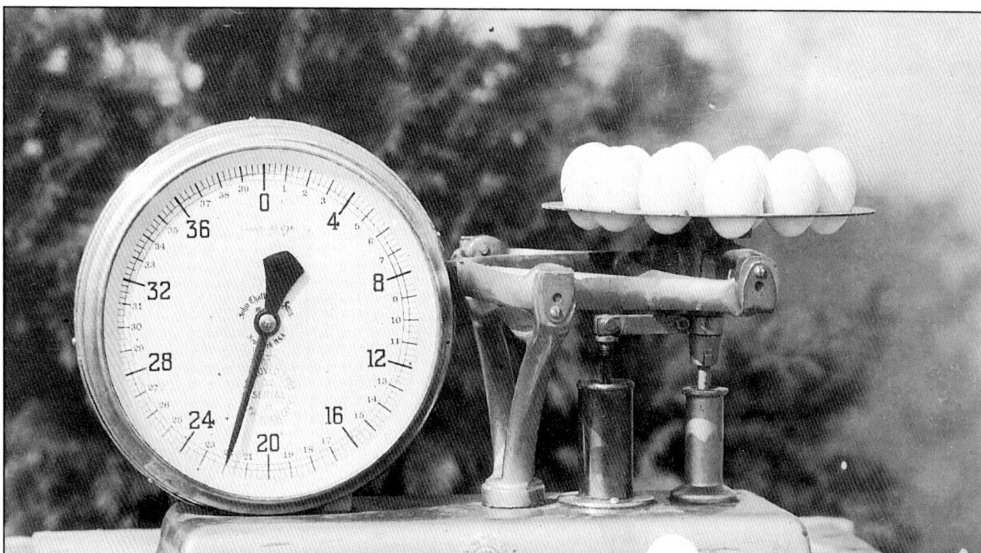

Featured here is an egg scale. It was used in the Poultry Department for a 1920s egg-laying test that recorded the average weight of a group of eggs. Later, eggs were weighed individually on a single-egg balance. In 1920, the state appropriated money for the establishment of the New York State Egg Laying and Poultry Breeding Contest, which proved its value for many years to come. In 1929, Gov. Franklin D. Roosevelt signed legislation to provide funds to replace the old houses with new ones and continue the contest.

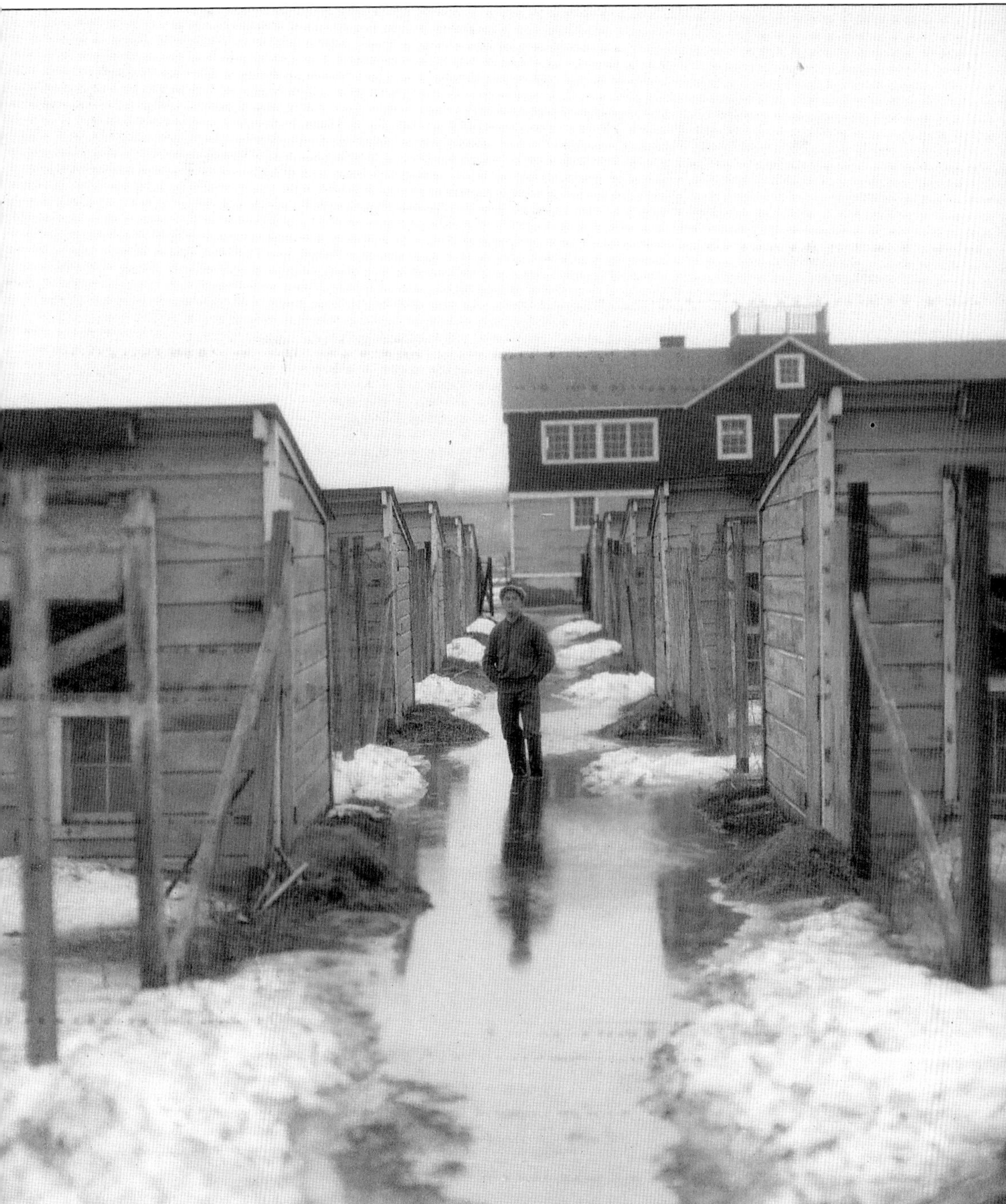

The Poultry Department's physical plant was equipped with a number of modern colony houses as well as a New Jersey multiple-unit house and another known as a "Cornell" laying house. By using these houses, students are given individual instruction for egg production and breeding. This student pauses for a moment while carrying out an assignment for poultry management. The 1921–1922 institute catalog listed four courses of study: Poultry Management, Poultry Judging, Advanced Poultry Management, and Incubation and Brooding.

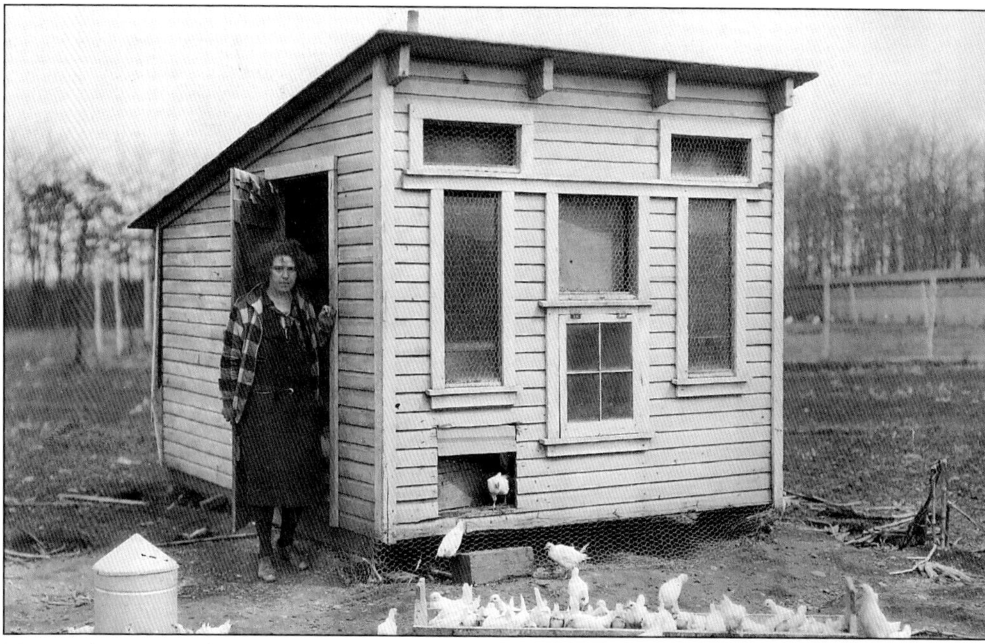

This student is standing at the door of an egg-laying pen at the institute's poultry range in 1925. She is required to complete the work satisfactorily in feeding for egg production and breeding. Since all students must develop the virtue of individual responsibility, she must take care of the colony house assigned to her.

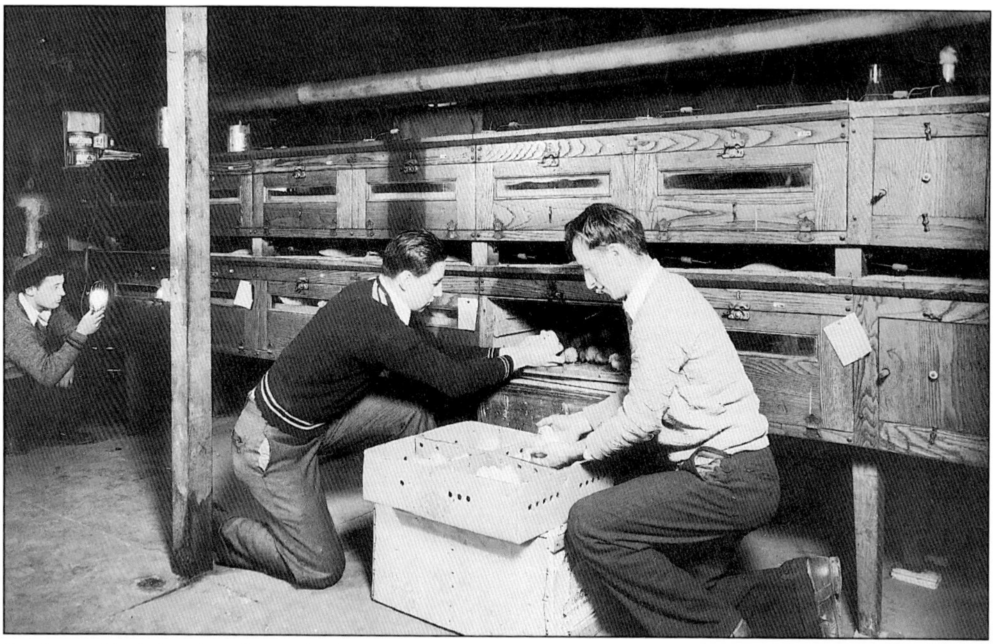

Students find that hatching chicks is a fascinating task. When WWI ended in November 1918, the Bureau of Rehabilitation, working with the Federal Board of Vocational Education, began sending veterans to Farmingdale to enroll in various courses of study. More than 225 students, such as the ones in this photograph, took the regular course of study in agriculture, farm mechanics, animal husbandry, or poultry science.

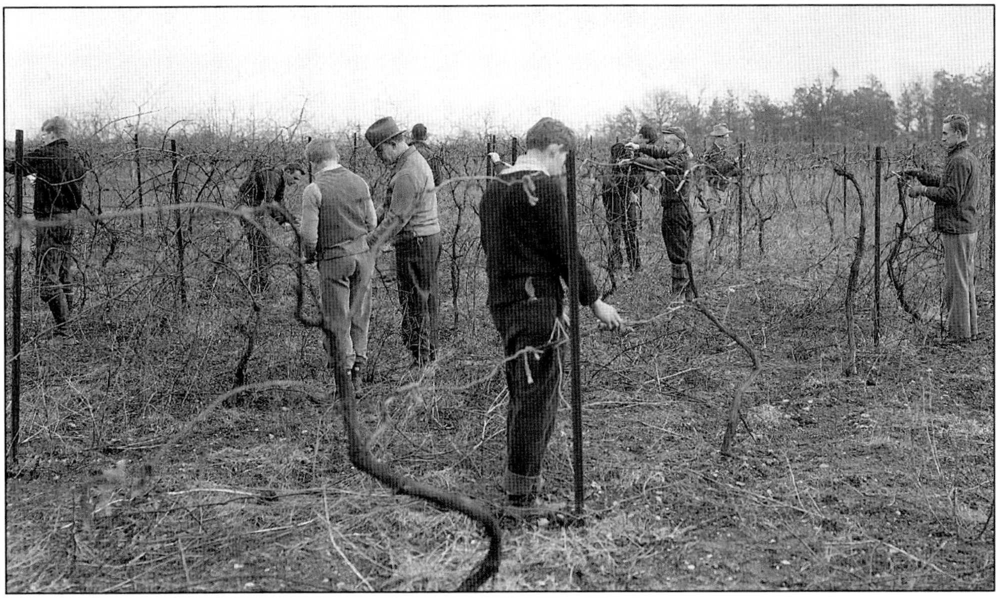

Horticulture students are pruning and tying grapevines in the institute orchard in 1930. Fordyce C. Deitz is the man in the left center with hat on. Deitz was made head of the Horticulture Department in 1924 and chief instructor of all fruit courses. At this time, the Horticulture Department offered such course titles as Vegetable Gardening, Fruit Growing, Floriculture, Landscaping Gardening, Farm Forestry, and Beekeeping.

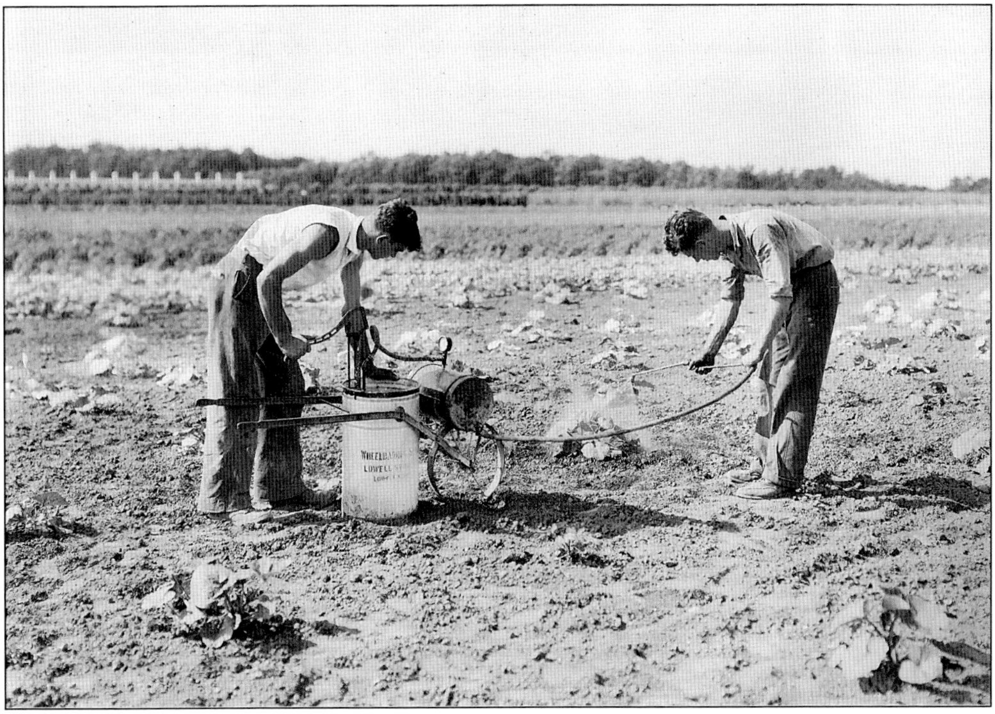

Two institute students are spraying melons with a hand pump in 1929. An important part of their educational experience was learning how to control diseases and insect pests. They are applying this skill in an agricultural assignment.

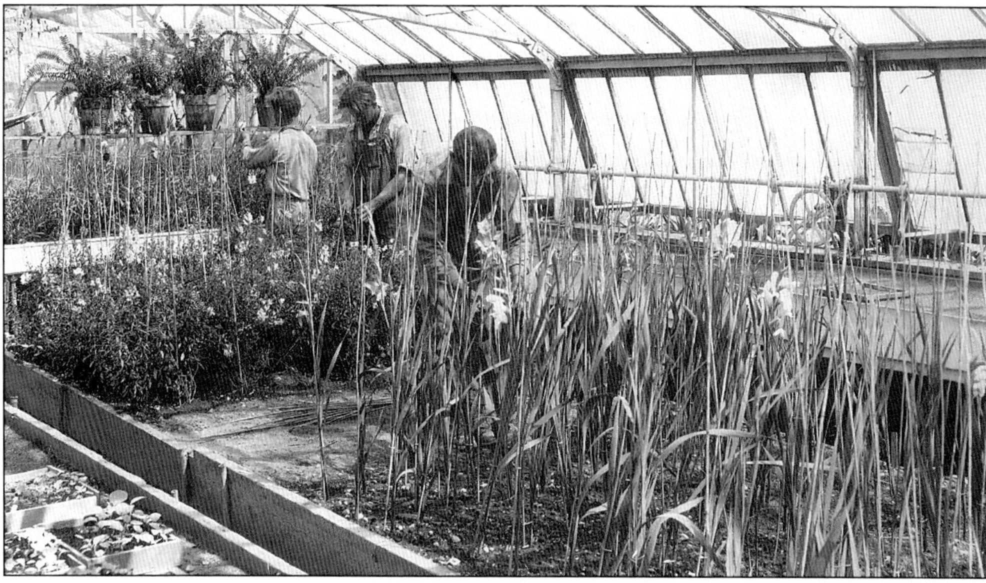

Students are cultivating flowers in the old greenhouse in the top photograph, while below snapdragons and sweet peas are growing. There were several greenhouses, as they were added on to the original structure when greenhouses were donated to the institute from several Long Island estates. The dome was part of a conservatory donated in 1932 from the Arnold Estate in West Islip and was reconstructed next to the original greenhouse in 1943. Two wings of the conservatory had been donated by the DeForest Estate in Cold Spring Harbor in 1934. Because of the maintenance costs, especially utility expenses, the old greenhouse was torn down in the 1980s and was replaced with a new one.

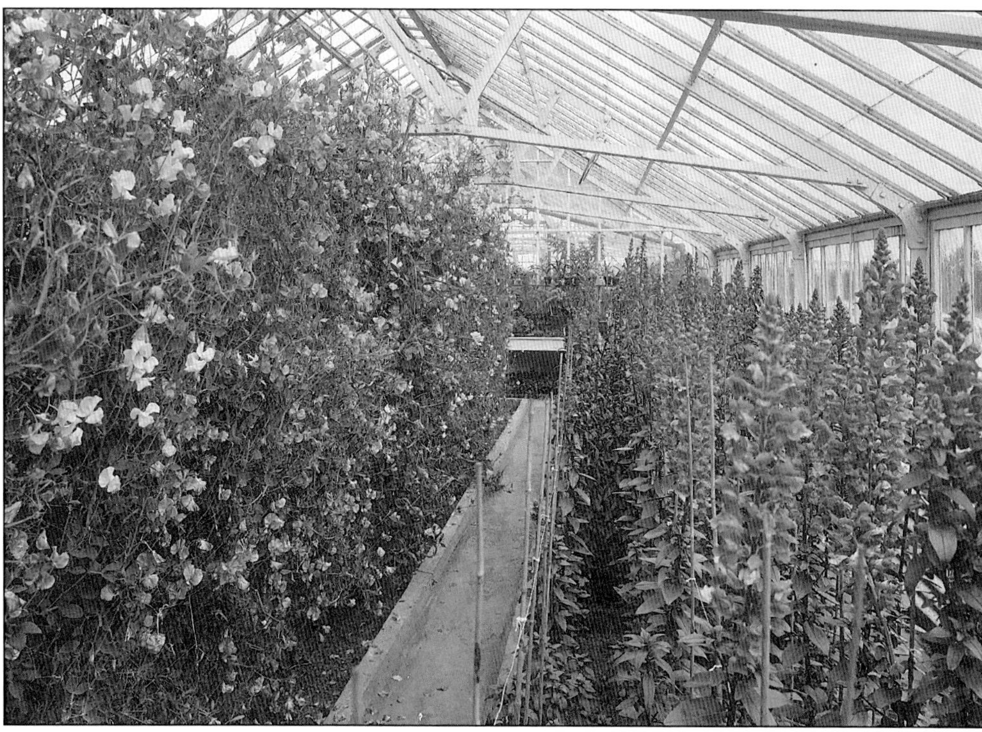

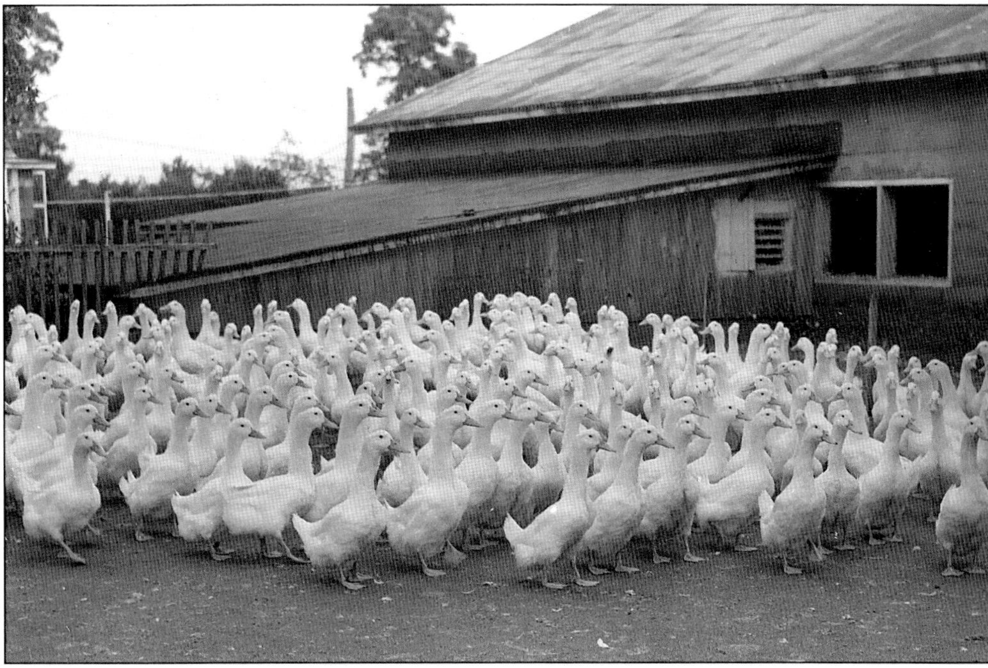

Long Island has been famous for its production of high-quality ducks. This 1930s duck farm is in Center Moriches, where Arthur Schoener, a student of the institute, was employed. Faculty member Locke James made an evaluation of Shoener's work at the duck farm. Such a procedure ascertained the student's effectiveness on the job and therefore completed the evaluation of his work.

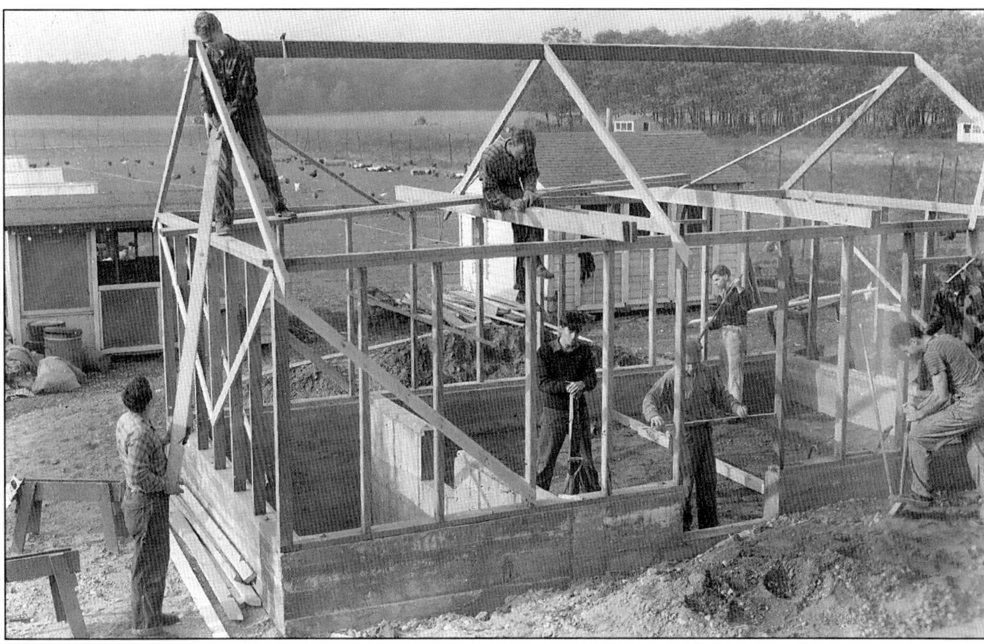

Students are constructing a storage pen and coal bin in the Poultry Plant area in 1935. Many skills were learned from this on-the-job assignment: carpentry, surveying, engineering, and concrete work. Thus, students combined theory and practice under the supervision of an instructor.

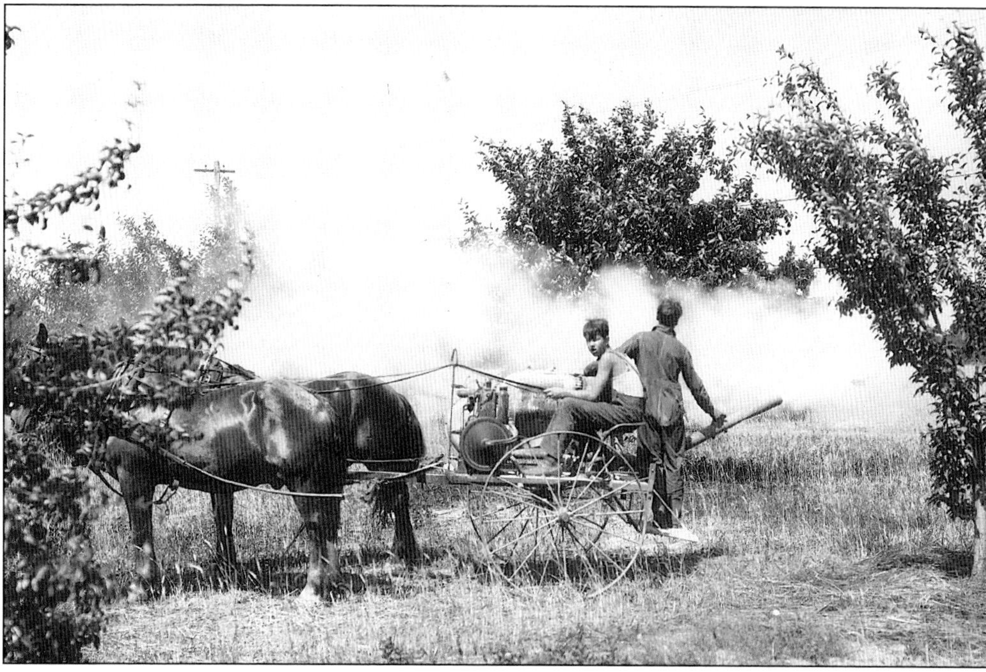

These horticulture students are applying their knowledge and technique learned in the classroom in the process of spraying, pruning, planting, thinning, and harvesting. The fruits that are considered include the following: pomaceous fruits, such as apples and pears; drupaceous fruits, such as peaches, plums, and cherries; small fruits, such as strawberries, raspberries, and blueberries; and grapes. By 1940, facilities in the horticultural program included shrub collection, a pinetum, gardens, over 5,000 square feet of greenhouse space, a nursery, and seed beds. Combined with all the study of the theory of horticulture and agriculture, and its underlying sciences, was a maximum of actual fieldwork.

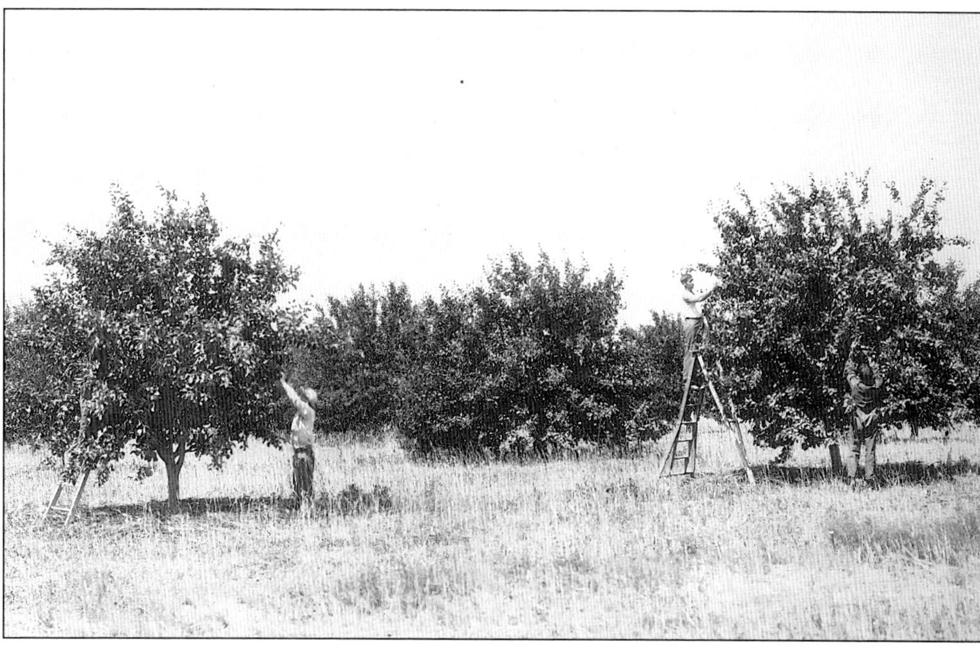

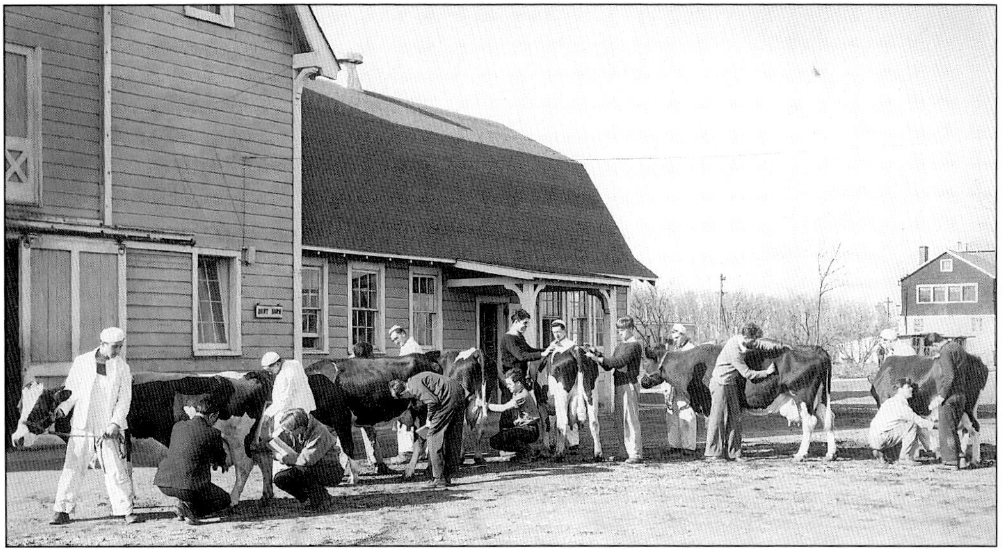

Students prepare animals for the annual livestock contest in 1931. The competition maximized the students' ability. At this time, Director Halsey B. Knapp believed that the assets of the institute land had to be adapted to the Long Island region and used in a variety of ways. Moreover, much of the inventory of the institute contributed to the success of the educational mission. There was a herd of cattle, chiefly Holstein and Jerseys; a herd of Berkshire and Duroc Jersey swine; a flock of Shropshire sheep; a flock of 2,000 laying hens; a 20-acre fruit plantation; several acres of gardens under irrigation; five teams of horses; and all the leading makes of farm and garden equipment.

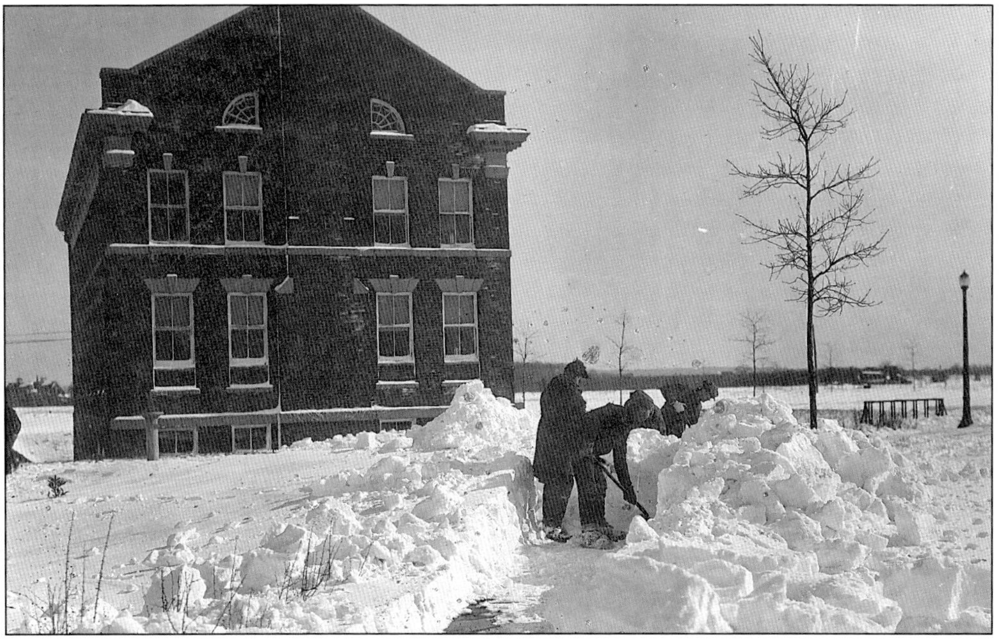

In this winter scene in the mid-1930s, students are shoveling snow to clear a path to Cutler Hall in the background. The expanse of land presented an unhurried scene that no longer exists on Long Island. Also, it is evident that the students at that time performed functions beyond the normal educational requirements. Such a fact even applied to the faculty.

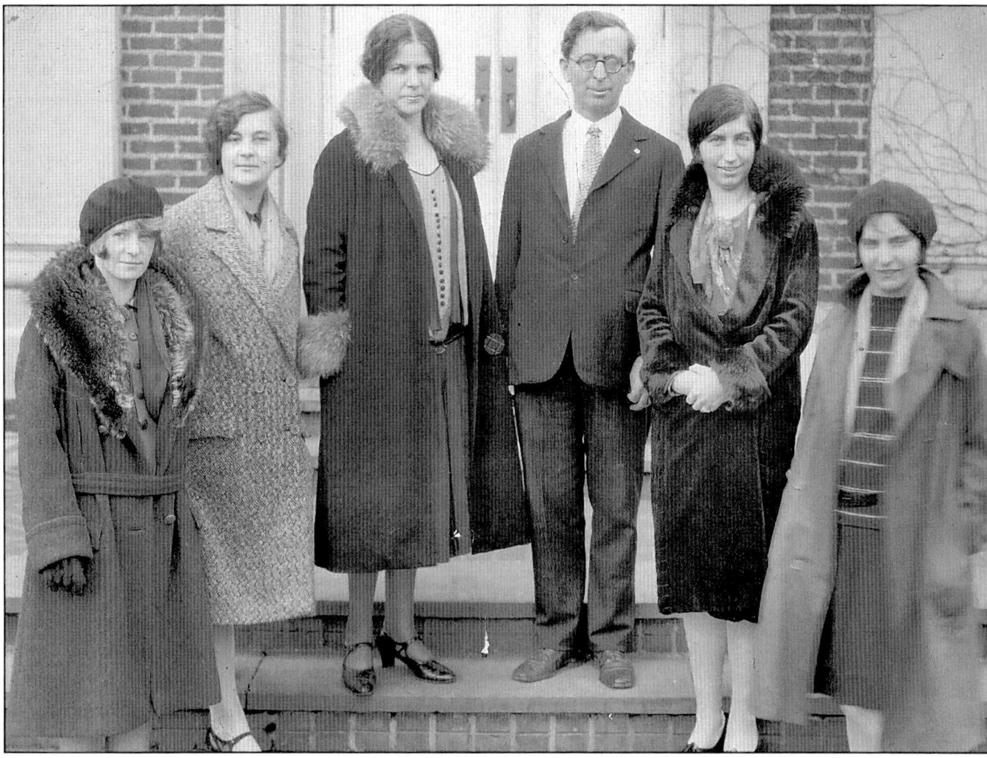

Part of the success of the institute was due to the hardworking staff members who remained in the background. In this 1927 photograph, the office staff poses together in front of Cutler Hall. They were loyal to Director Knapp and committed to carrying out the mission of the institute. Note the women's style of clothing and how it differs from contemporary style.

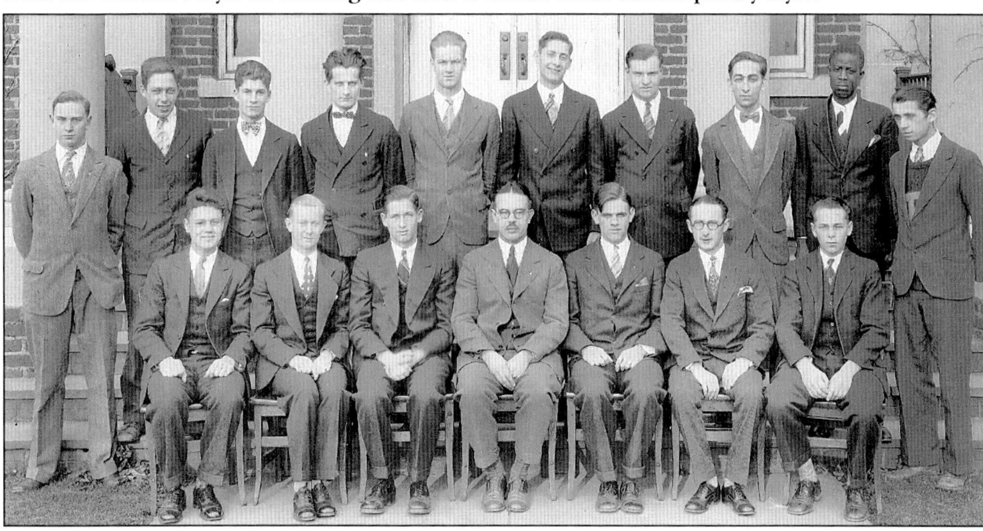

The graduating class of 1929 poses in front of the horticulture building (Hicks Hall). The men's formal style of clothing has changed very little in more than seven decades. While students came to the institute in 1930 primarily from New York State, the largest number coming from Long Island, there were students enrolled from such distant places as Rhode Island, Massachusetts, Connecticut, New Jersey, Pennsylvania, Egypt, Greece, Guatemala, Romania, and Bulgaria.

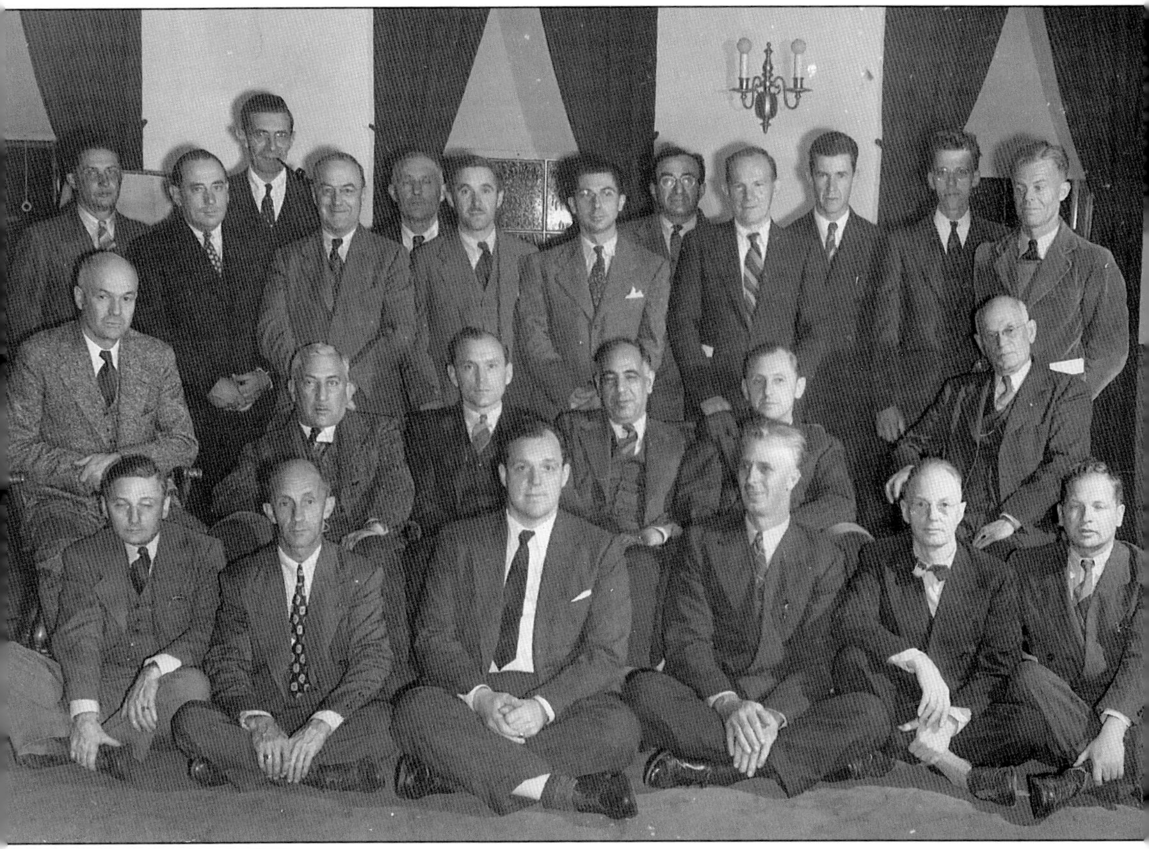

This rare group photograph of the faculty in 1938 reveals an all white male identity, not unusual for the period, although the student body was fully integrated. Shown, from left to right, are the following: (front row) Horton, Cutler, Roesch, Patterson, Hersman, and Pyenson; (middle row) Knapp, MacDougall, Foote, Musa, Wedell, and Stephens; (back row) Lewis, Stockbridge, Franke, Nevelle, Ingham, Rissmeyer, Wicks, Scarci, James, Fairbanks, Goetz, and Gray.

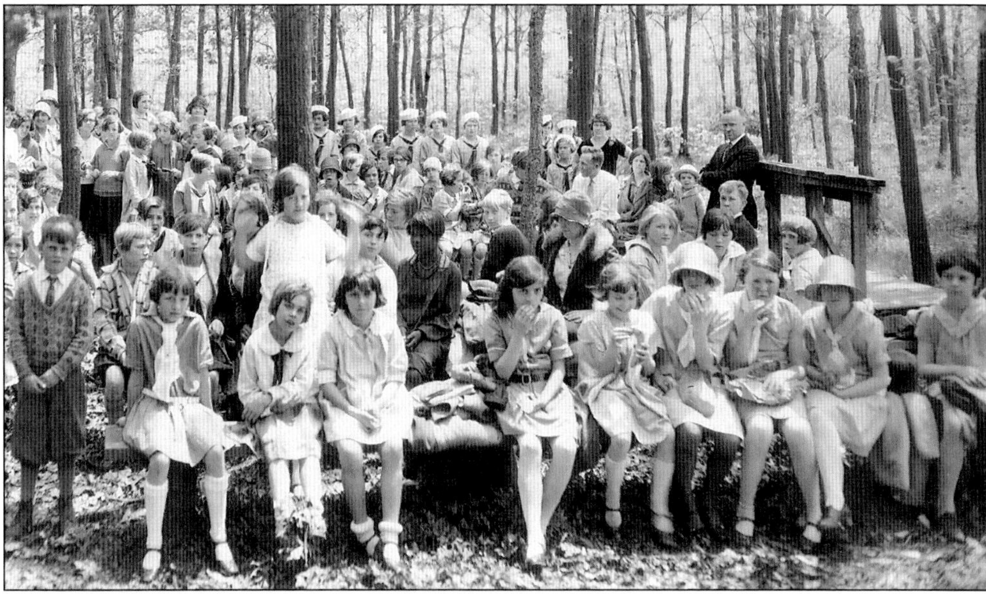

A large group of 4-H children is in the institute's wooded area beyond the poultry plant in 1931. They have gathered for a visit from Gov. Franklin D. Roosevelt during an Open House Program. Governor Roosevelt went on to win the presidential election in 1932. Outdoor classes also were held on this spot when weather permitted.

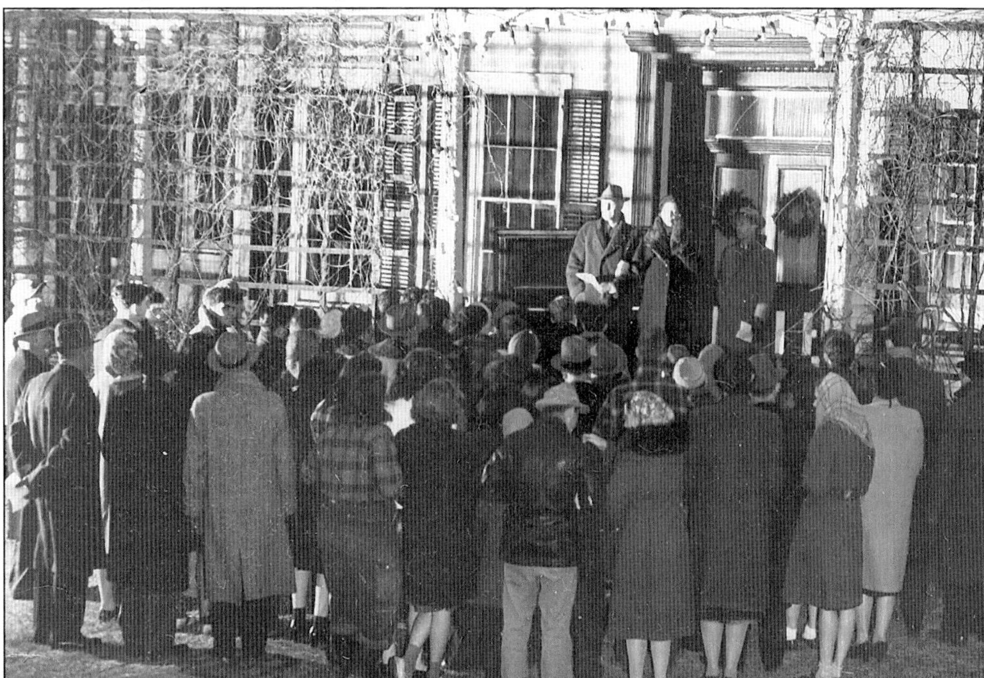

In this late-1930s photograph, students and faculty present Director Mrs. Knapp with a carol around Christmastime in front of the Mott House. Knapp returned the greeting with a Christmas message. The faculty and student body were small enough at that time to enjoy an event in this way.

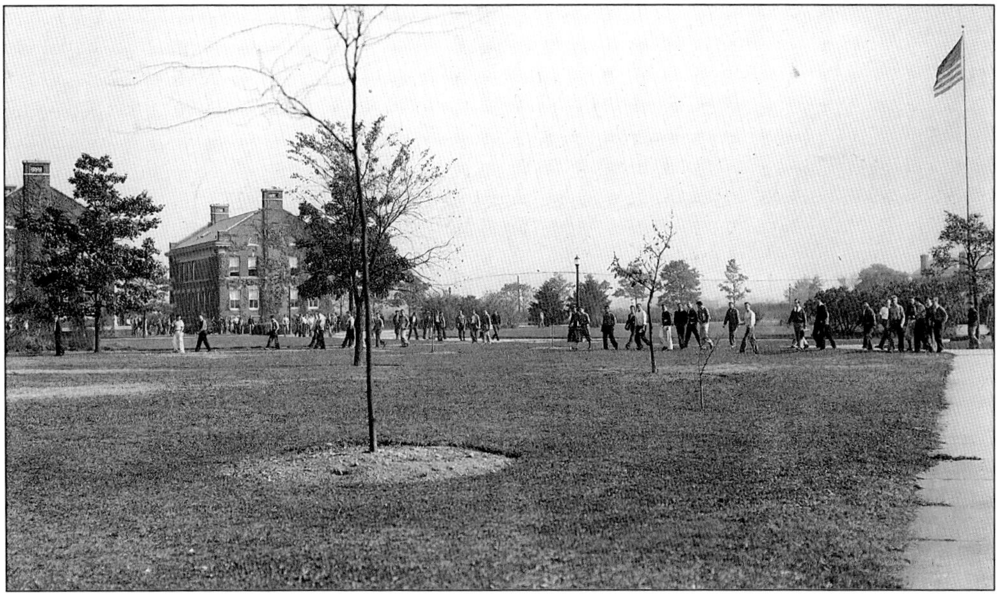

This wide campus view shows students changing classes in the early 1930s. The photograph was taken from the west side of the circle, looking toward Hicks Hall (left), Cutler Hall (center), and the Director's Cottage (extreme right). The students are moving in an orderly manner and appear very collegiate. The flagpole is to the right.

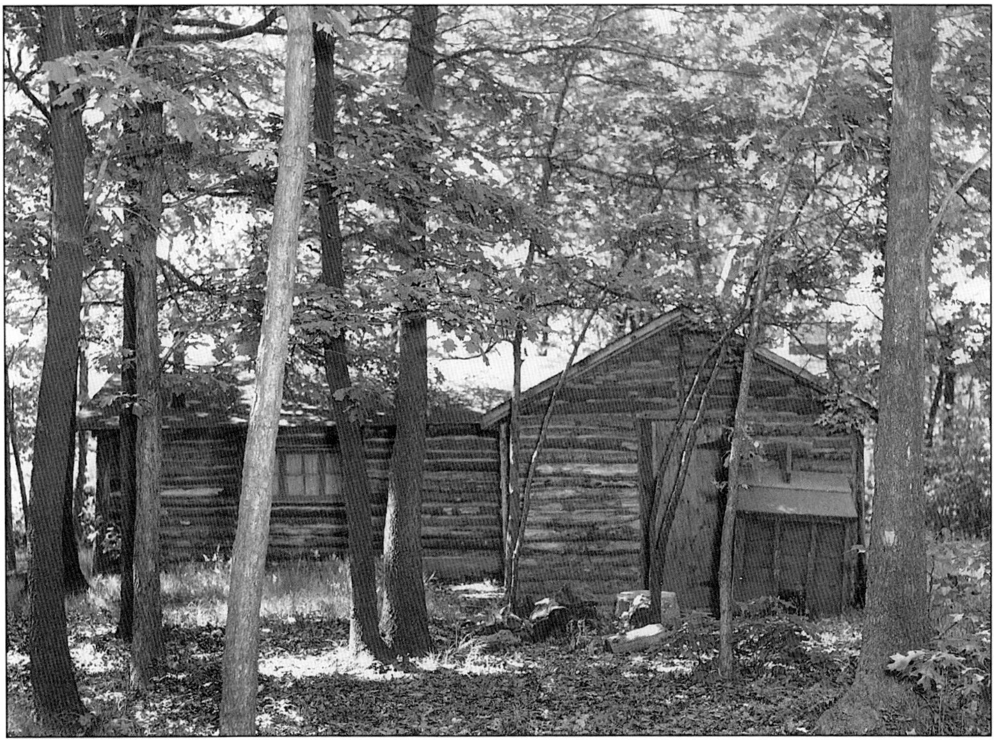

This unique log cabin stood in the secluded woodland at the edge of the campus. It was built in 1955 by students and faculty to offer an escape from the activities of study and work. The cabin featured a kitchen, two fireplaces, and a nearby picnic area. Because of a fire, it no longer exists.

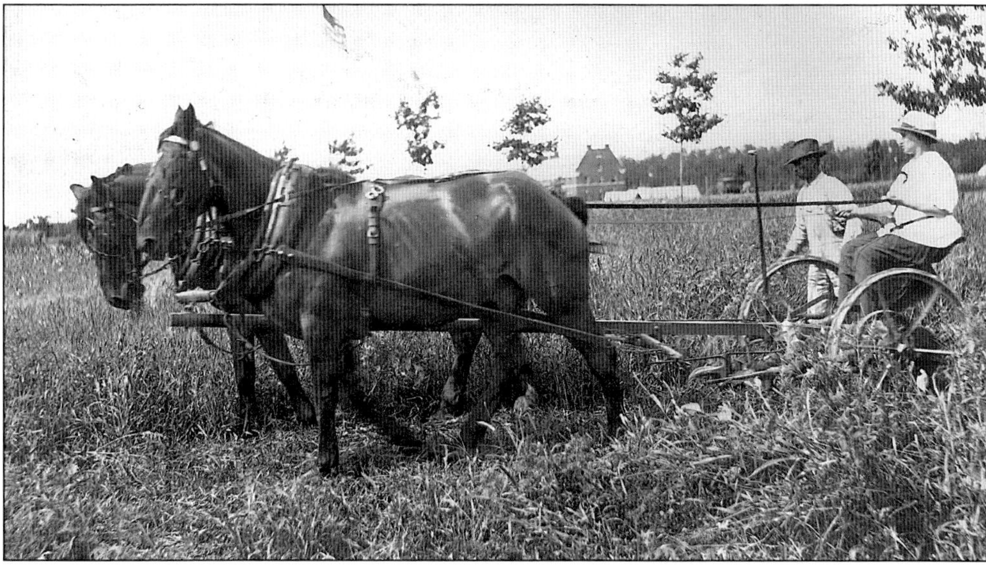

A female student receives instruction in mowing in the 1920s—not an unusual occurrence at the institute, since large numbers of women enrolled in regular and special courses. Hooper Hall, then a dormitory, is visible in the background. Technical education was supplemented by academic courses such as English, Farm Arithmetic, Economics, and Civics and Citizenship.

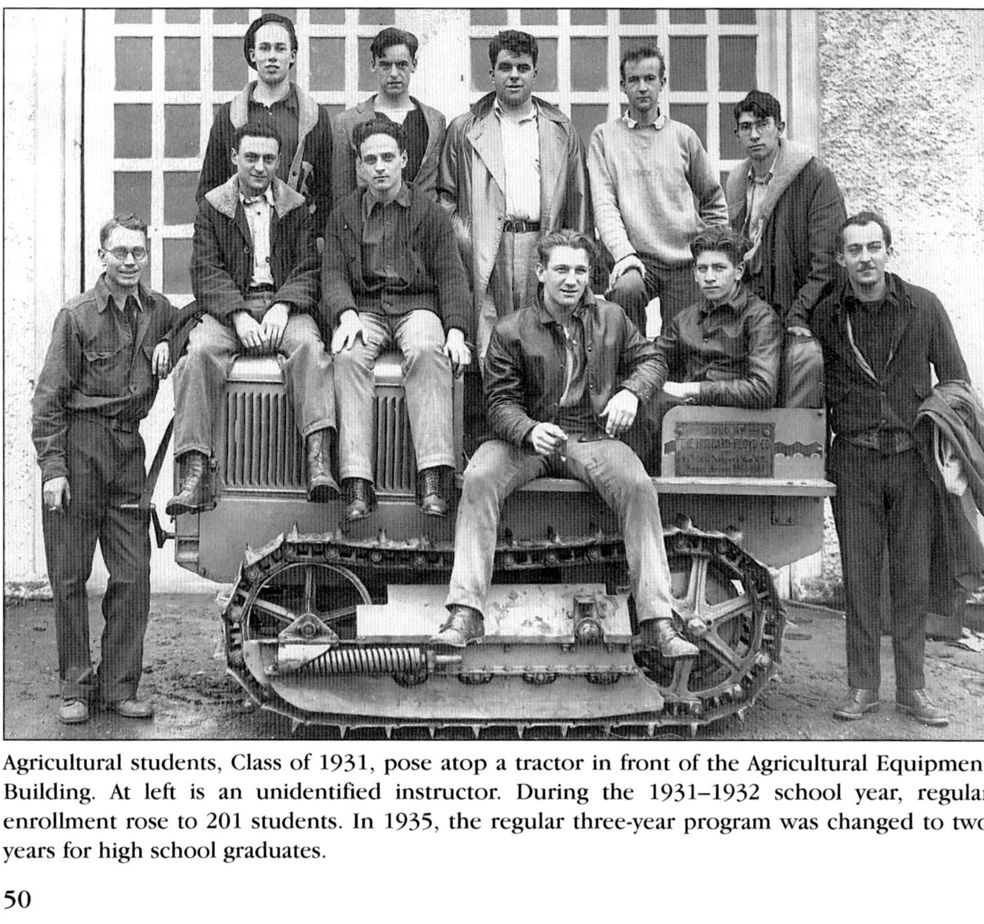

Agricultural students, Class of 1931, pose atop a tractor in front of the Agricultural Equipment Building. At left is an unidentified instructor. During the 1931–1932 school year, regular enrollment rose to 201 students. In 1935, the regular three-year program was changed to two years for high school graduates.

Three

THE GROWTH OF THE 1940S AND 1950S

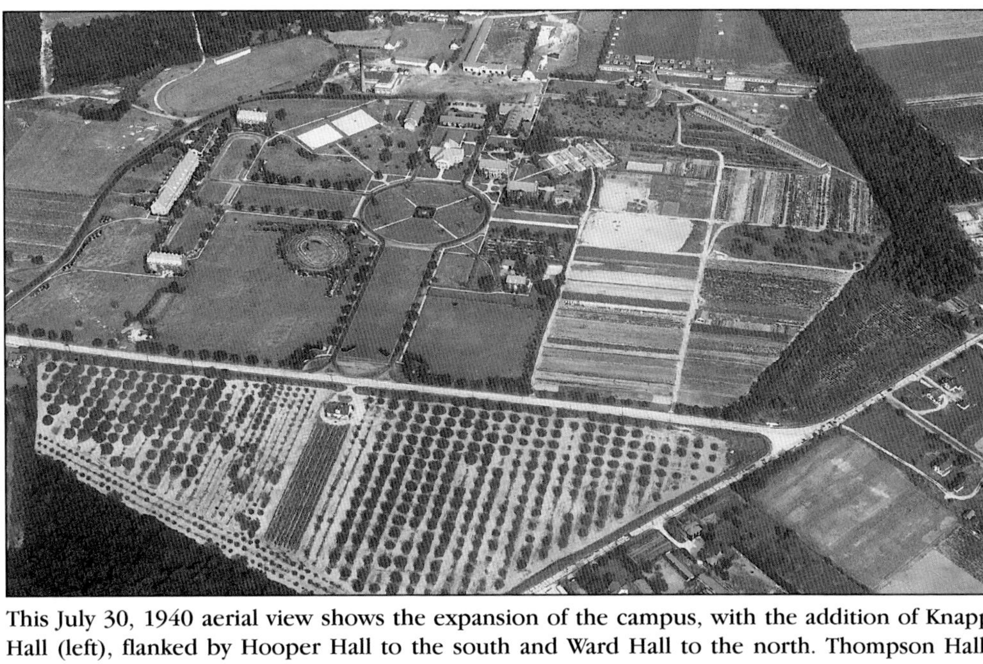

This July 30, 1940 aerial view shows the expansion of the campus, with the addition of Knapp Hall (left), flanked by Hooper Hall to the south and Ward Hall to the north. Thompson Hall, the administration building, is in the center at the top of the circle. To the right of Thompson Hall are Hicks Hall and Cutler Hall. To the lower right of the circle is the Director's Cottage. The greenhouses are to the right of Thompson Hall. Melville Road, on the southern border of the campus, runs west to east into Route 110. The total 1940 population of Nassau County and Suffolk County had increased to 604,103—considerably less than the 2.7 million population today. The photograph demonstrates the continuing agrarian pattern of the region. There are very few homes in the surrounding area.

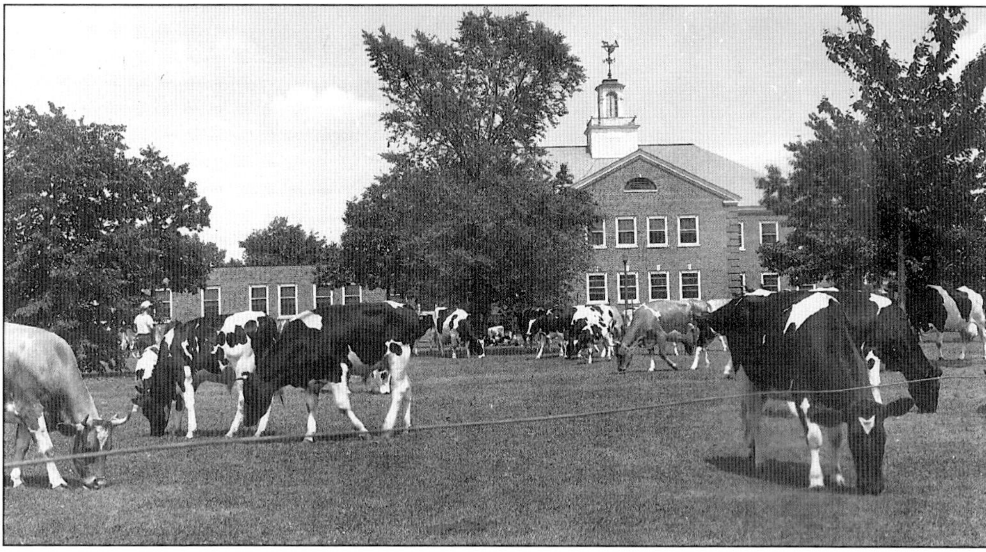

Livestock are grazing on the institute grounds in 1940. Thompson Hall, with cupola, is in the background. Then serving as the administration building, Thompson Hall was built at a cost of $124,388; it was dedicated on October 30, 1937. The governor of New York State, Herbert Lehman, attended the ceremony and identified George Lincoln Thompson as the "father of the institute." Senator Thompson introduced legislation that provided for the establishment of the school in 1912. The director's office, the library, the main office, the animal husbandry laboratories, and classrooms were housed here.

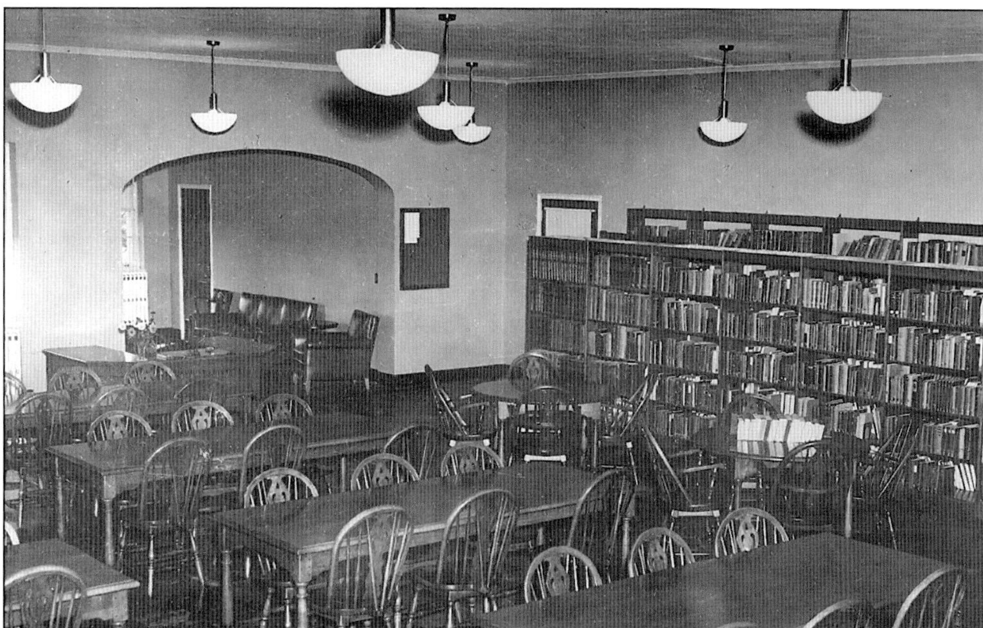

The institute's original library was located on the second floor of Thompson Hall in what is now Room 215. The library moved to Whitman Hall and, later, to its permanent location in Greenley Hall. Today, the library possesses an interesting collection of rare books, and the college archives are kept there.

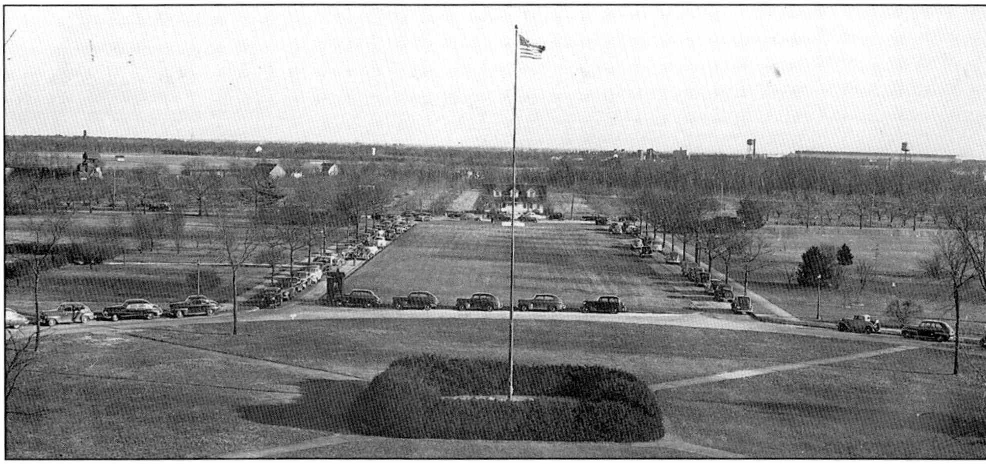

This photograph of the campus entrance was taken from the tower in Thompson Hall during the Country Life Program in 1949. The circle has become a permanent fixture and allows one to become oriented to the campus. The visitors' cars are parked neatly, with more of them entering at the left.

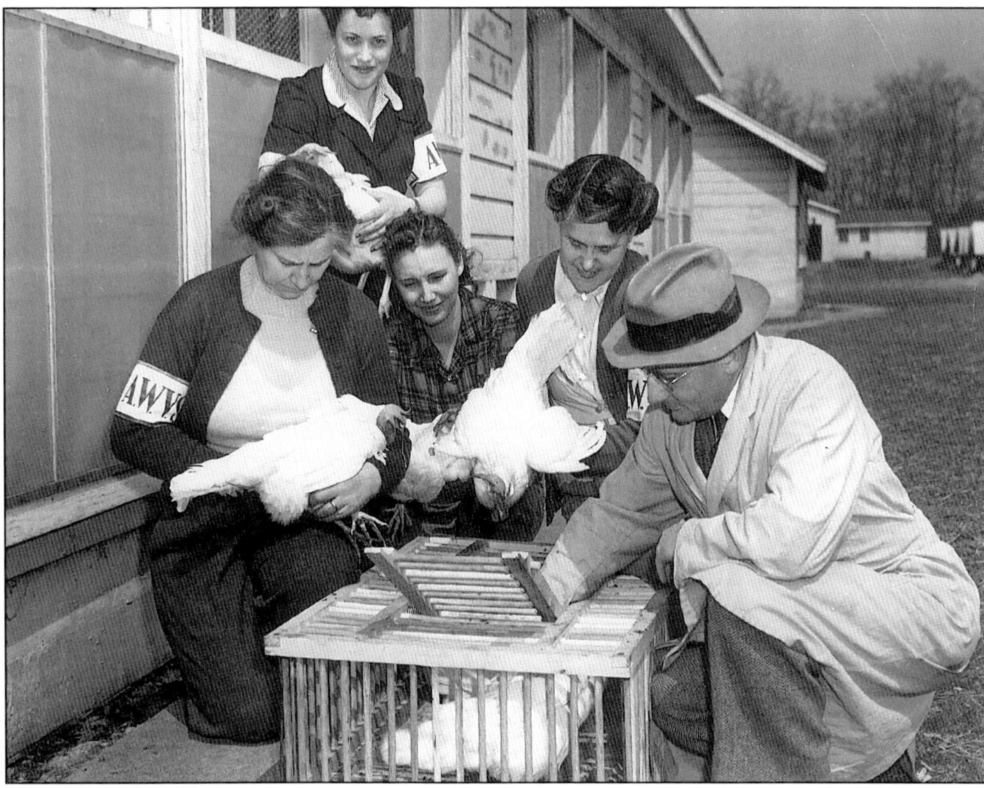

These special students are studying poultry raising in the early 1940s under D. Hart Horton, who was the head of the Poultry Department from 1927 to 1957. Horton Hall, named in his honor, is the present administration building. Through Horton's efforts, the poultry facilities were modernized, specifically the brooder houses, laying pens, incubators, and killing room. These women students were volunteer agricultural students and were contributing to the American war effort during WWII.

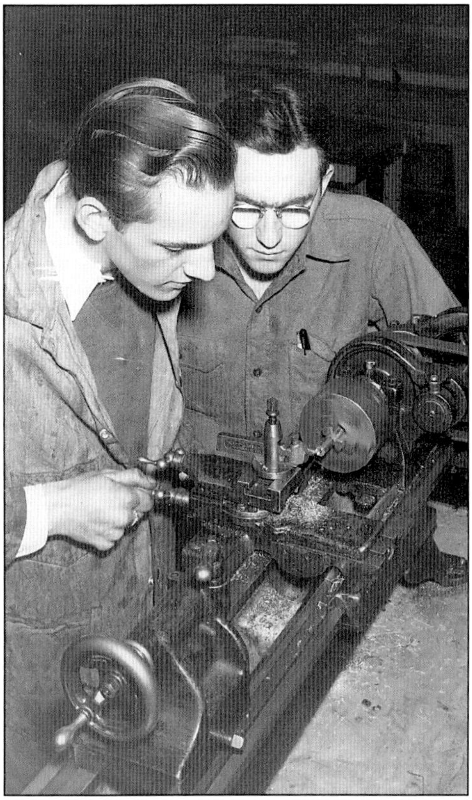

Two students in the Agricultural Equipment Building are applying their skill at a bench lathe during a Country Life Program in 1940. Under normal circumstances, students worked in small laboratory classes under the close supervision of an instructor. The educational philosophy of Director Knapp and his faculty was to have the students become proficient by performing the same operations over and over again, always seeking improvement until skill replaces awkwardness and satisfaction comes to a job well done.

Captain D. Robert MacDougal instructs students in the Agricultural Equipment Building Laboratory in 1940. Since instructors worked with small groups of students, a mutual respect developed among them. The instructors had to be expert at what they taught. Mrs. MacDougal was Director Knapp's secretary for many years.

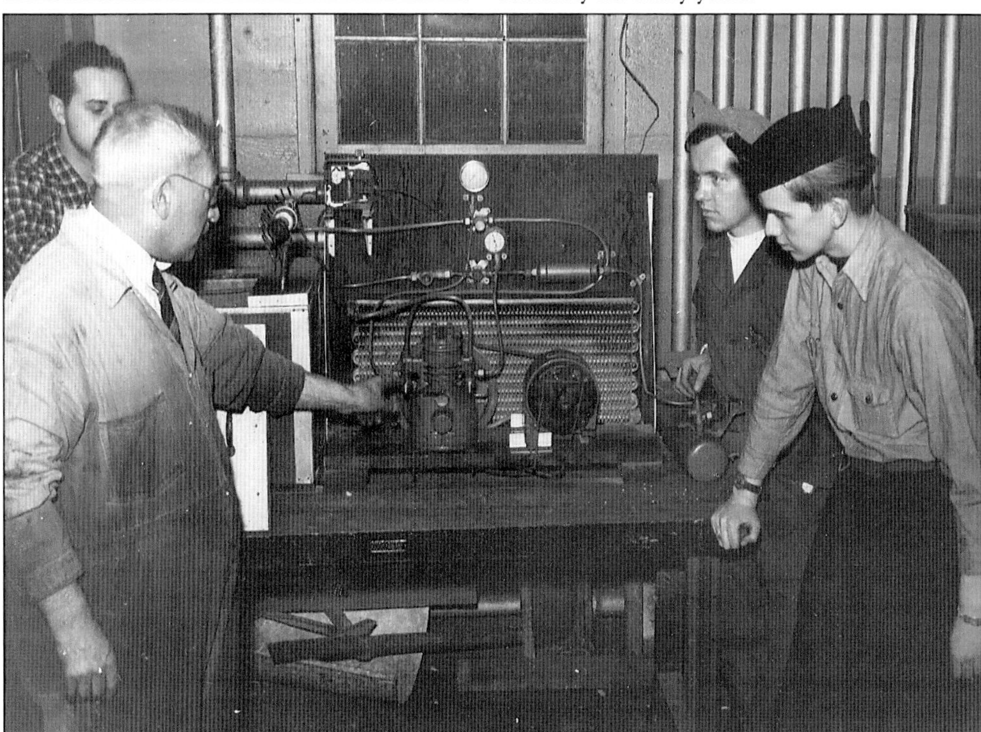

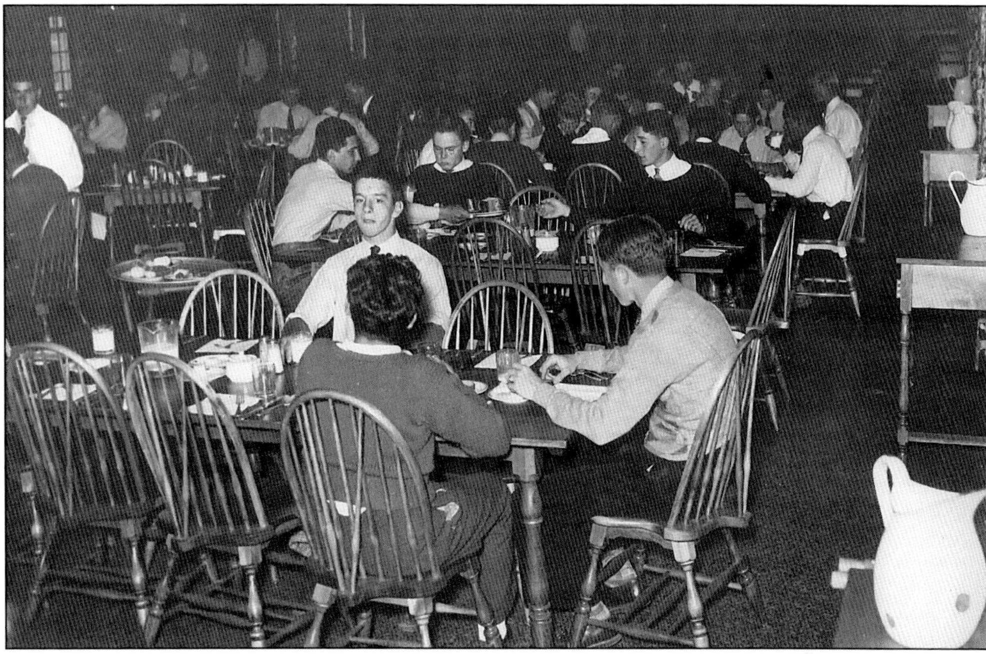

Students are at dinner in the dining hall of Knapp Hall, which was completed in 1937 at a cost of $226,905. It was named to honor Halsey B. Knapp, who guided the school successfully as director during its early years of growth, from 1923 to 1956. Note the formal pattern of the tables and chairs and that the students are dressed in white shirts and ties. They are drinking milk that was produced at the school dairy. Strict discipline was expected by all during the 1940s.

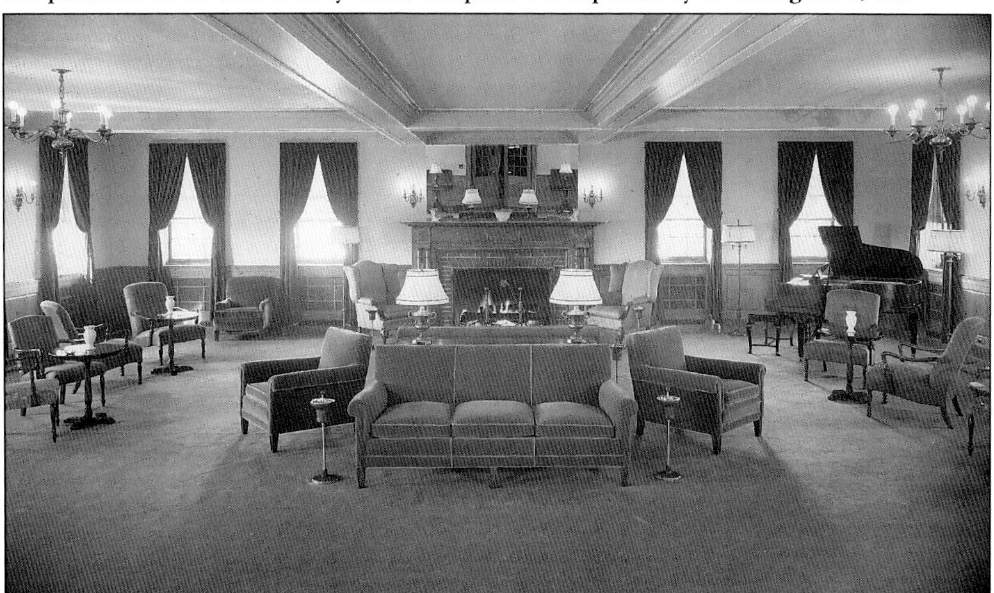

This lovely room is the Knapp Hall Lounge as it looked in 1940. Faculty meetings were held here, as well as lectures, classes, and social gatherings. It also served as a reading room. Note the piano, fireplace, and mantle. The room has been converted into the Fireside Lounge and is used for special functions.

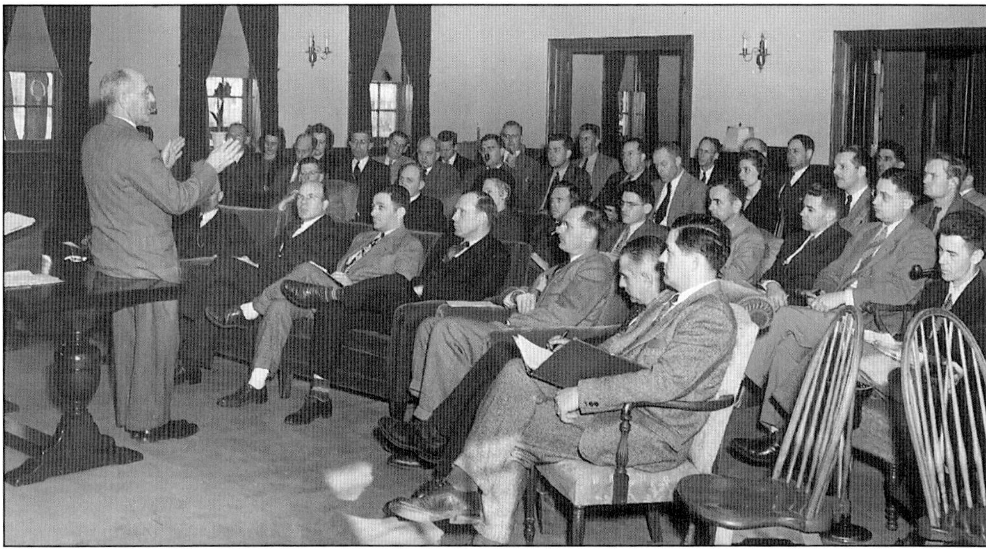

Prof. Lynn Emerson of the Cornell University faculty conducted an in-service course in the Knapp Hall Lounge in 1950. Attendance included all the faculty at the institute. The course, and many like them, was central to Director Knapp's philosophy that the faculty must constantly upgrade their knowledge.

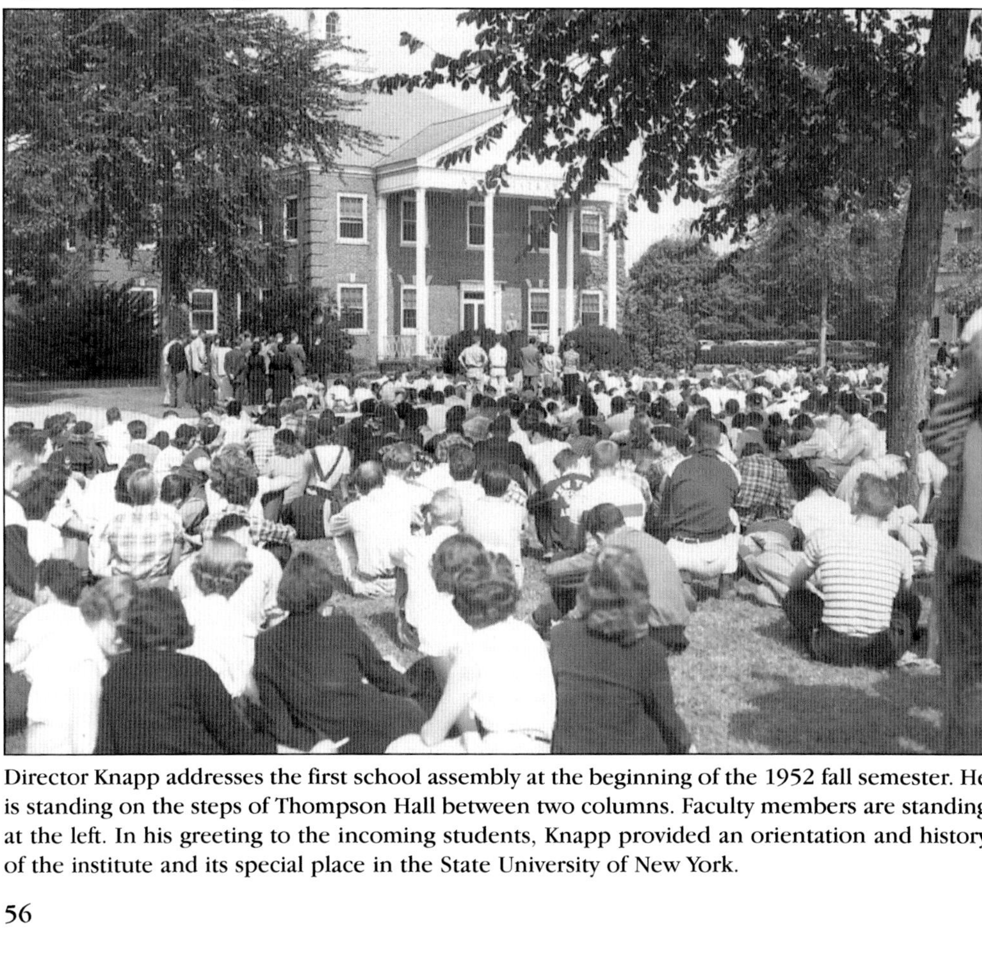

Director Knapp addresses the first school assembly at the beginning of the 1952 fall semester. He is standing on the steps of Thompson Hall between two columns. Faculty members are standing at the left. In his greeting to the incoming students, Knapp provided an orientation and history of the institute and its special place in the State University of New York.

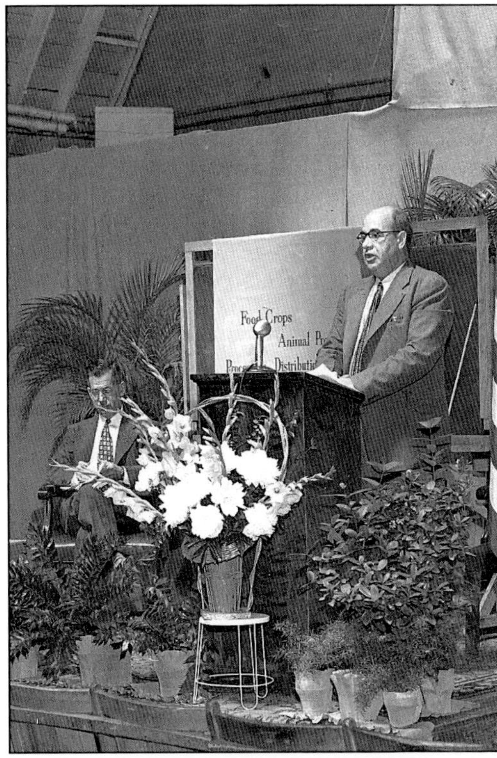

Prof. Rollo Wicks, Canton Agricultural and Technical College, served as chairperson for the general meeting of the two-year College Conference in 1950. The scene is in the old gymnasium-auditorium, now the bookstore.

Director Knapp presents the winning trophy to a student in the livestock contest at the Country Life Program in the late 1940s. The program remained popular through the years as the public supported it with large numbers of visitors in attendance. It was originally started in 1920 by the Farm Mechanics Department and was called the Farm and Home Equipment Show. During the next decade, other departments participated and put on their own displays and demonstrations. The event soon became know as the Country Life Program. As always, the entire faculty was in attendance to provide demonstrations and answer questions.

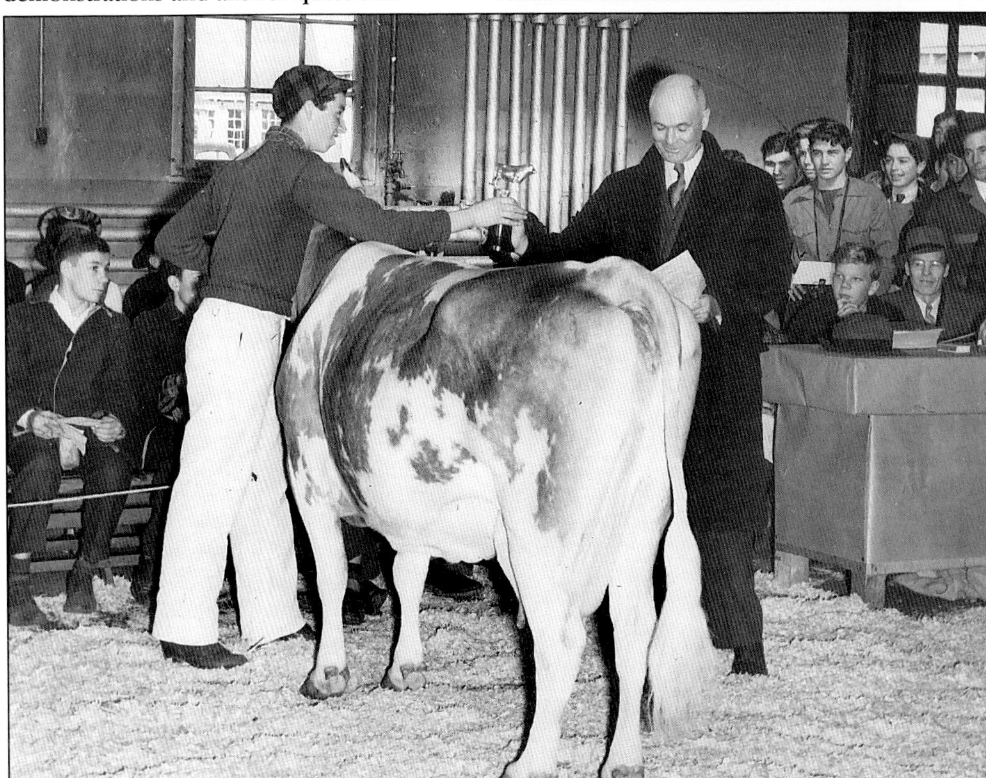

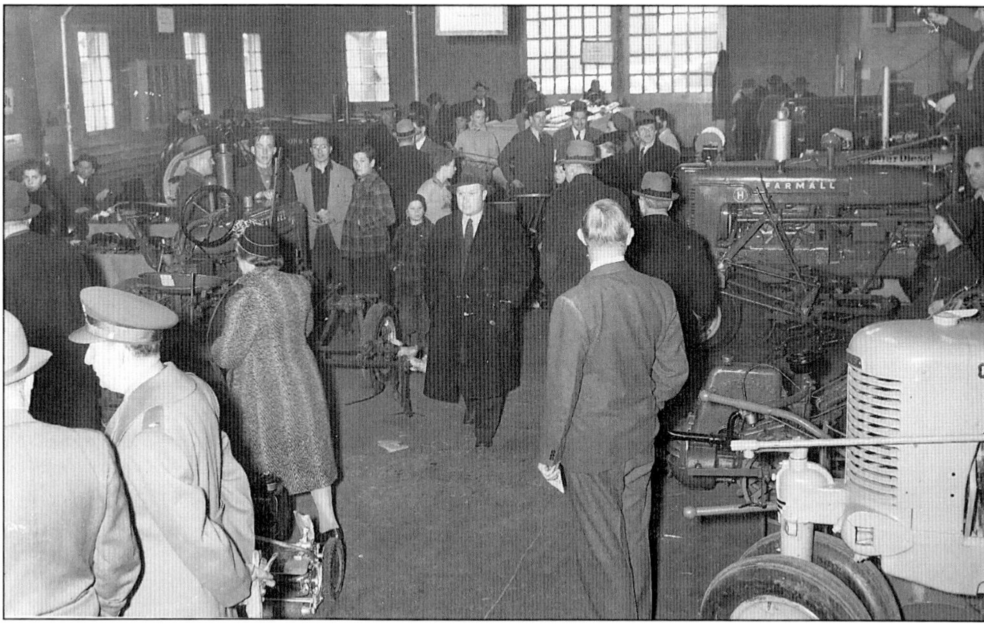

A large crowd gathers in Agricultural Equipment Building during the Country Life Program immediately after WWII. Among the many features during this four-day program were a Victory Garden; the Annual Farm and Home Equipment Exhibit; the Long Island Baby Chick and Egg Show; and Farm Machinery and Tractor Repair. The Country Life Program had been curtailed during WWII.

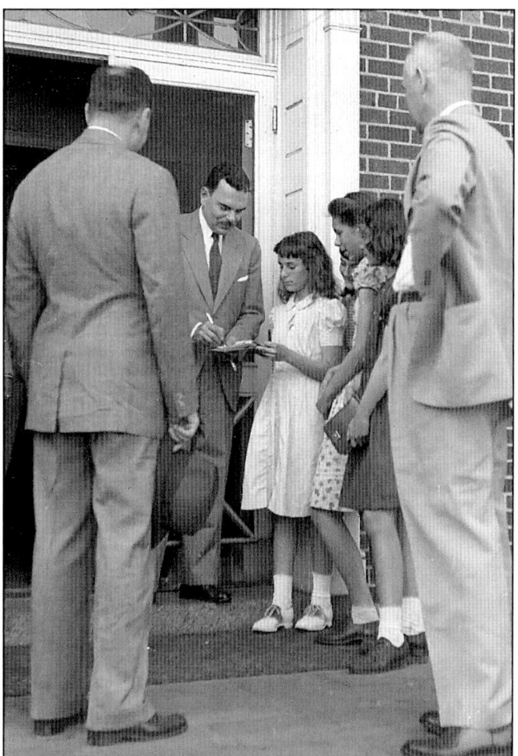

On June 12, 1947, Gov. Thomas E. Dewey visited Nassau County to inspect the state housing and educational facilities for veterans of WWII. He visited the Campus Village at the institute, where veterans and their families lived while they studied. He entered some of the homes and greeted the residents. He expressed satisfaction with what he saw. Governor Dewey retired to Thompson Hall for refreshments and signed autographs as he left the building. Governor Dewey is second from left. Director Knapp is at right.

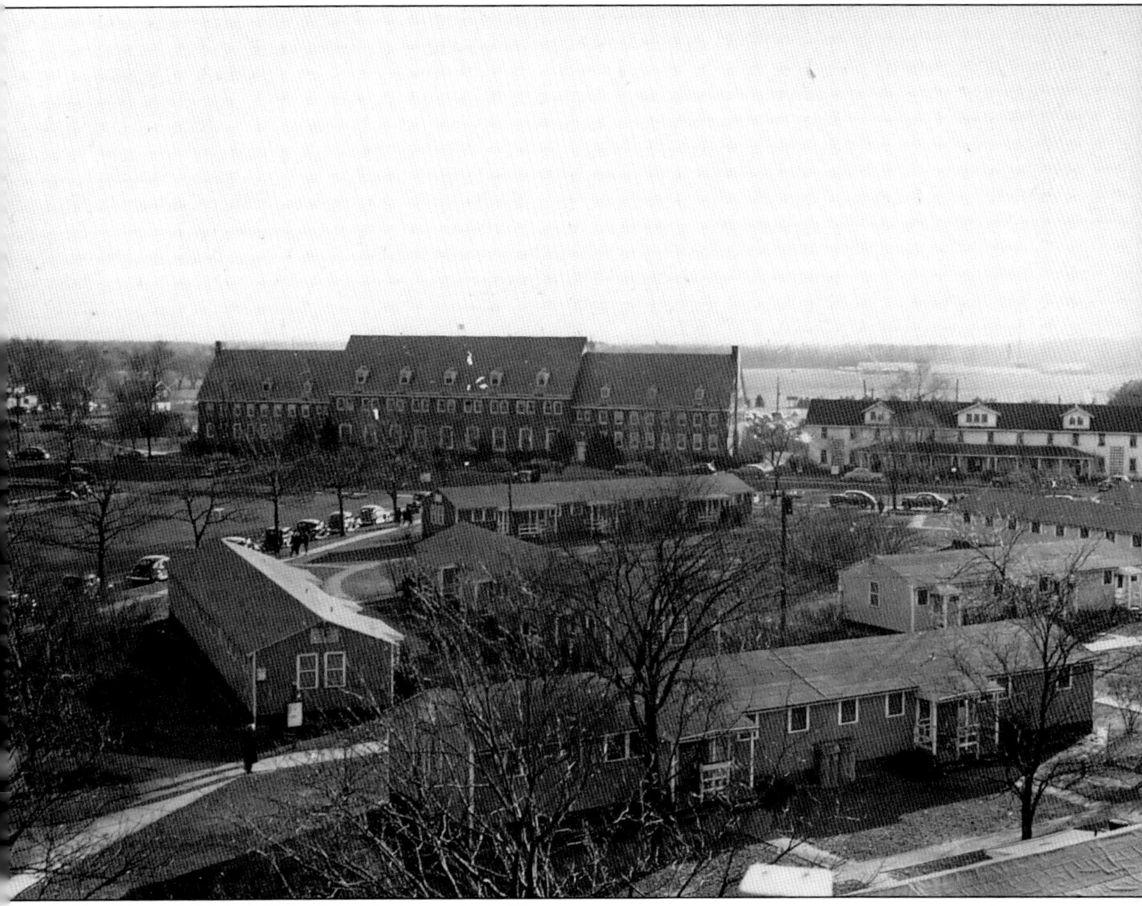

This is a panoramic view of the Campus Village from the tower of Thompson Hall in 1949. The Campus Village included temporary apartments for WWII veterans and their families in the area where Whitman Hall now stands. Knapp Hall is in the background, left center. To the right of Knapp Hall is a dormitory that was later demolished. This miniature community lasted from 1946 to 1956, helping to relieve the postwar housing shortage. The 1948 yearbook described the Campus Village as representing "a wide range of family life, from newlyweds to old married folk of ten years. The present population is 35 families, which includes 20 children. The birth rate is undoubtedly the highest in the country."

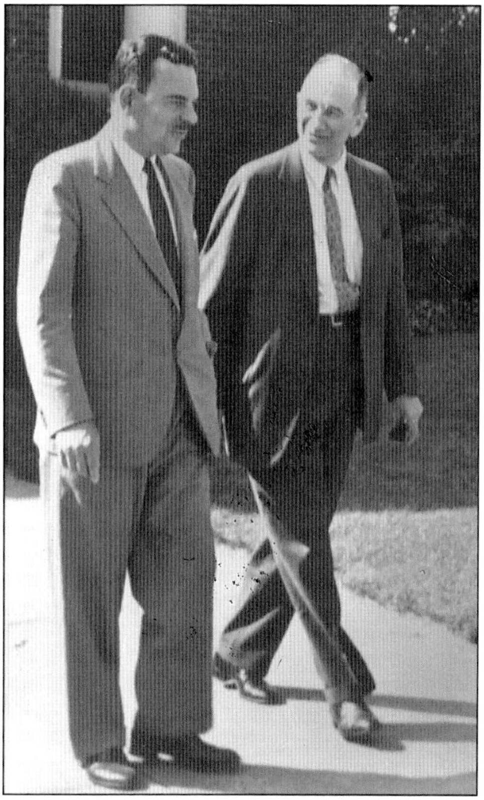

Gov. Thomas E. Dewey and Suffolk County Republican party leader Rep. W. Kingsland Macy leave Thompson Hall to visit other parts of the campus on June 12, 1947. Dewey had been defeated by Pres. Franklin D. Roosevelt in the 1944 election. He again received the presidential nomination in 1948 and was defeated again, this time by Harry S. Truman in the greatest political upset in national politics. Everywhere Dewey went on campus, he was introduced as "the next president of the United States."

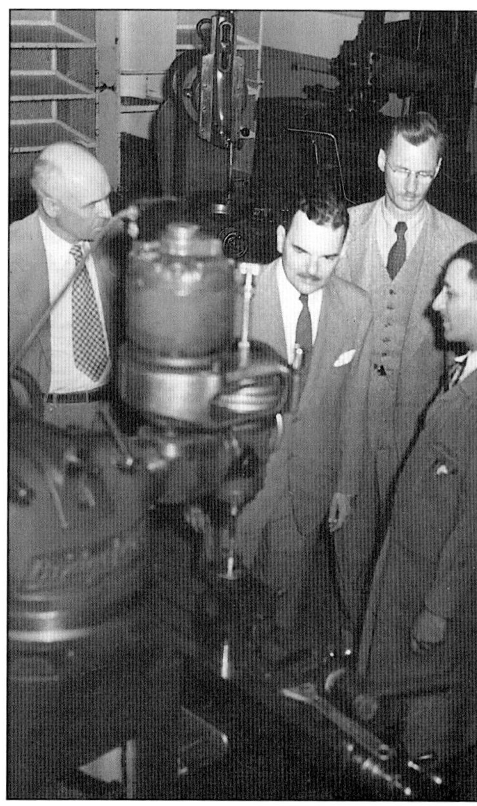

Governor Dewey remained on campus to visit this laboratory with the latest instructional equipment displayed. Shown, from left to right, are Knapp, Dewey, David W. Allee, William Nastri, and Herman T. Stichman. Allee was the head of the new Industrial Technical Division, which had been established in 1946 on Conklin Street, Farmingdale. Nastri was an instructor, and Stichman was the New York State housing commissioner. Upon leaving the campus, Governor Dewey expressed satisfaction with school and its facilities.

A student picks peaches in the orchard during the 1941 harvest. The Fruit Growing course was taught by Prof. Norman Foote, who was born in Malone, New York, and graduated from Malone High School, West Nottingham Academy in Maryland, and Cornell University. According to the 1940–1941 horticulture catalog, the course addressed the planting of orchard and small fruits in the landscape, recognizing both utility and ornamental values. Other elements of the course included the selection of varieties, cultural requirements, and training and practice in pruning and thinning.

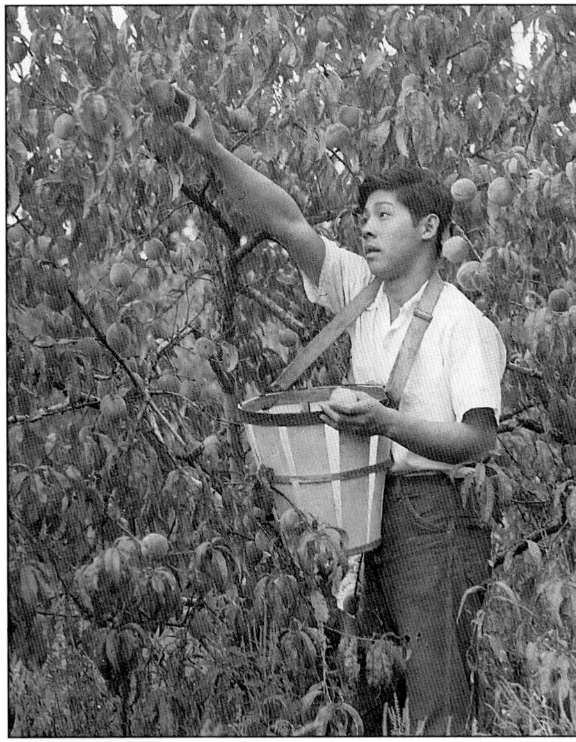

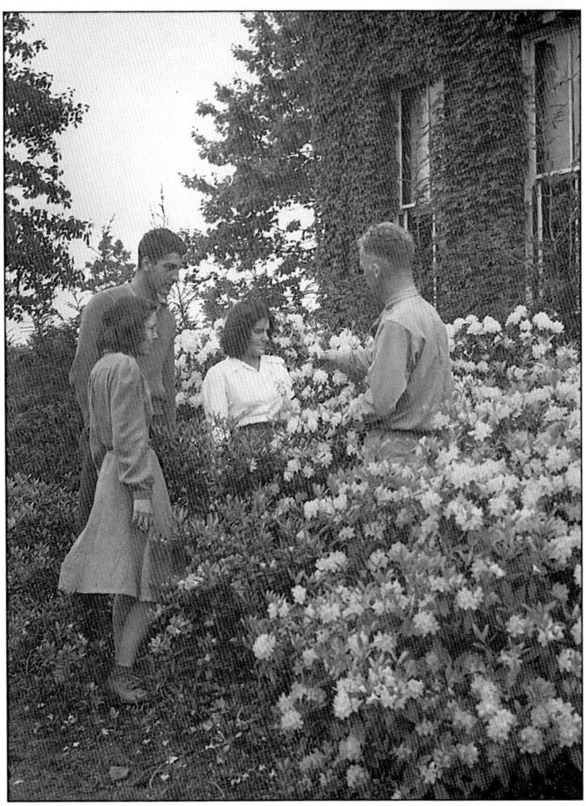

Prof. Harvey Gray, right, guides three floriculture students in designing flower borders through the medium of drawing. The garden schemes featured annuals, perennials, and bulbs and emphasized color, light, height, texture, and cultural demands. The young woman to the left of Professor Gray is Mary Izzo, daughter of an early-1920s graduate of Farmingdale.

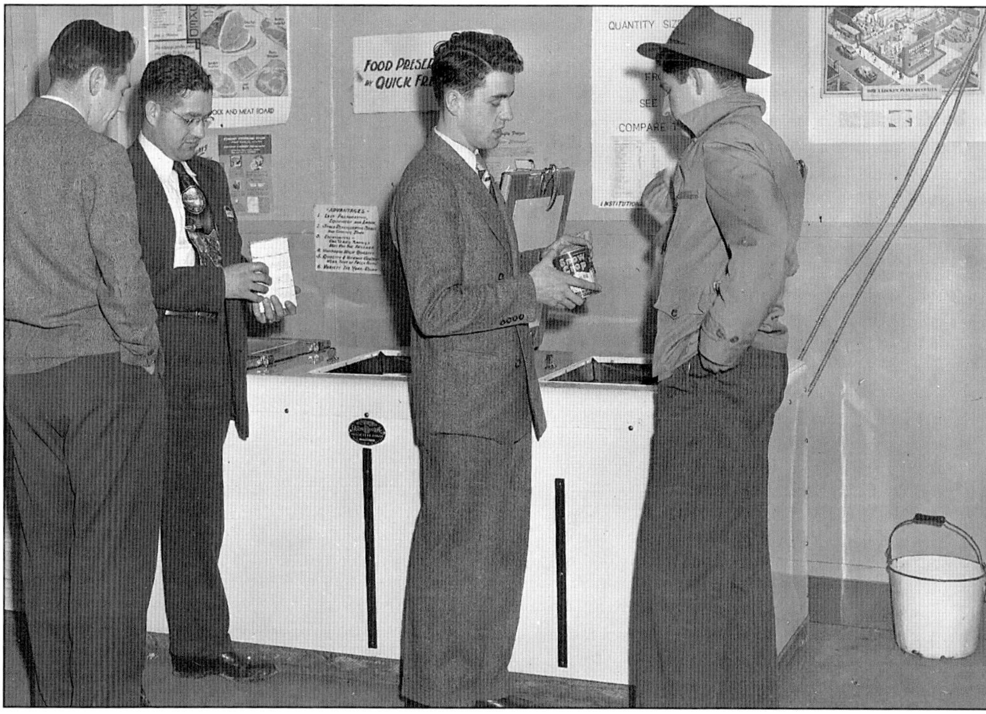

The 1950 Country Life–Open House Program was held for three days: February 23, 24, and 25. This exhibit and demonstration was named "Frozen Foods: Preparation, Packaging, and Storage." An instructor and three students are examining commercial packages of frozen foods. Shown from left to right are T. Hunter, George Silvera (instructor), R. Degenhardt, and J. Rueckheim.

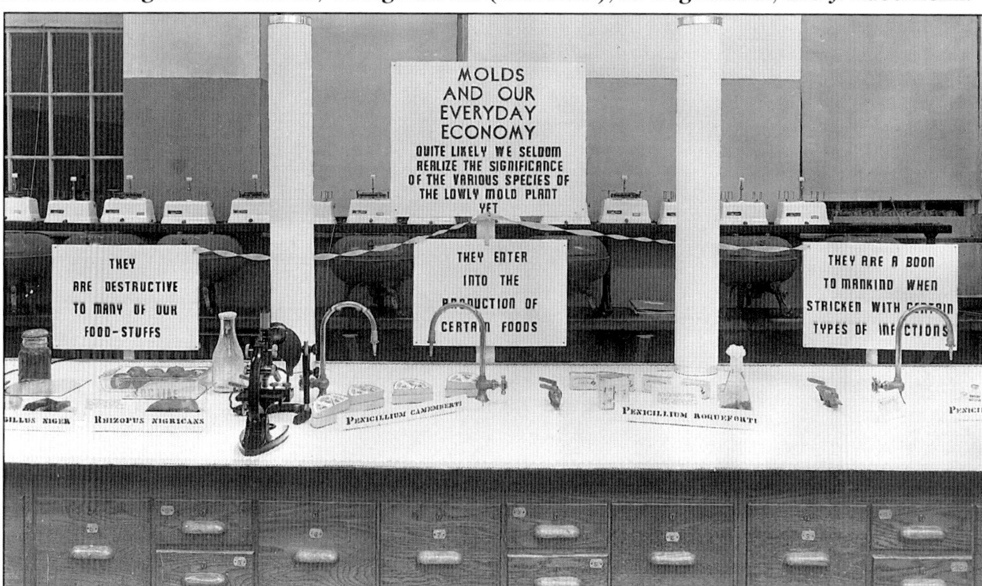

The 1950 Country Life–Open House Program presented this exhibit entitled "Molds and Our Everyday Economy." It was prepared by students in the bacteriology class and presented in a laboratory in Thompson Hall. The three types of molds were exhibited: those destructive of foodstuff; those used in the production of certain foods; and those used for medicinal purposes.

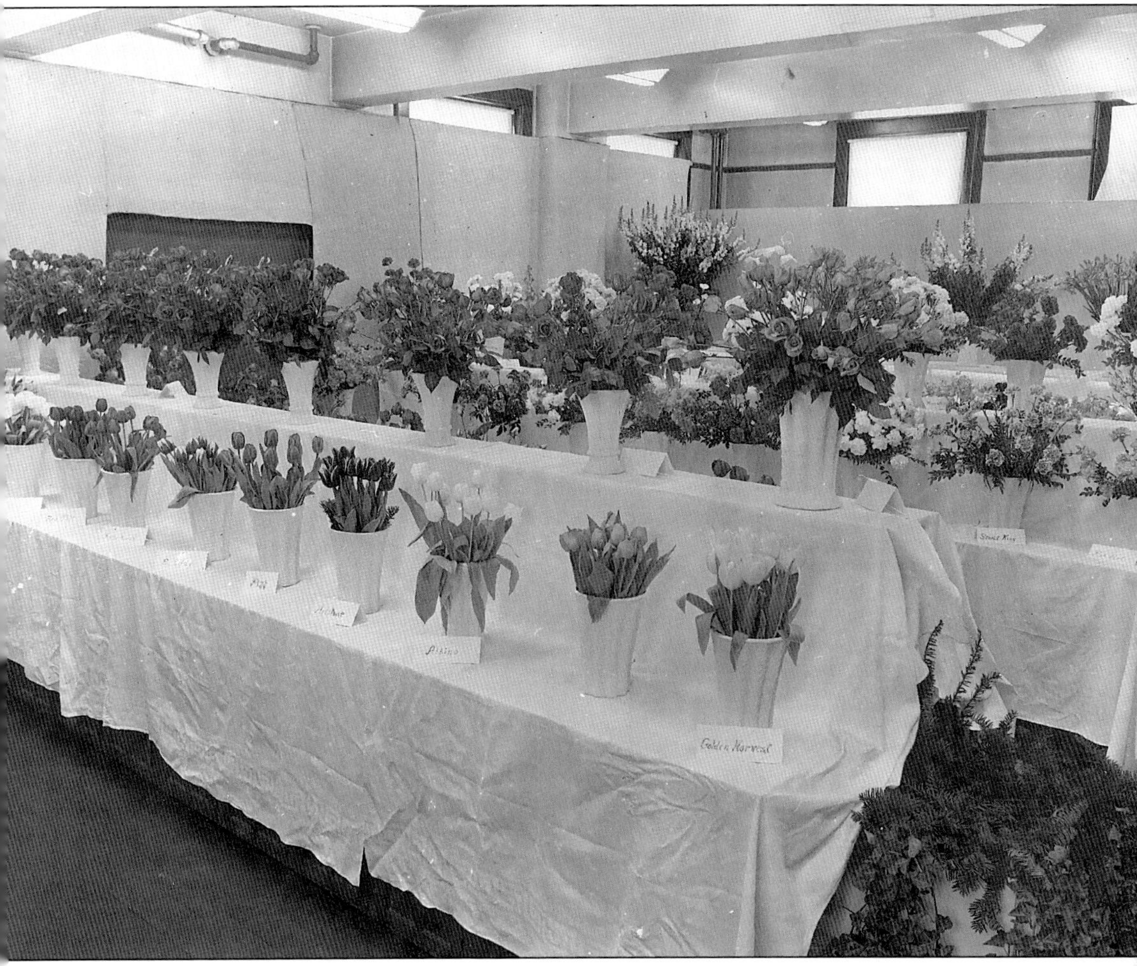

The Long Island Flower Industry participated in the 1950 Country Life–Open House Program. More than 50 Long Island flower growers exhibited many varieties of flowers that they cultivated. The exhibit was prepared by the institute's horticulture students who were majoring in floriculture. Graduates in the program began successful flower shop enterprises.

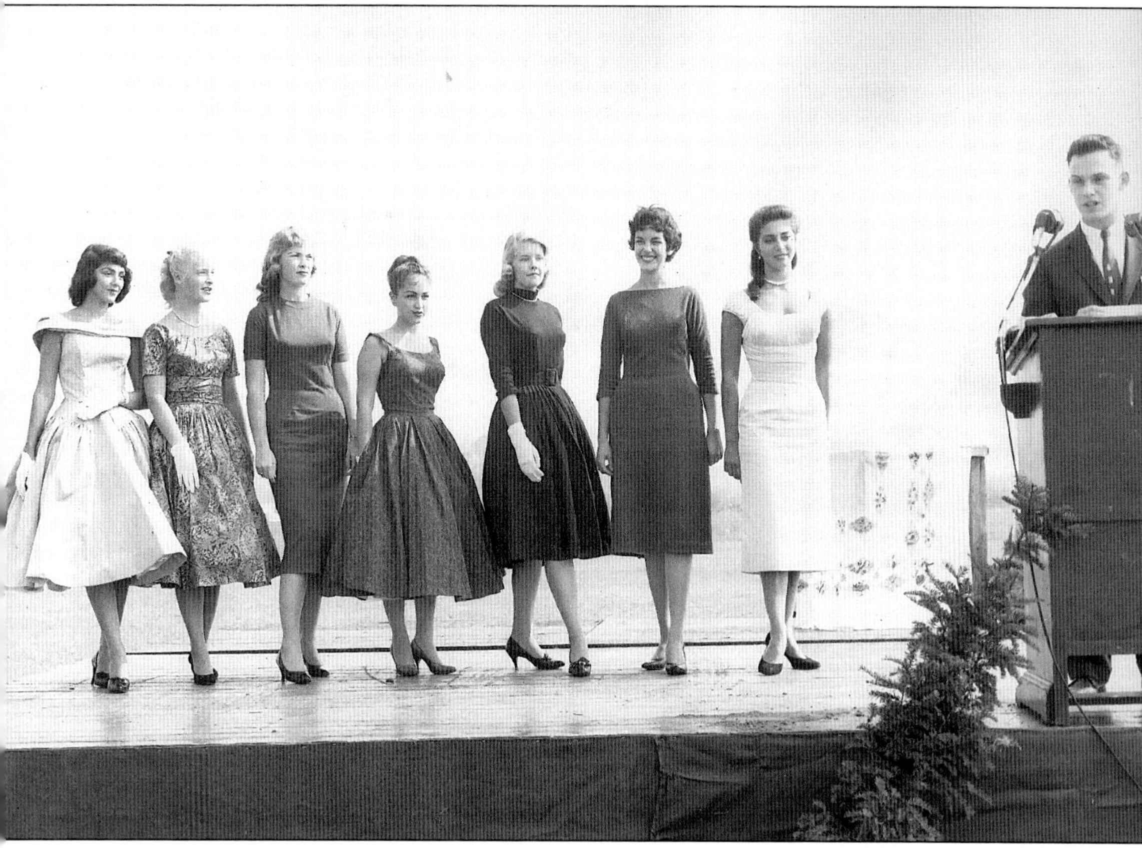

The queen pageant contests were the most popular attractions at the collegiate level. At Farmingdale, during the 1950s, many queen contests were held. In addition to the Homecoming Queen selection, the most popular was the Chrysanthemum Queen Contest, held in the fall semester, and cosponsored by the Ornamental Horticulture Department and the Long Island Chrysanthemum Society. The person selected to be the Chrysanthemum Queen served as the guest of honor at the Annual Chrysanthemum Show. The young women in this scene on campus are competing for the title.

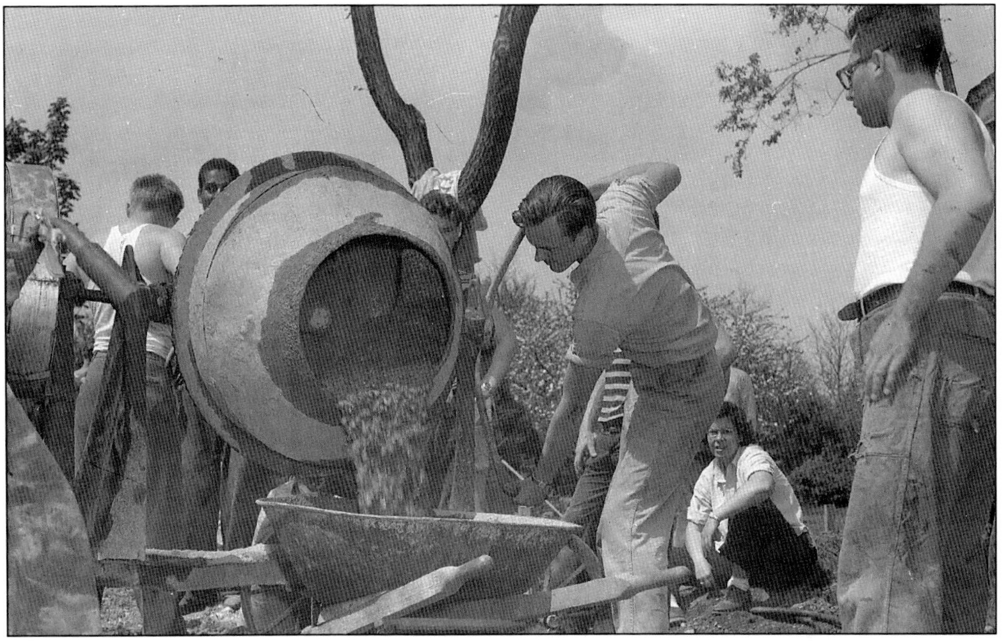

These horticulture students are completing a concrete construction project in the spring term of 1948. They are building garden architectural features for landscape planning and construction. They have accumulated knowledge in garden materials with special attention to methods of construction. Annual tuition for these New York State students was free; for out-of-state citizens, the cost was $100.

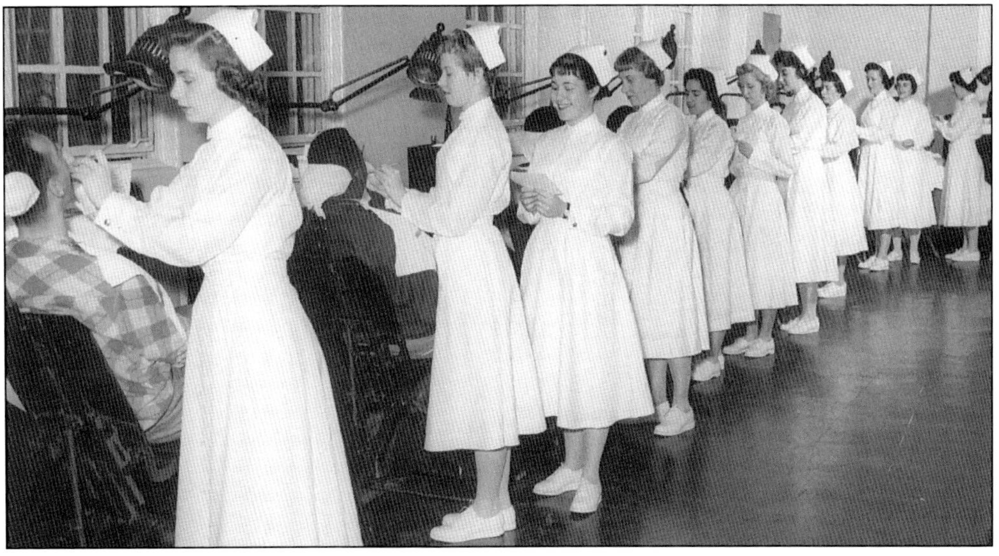

The first dental hygiene class was accepted in the 1946 fall term at the institute. It has since become one of the most successful programs on campus, with a constant oversubscription of applicants. The student dental hygienists gain practical experience by treating volunteer patients on campus. Arrangements also were made to have the dental hygiene squad go to such places as the Hicksville public schools and the Grumman Aircraft Corporation to give prophylactic treatments to patients. In this photograph, dental hygiene students are providing treatment at the Veterans Administration Hospital in Northport, Long Island, on November 14, 1957.

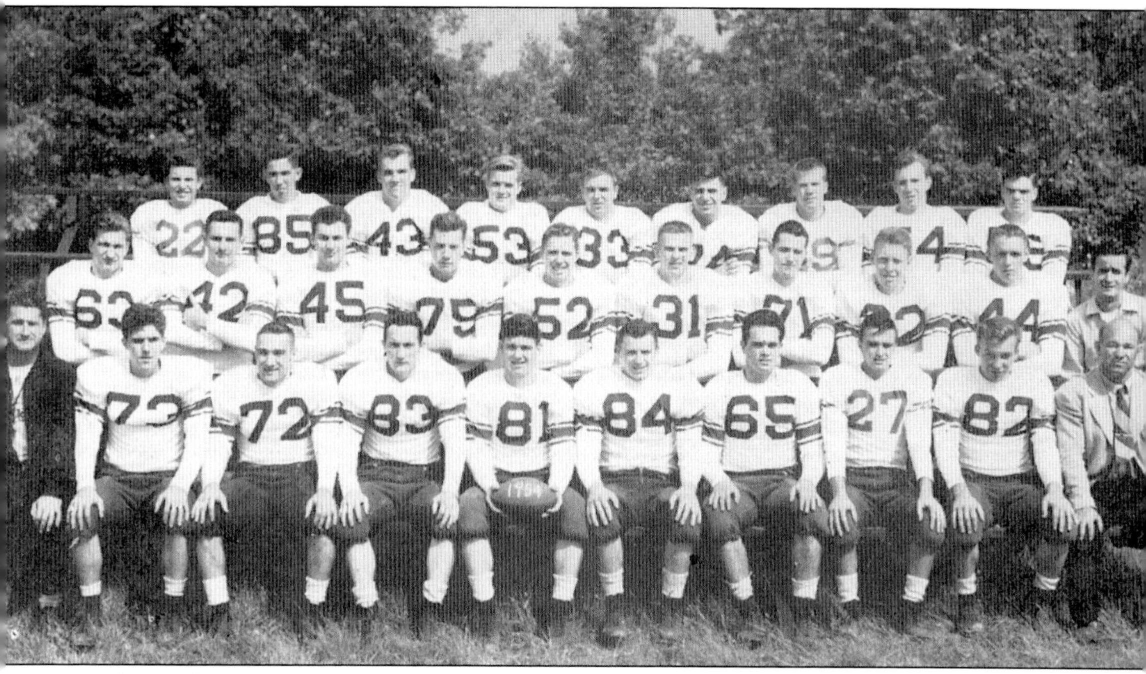

The 1954 football team poses for this group photograph. Coach Tom Watt (far left, front row) became athletic director in 1964 and continued until 1980, when he retired. Shown, from left to right, are the following: (front row) coach T. Watt, J. Boyd, M. Boyle, A. Lain, C. Godwin, D. Purshall, J. Valentino, A. Gody, R. Dobec, and coach ? MacArthur; (middle row) J. Hoffer, F. Bartol, R. Gunderson, C. Riddleburgh, E. Burtis, R. Schleiter, E. Sutphin, W. Schlegel, R. Weisner, and manager J. Frey; (back row) P. Hiltenbrand, K. Walch, J. Richardson, D. Biegner, D. Pennington, J. Hubbard, A. Askeland, C. Heinzerling, and F. McMurphy.

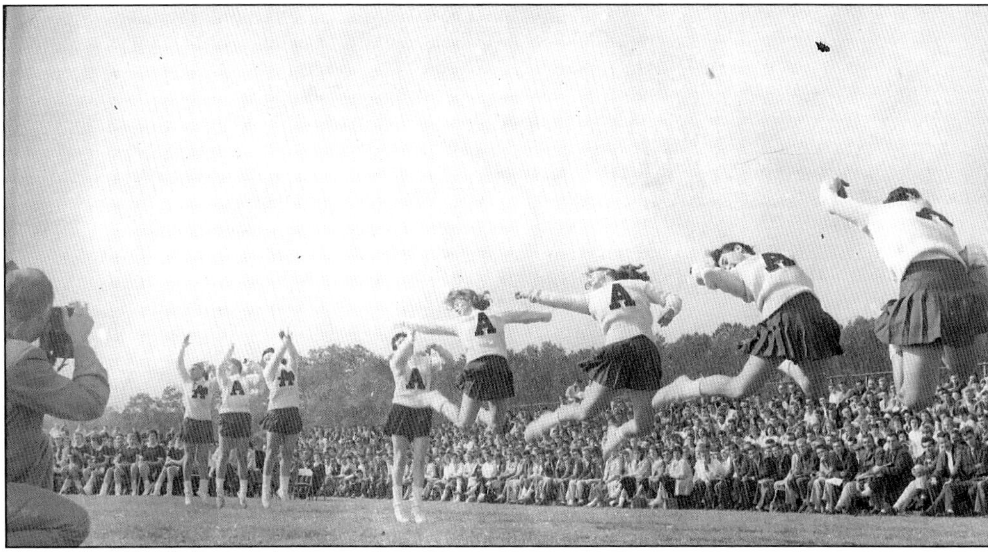

Cheerleaders perform during halftime at the Homecoming Day football game in November 1954 at the Long Island Agricultural and Technical Institute (the name adopted in 1946). In addition to the football game, a cross-country meet and a soccer game were other events that took place. The many school clubs also paraded on the field during halftime, and a children's beauty contest was inaugurated.

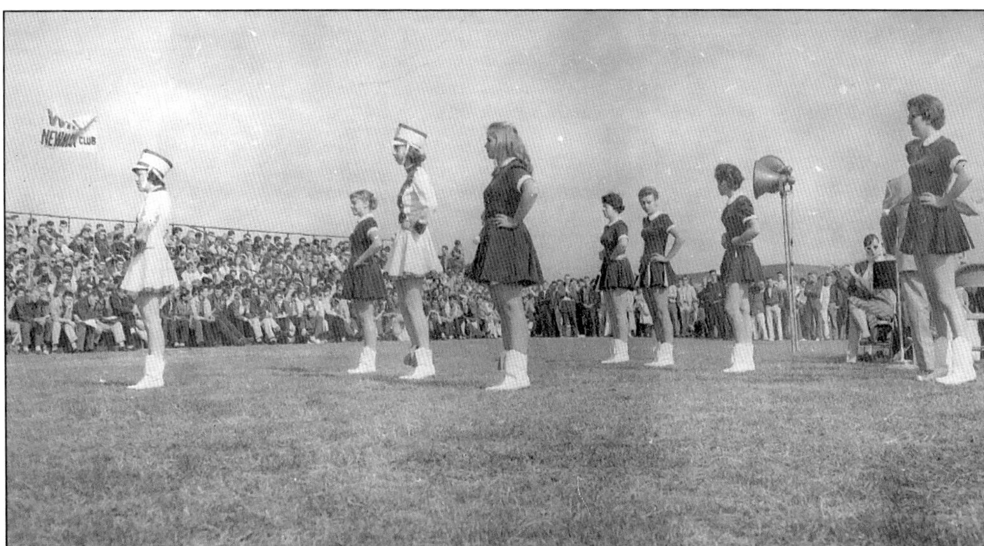

Cheerleaders at the 1958 Homecoming Day inspire school spirit during the football game as part of this gala occasion. Other Homecoming Day activities included alumni tours of the campus, a dinner, and dance. As they mingled with students and faculty, returning alumni were fascinated by the changes that had occurred since they had graduated.

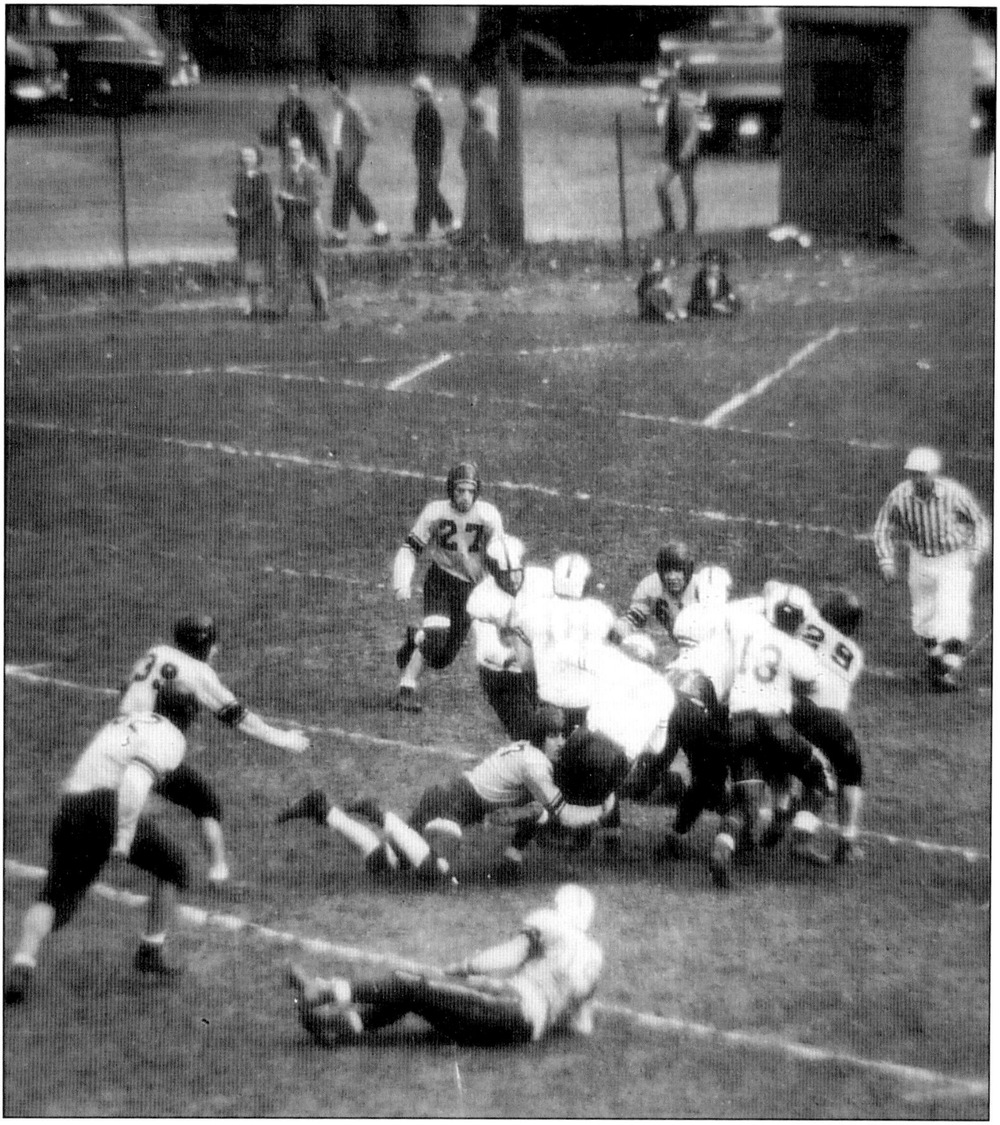

From 1943 to 1945, there were no athletic teams in competition because of WWII. In this action scene, the football team is taking on one of its rivals in 1950. The football program was traditionally one of the strongest for Farmingdale, but it was dropped in 1963 for three reasons. First, the participation level had declined, making it difficult to field a team. Second, the budget was getting tighter as other sports were added to the program. Third, with the athletic program about to join the National Junior College Athletic Association, it was difficult to find other competitors that were members of the NJCAA. The student body was unhappy over the decision to drop football.

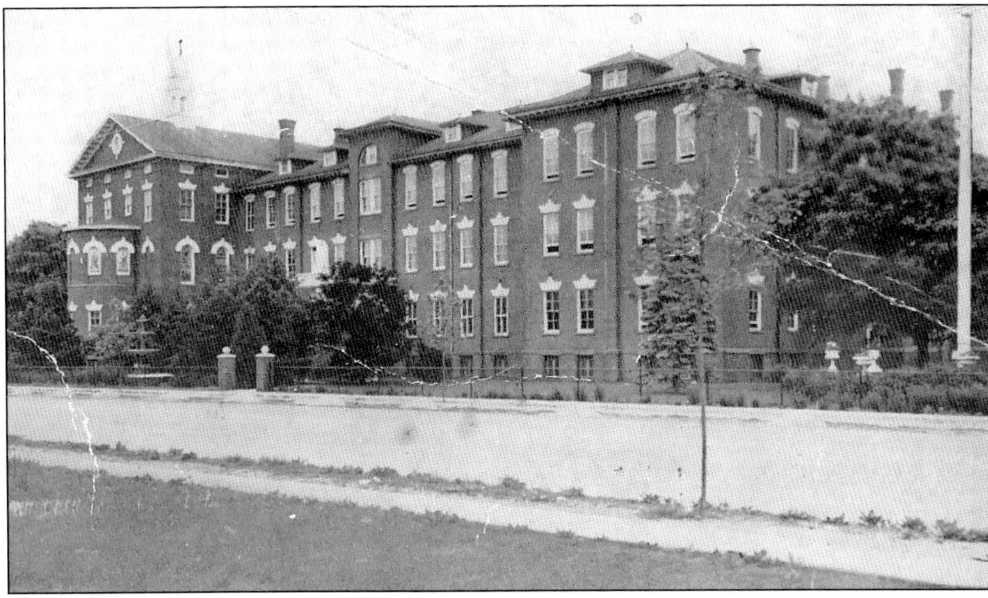

The Industrial Technical Division began in 1946 at 520 Conklin Street in the village of Farmingdale because the facilities were inadequate on the main campus. Director Knapp rented the old Nazareth Trade School, shown here, from the Farmingdale school district for $10,000 a year. It had been run by the Dominican Sisters for underprivileged children and orphans. The building was closed in 1956 and was later demolished.

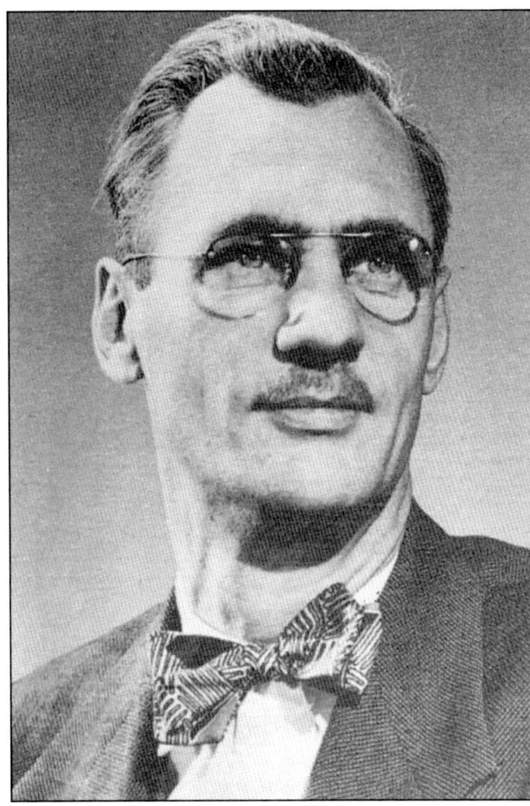

David W. Allee (1909–1985) became the first director of the Industrial Technical Division at Farmingdale. Born in Minneapolis, he received a civil engineering degree and gained considerable vocational, industrial, and teaching experience. Allee guided the development of course work and hired a talented faculty. The students who graduated, at first mostly WWII veterans, easily found employment in the burgeoning postwar economy.

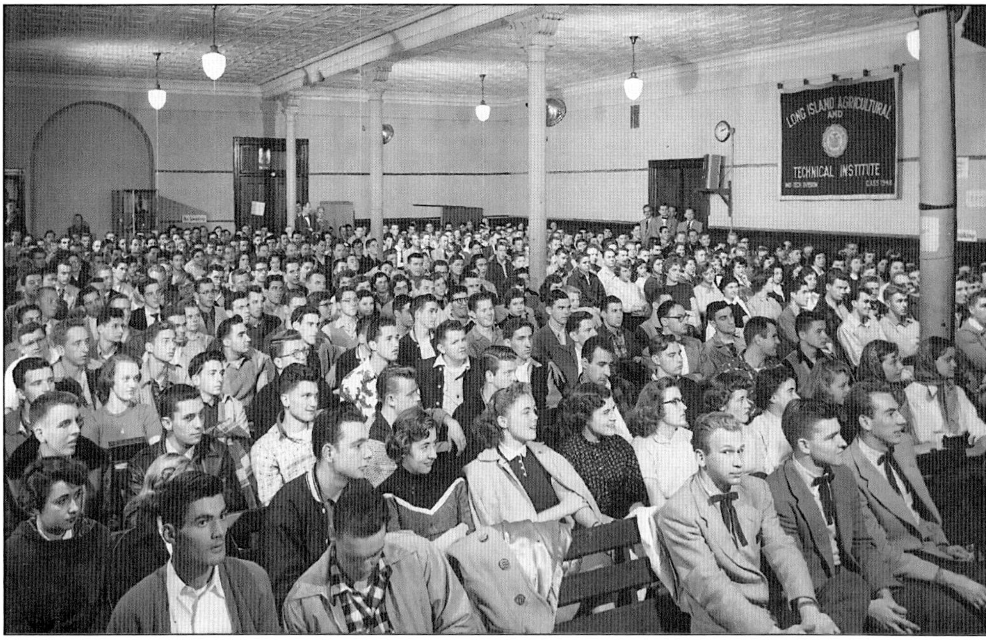

This composite student body photograph was taken at the Conklin Street School in early 1948 during an assembly. In the distant background, leaning against a column is Director David W. Allee. His philosophy of education was similar to Knapp's: technical education rested on an integrated sequence of courses with lecture instruction, but with an emphasis on laboratory and experimental work. It differed from vocational education by its advanced level of subject matter, and its focus on practical application of the engineering sciences and technology. This scene affirmed the Industrial Technical Division's immediate success.

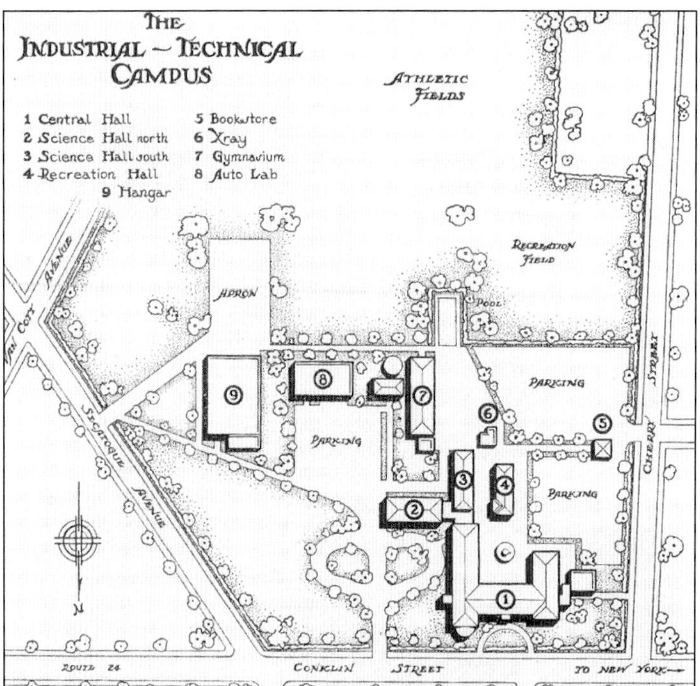

This is the layout of the Industrial Technical Division in the village of Farmingdale as it looked in 1948. It no longer exists. The building referred to as the "Hanger" (No. 9 on the map) was moved to the main campus, where it served as a bookstore, gymnasium, and assembly hall. Today, the Hanger is the Allard Field House, named for Gerald Allard, athletic director from 1929 to 1964.

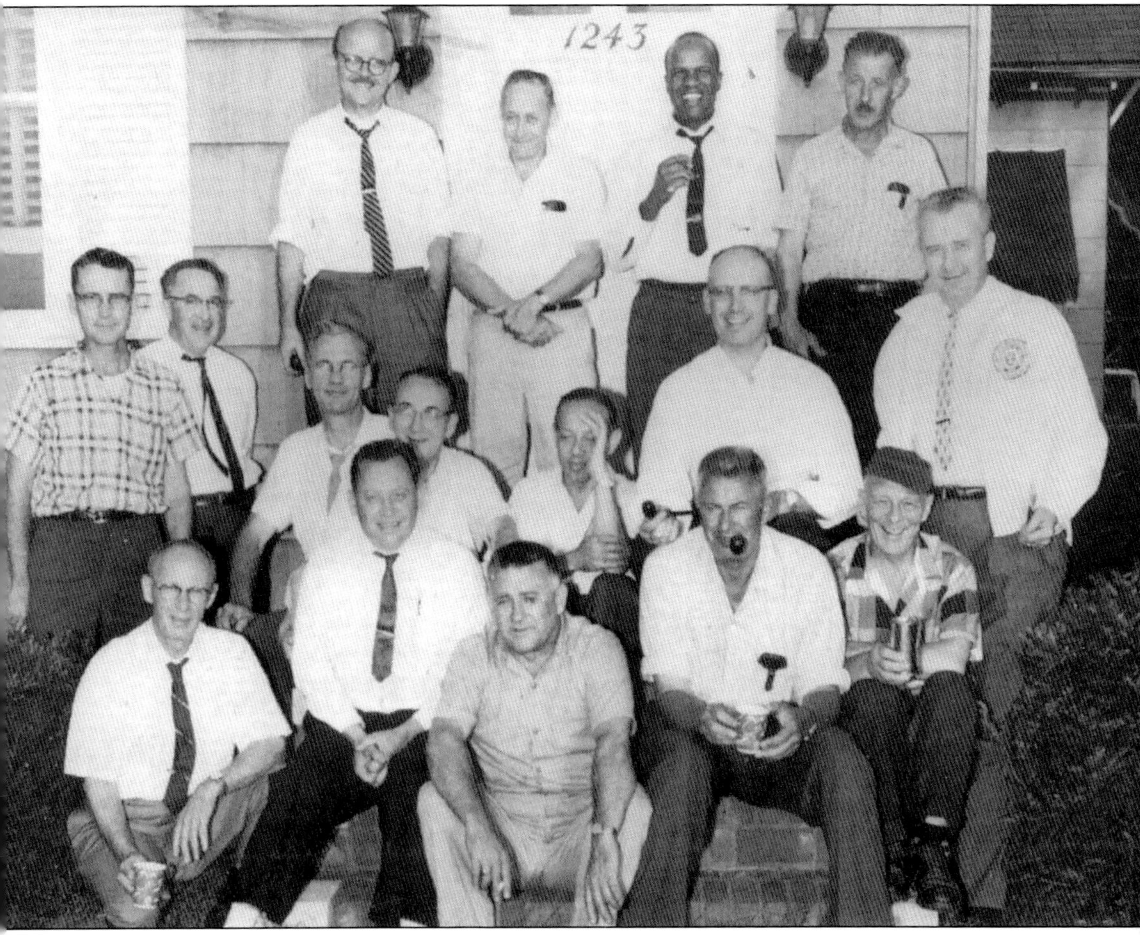

The original faculty that contributed to the success of the Industrial Technical Division at the Conklin Street School gathered in 1947 in Farmingdale for this group picture. They developed such a great rapport among themselves that they formed the "520 Club" and continued to meet together for many years to come. Shown, from left to right, are the following: (front row) Don Waite, Jack Coogan, Al Hraba, Walter Truex, and Ed Roberts; (middle row) James Irwin, George Drennan, David W. Allee, Carl Judd, William Haydu, Bert Willenbrock, and Ray Bowman; (back row) Raynor Wallace, C.D. Thomson, Al Perry, and Viggio Hansen.

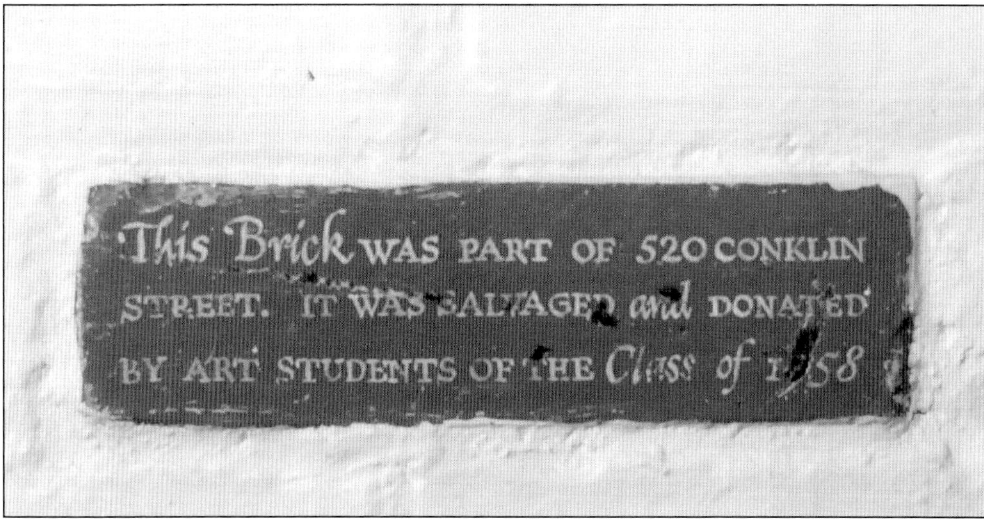

This image of a brick was hand-lettered by Prof. Thomas Greeley of the Art Department in 1958. The brick was taken from the Conklin Street School when it was being torn down in 1958 and was placed in Conklin Hall on campus. It says, "This brick was part of 520 Conklin Street. It was salvaged and donated by art students of the Class of 1958."

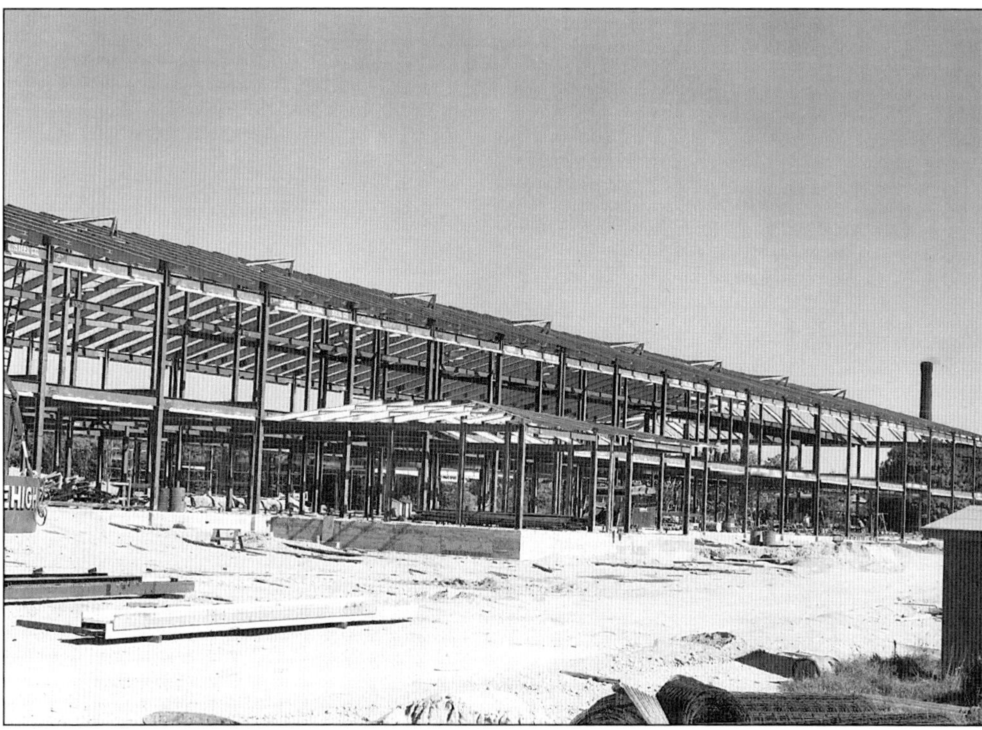

This photograph shows the construction of Lupton Hall in 1951–1952. The Conklin Street School was closed gradually. On the main campus, Lupton Hall, which was to house the Technical Division, opened in the fall of 1952. David W. Allee moved his office there. By this year, a clearer identity had been established in the school's new name: the Long Island Agricultural and Technical Institute.

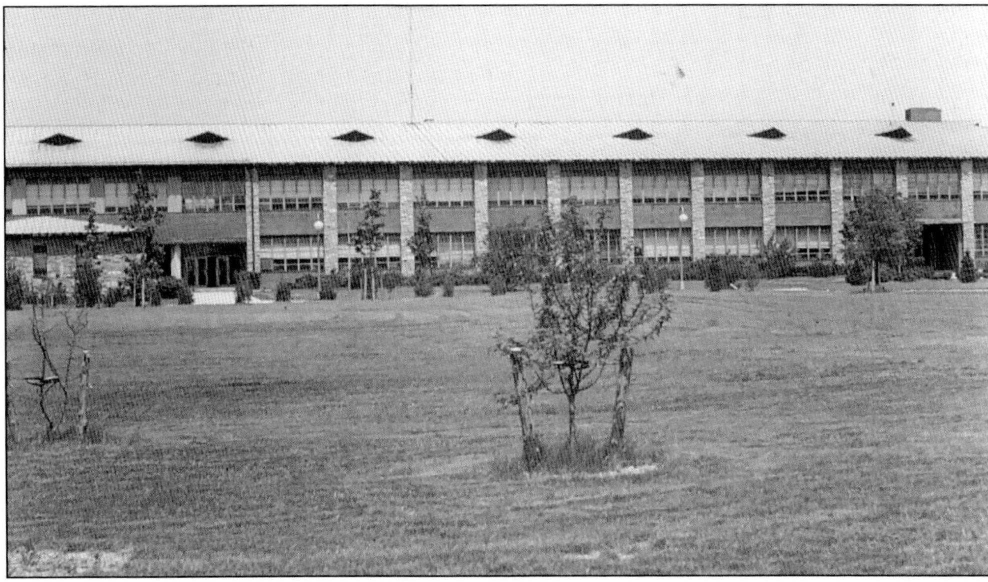

Lupton Hall stands proudly as the center of technical education soon after its opening. The building was named for John M. Lupton of Mattituck, Long Island, who should be considered a "father" of the college. Lupton twice served in the State Assembly, where he twice introduced bills to establish a school of agriculture on Long Island. The bills failed to pass.

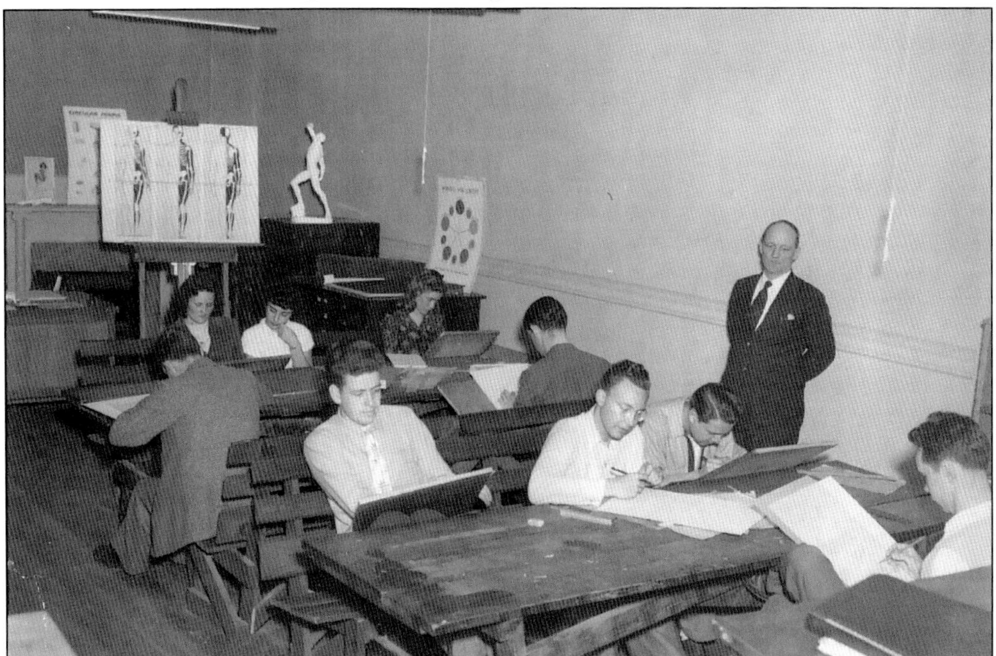

These Art and Advertising Design Department students are working under the watchful eye of instructor Ed Roberts, standing at right. The program offered a course of study for men and women training for jobs in the advertising field, such as advertising layout, illustration, cartooning, lettering, photograph retouching, fashion illustration, and window display. Three students are identified: Judson Snyder, left center, with tie; Dom Trotta, directly in front of Roberts; and Dottie Faulkner, rear row, third from left.

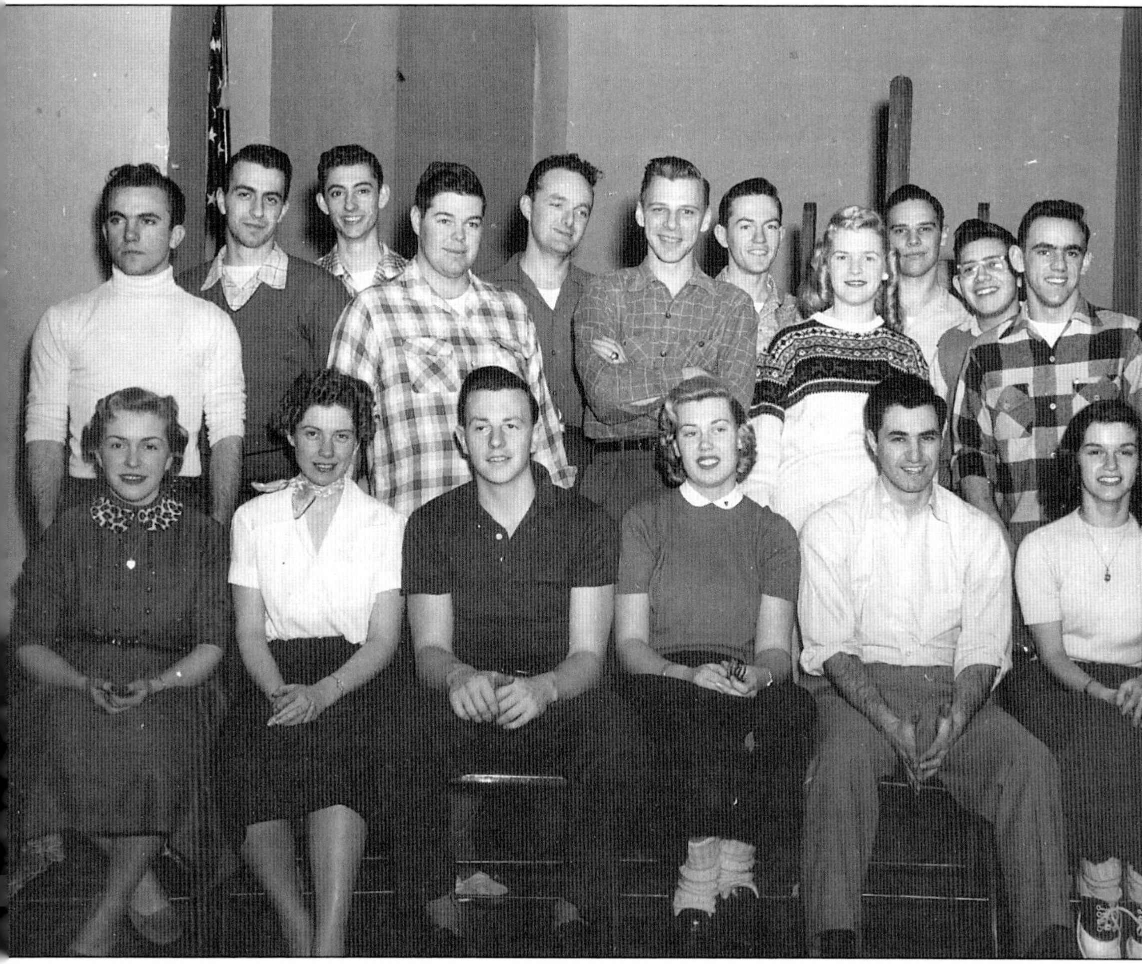

These students are part of the Art and Advertising Design Department, Class of 1956. The curriculum began in 1946 at the Conklin Street School and moved with the rest of the Technical Division to expanded facilities on the main campus. Shown, from left to right, are the following: (front row) Joan Collins, Pat Hall, Larry Butcher, Barbara Heitman, Dick Bird, and Mary K. August; (back row) Gary Anderson, Mike Delucia, Dick Fuller, John Dahlman, Chuck Hall, Ted Blake, Dick Barry, Ellie Carson, Walter Anderson, Tom Bruno, and Don Beyer.

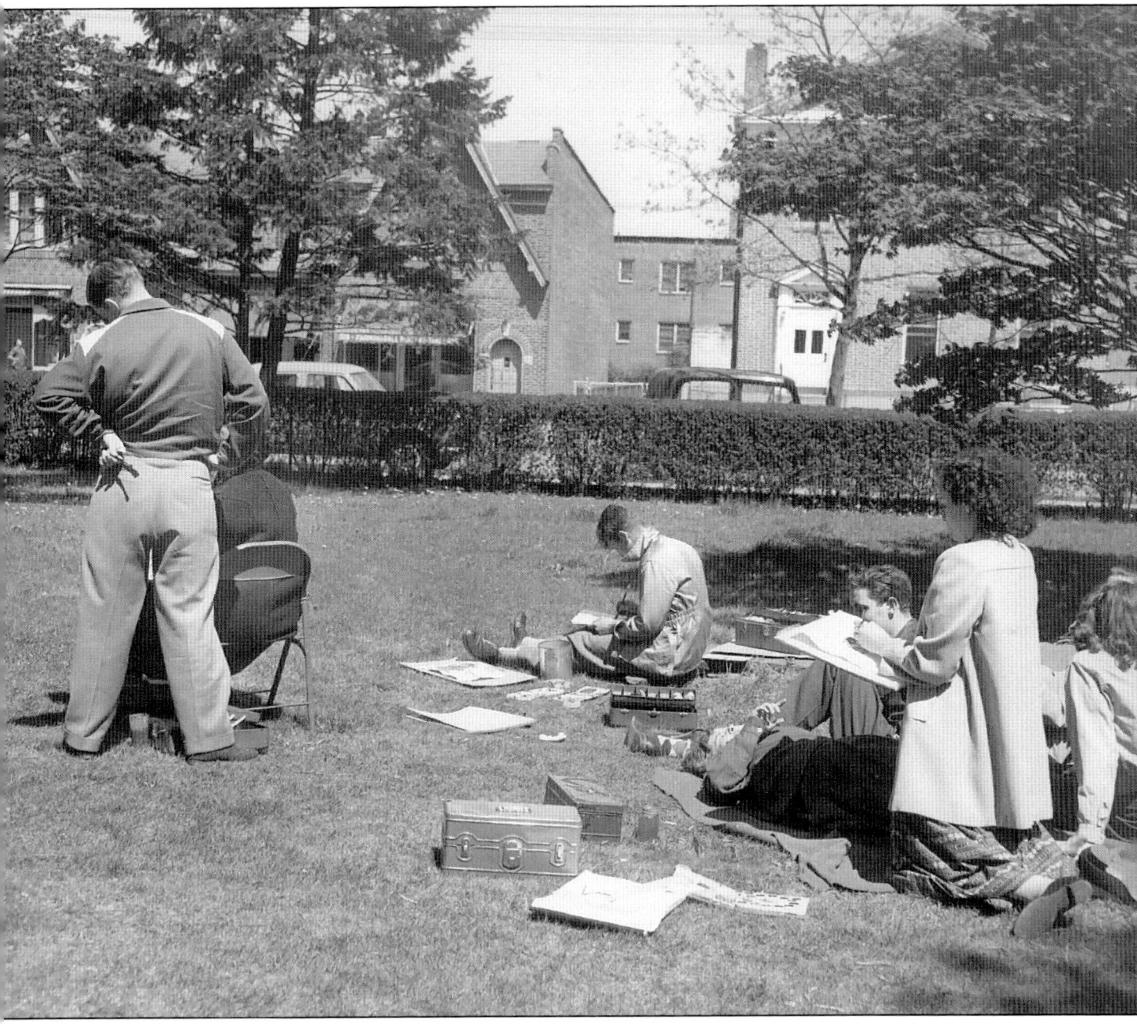

These students are working on an outdoor assignment in the village of Farmingdale in 1951. They are enrolled at the Technical and Industrial Division of the Conklin Street School. It was important for them to capture the light, movements, and activities of the inhabitants of the community. With equipment lying on the ground, they are focused on their work. The village of Farmingdale has always been hospitable to the college students and faculty, and the college has always sought to cooperate with the community.

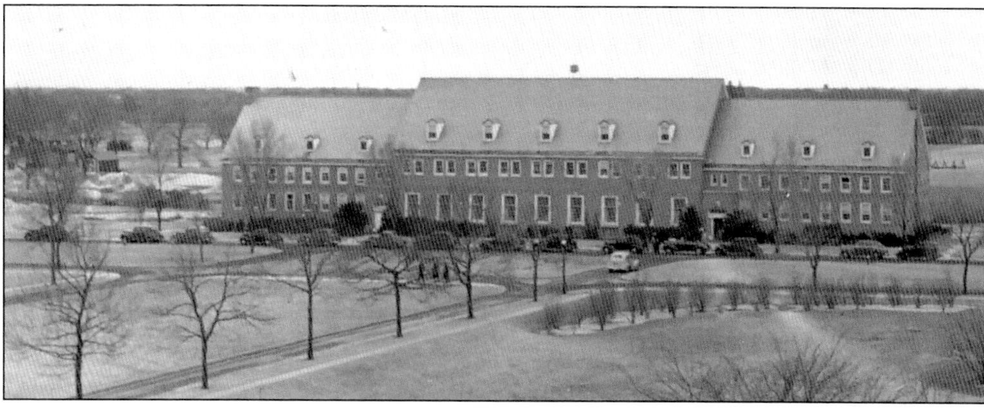

Knapp Hall stands by itself in the 1940s, surrounded by an expanse of land. The view is from Thompson Hall, looking west. The open land in the right foreground is now occupied by Whitman Hall. Halsey B. Knapp was director from 1923 to 1956, greatly influencing the development of the school. Knapp Hall has served as a dormitory, dining hall for faculty and students, faculty offices, and as a place for dances and other special events. The Knapp Hall Lounge has been converted into the Fireside Lounge.

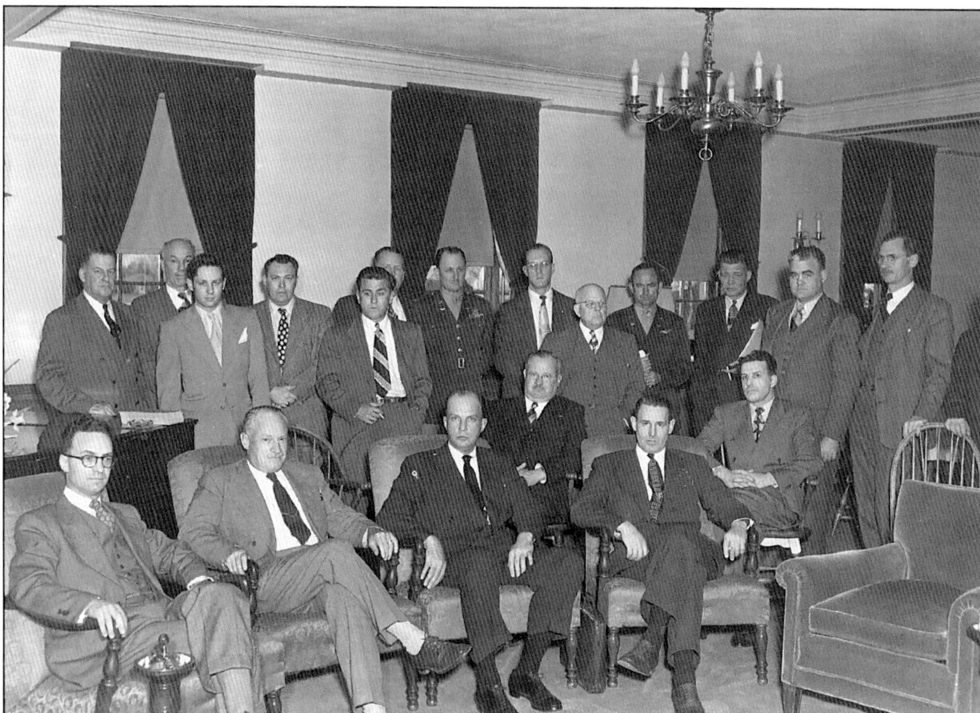

A visiting group representing the aviation industry is meeting with the Aircraft Operations Department in the Knapp Hall Lounge in 1948. Director Knapp is standing, second from left. Director of the Technical Division, David W. Allee, is standing at right. In order to keep the instructional program current and responsive to the needs of industry and business, the college has relied on departmental advisory committees, which serve in a consultative capacity. Because of the ever-expanding mission of the school, by 1960 its name had been changed again to the State University Agricultural and Technical Institute. This mouth-filling name was quickly abbreviated to SUATI.

Four

The Charles W. Laffin Years: Transition

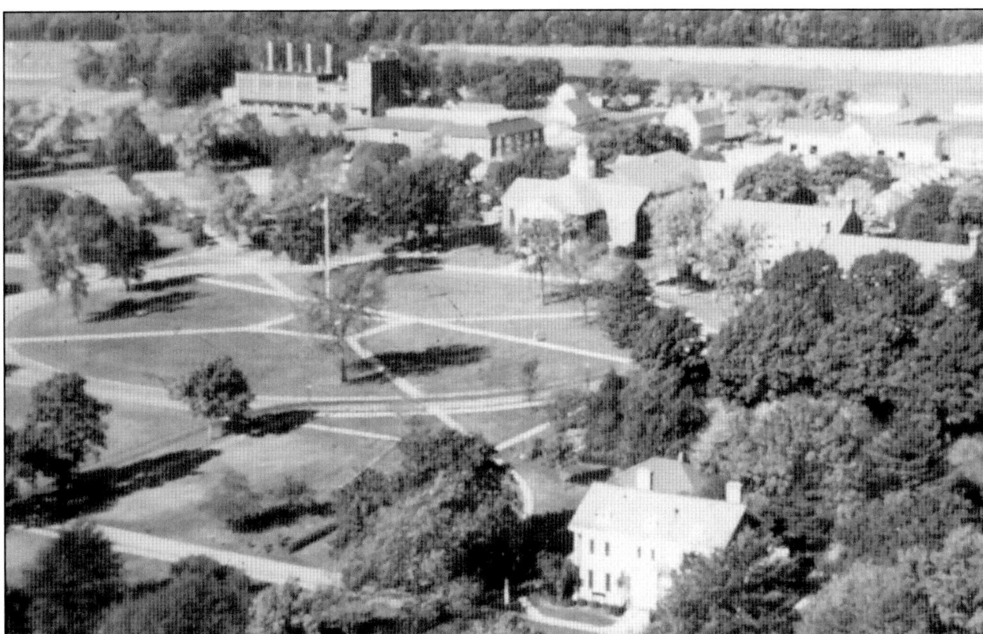

This 1965 aerial view of the campus shows increased growth and development, but it still retains a bucolic appearance. The new power plant with four smokestacks is in the background on the left. Conklin Hall, to the right of the power plant, has had its smokestack removed and has been converted to classroom and office space. The circle with flagpole at left center remains the most distinguishable feature. Thompson Hall, with cupola, is at the top of the circle, and Hicks Hall and Cutler Hall, barely visible, are to the right. The Director's Cottage is clearly visible in the lower center right. Knapp Hall, Ward Hall, and Hooper Hall are to the left, but are not shown.

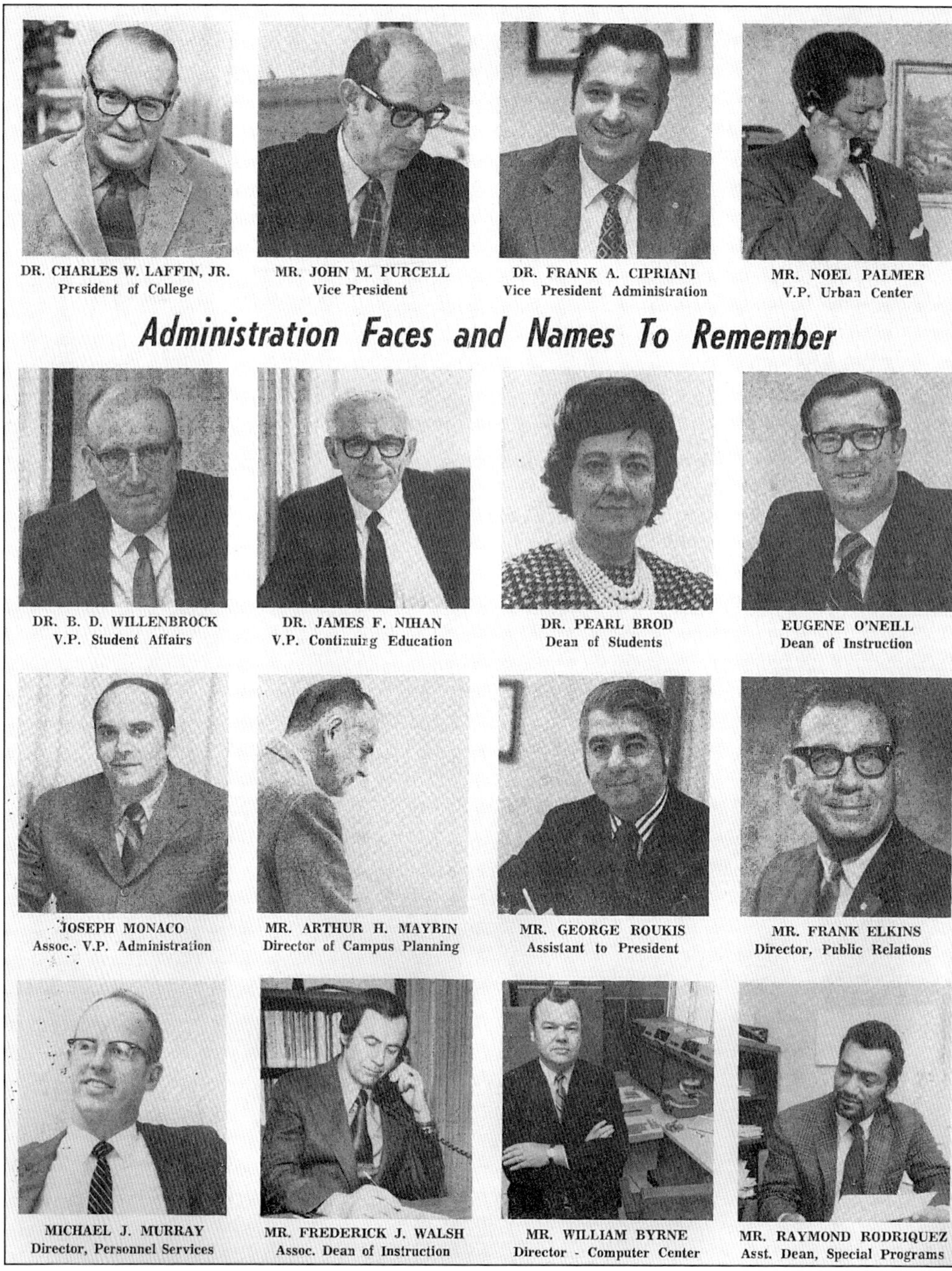

DR. CHARLES W. LAFFIN, JR.
President of College

MR. JOHN M. PURCELL
Vice President

DR. FRANK A. CIPRIANI
Vice President Administration

MR. NOEL PALMER
V.P. Urban Center

Administration Faces and Names To Remember

DR. B. D. WILLENBROCK
V.P. Student Affairs

DR. JAMES F. NIHAN
V.P. Continuing Education

DR. PEARL BROD
Dean of Students

EUGENE O'NEILL
Dean of Instruction

JOSEPH MONACO
Assoc. V.P. Administration

MR. ARTHUR H. MAYBIN
Director of Campus Planning

MR. GEORGE ROUKIS
Assistant to President

MR. FRANK ELKINS
Director, Public Relations

MICHAEL J. MURRAY
Director, Personnel Services

MR. FREDERICK J. WALSH
Assoc. Dean of Instruction

MR. WILLIAM BYRNE
Director - Computer Center

MR. RAYMOND RODRIQUEZ
Asst. Dean, Special Programs

The administrative leadership of the college in 1971 consisted of these 16 individuals. Frank A. Cipriani succeeded Charles W. Laffin Jr. to the presidency in 1978. However, Mauro Zulli, a longtime faculty member and department and division head, was appointed acting president in the interim, 1976–1978. Laffin was president from 1961 to 1976. It was during his tenure that the most dramatic changes occurred as the civil rights revolution, women's movement, and antiwar protests greatly affected campus life.

Charles W. Laffin served as president of the college from 1961 to 1976, succeeding Acting Pres. David Allee (1960–1961), who had succeeded William Medesy (1956–1960), who had taken over form Halsey B. Knapp. Laffin was a pioneer in the community college movement. A graduate of Colgate College, he earned a master's degree from Syracuse University, and a doctorate in education from New York University. He gained experience at various two-year colleges and was instrumental in organizing Nassau Community College in 1959, where he became its first vice president before coming to Farmingdale.

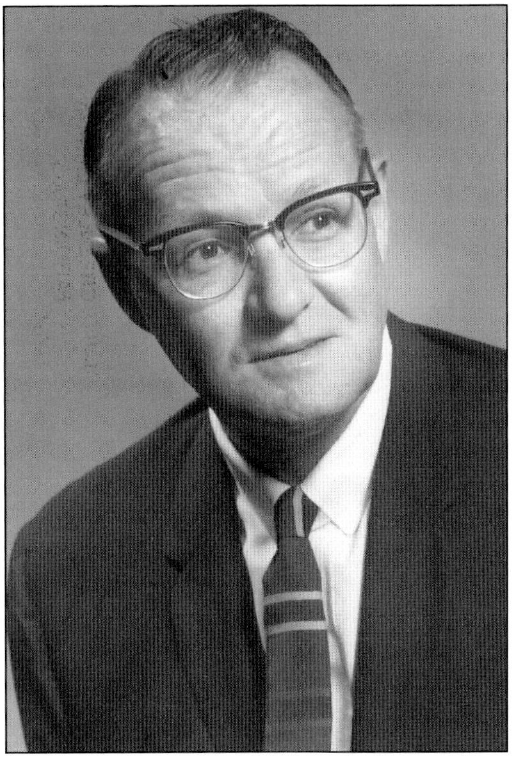

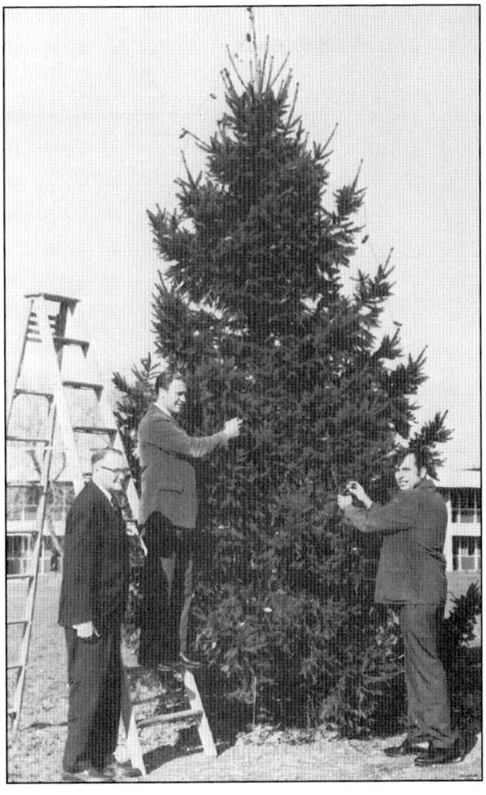

President Laffin is enjoying himself as he supervises the Christmas tree decoration in the holiday season of 1968. It was an eventful time for students as they decorated their dormitory rooms and campus, with faculty participating. In spite of the pressure of examinations, a spirit of joy and cooperation prevailed throughout the college. Laffin saw to it that no elitism existed among his faculty and staff.

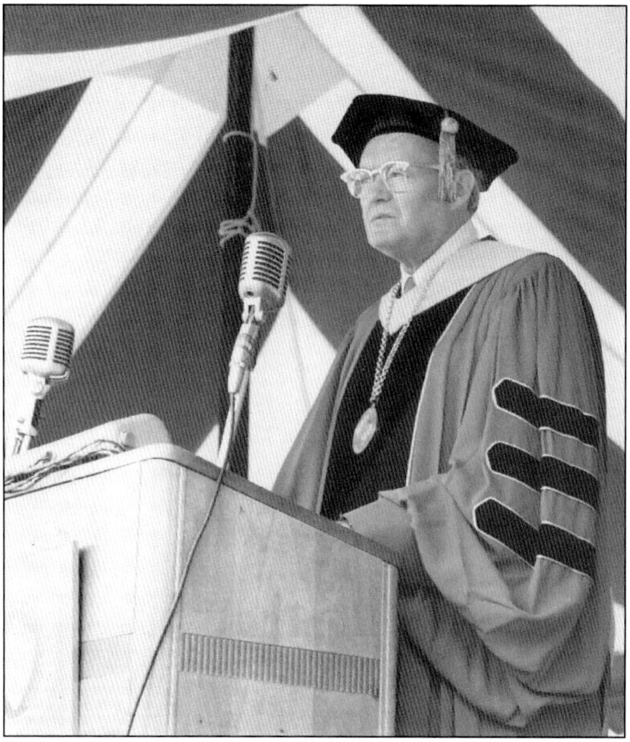

President Laffin addresses the graduating class at the 1970 commencement ceremony. Under his leadership, Farmingdale evolved from an agricultural institution with classrooms and laboratories to a more advanced career-oriented institution of higher learning. He helped to introduce 30 new curriculums that included every facet of modern technology and five educational opportunity centers throughout Long Island. He hired a distinguished faculty with advanced degrees, publications, and teaching expertise. In a 15-year period, he watched the 1961 college total enrollment grow from 1,676 to a 1976 enrollment of 6,800 day students and 7,700 evening students.

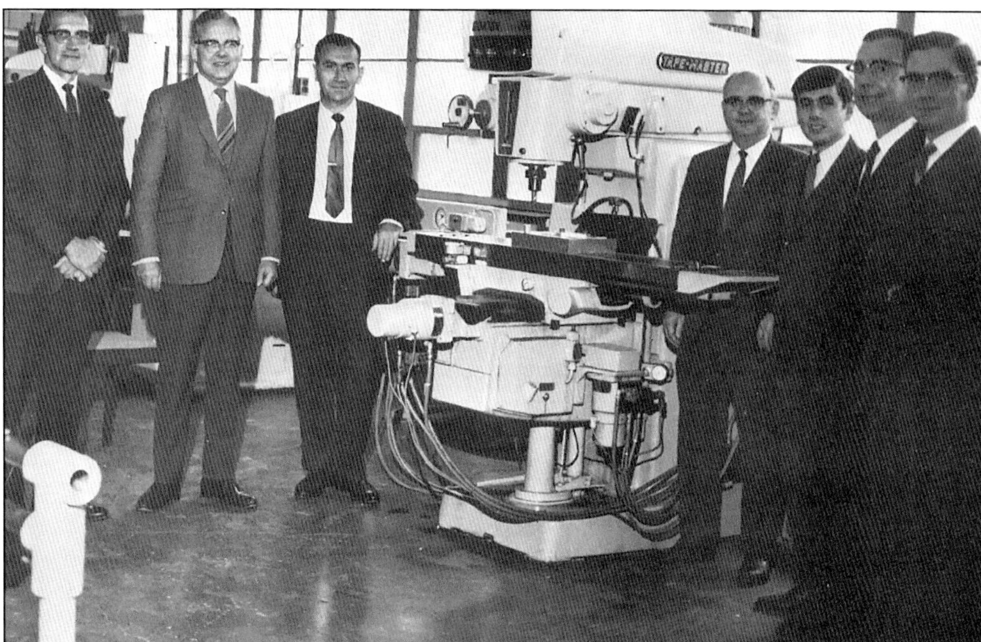

Faculty members of the Air Conditioning and Mechanical Technologies Department pose with some of the modern equipment used in the instructional program in 1969. Students who majored in the program prepared to enter an industry to make life more comfortable and to become manufacturing engineers, tool designers, and technical writers. Shown, from left to right, are C. Rakowski, F. Pyne, E. Mayer, R. Keegan, T. Campbell, W. Tobin, and R. Williams.

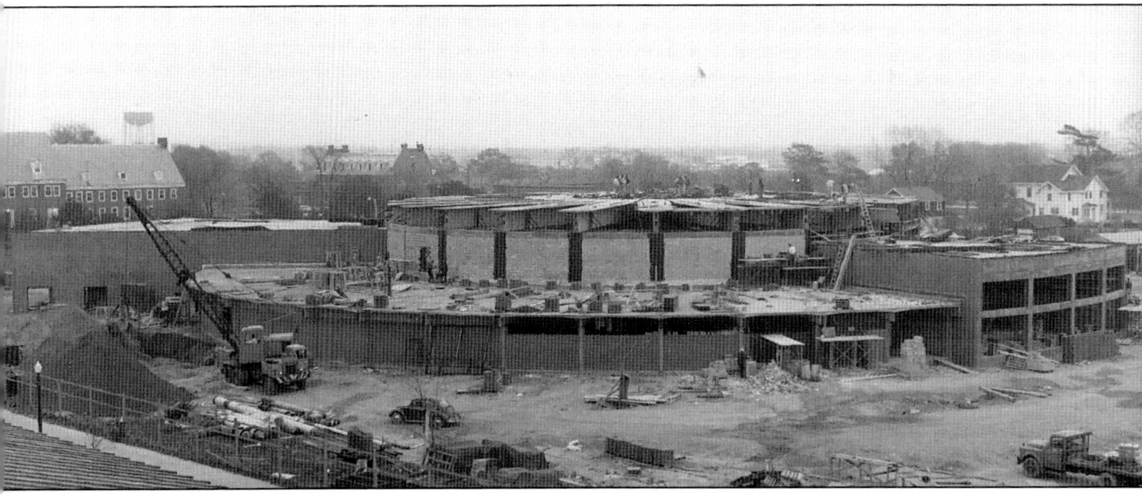

This campus view shows the construction of the student activities building, or Theodore Roosevelt Hall. The date is November 11, 1964. The building on the left is Knapp Hall, and to its right in the background is Hooper Hall. Note the circular pattern of Roosevelt Hall.

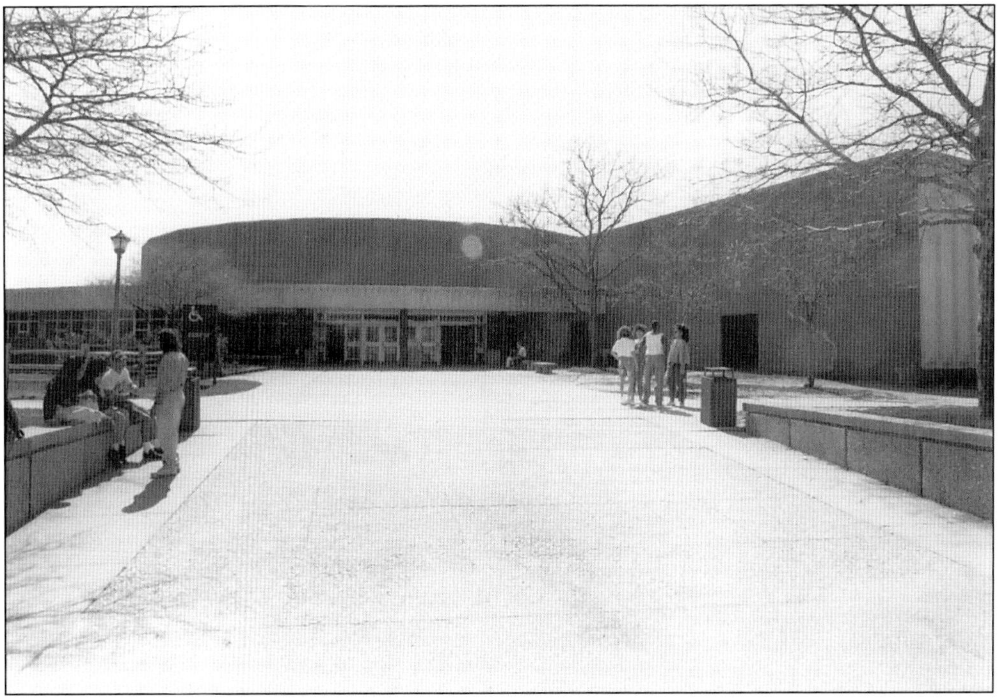

Students relax in front of Roosevelt Hall in this northwest view taken in 1970. Roosevelt Hall has been in operation since October 1965, as a College Union facility. It was used as a gymnasium until Nold Hall was constructed. The center of campus life, Roosevelt Hall has contained club meeting rooms, student lounge, recreation center, 400-seat theater-auditorium, and commuter lounge.

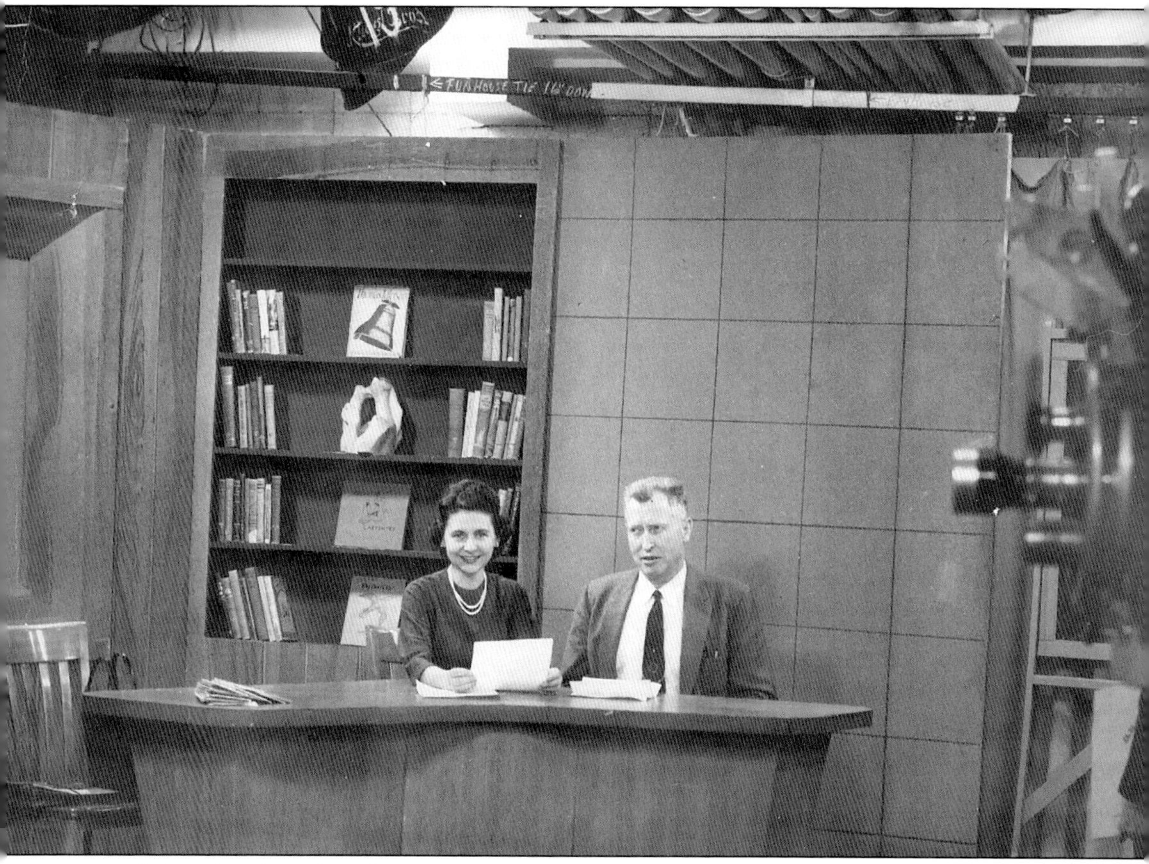

Prof. Ann Senyk and Prof. Horton Amidon of the Social Science Department—which was a part of the General Education Division at the time—are shown teaching a three-credit course, entitled Living Today, on New York City television station WPIX in 1968. Prof. Ronald Dougher, not shown, also participated in the planning and presentations of the lessons. Three hundred students enrolled for the course. Later, for the bicentennial celebration of the Declaration of Independence, Prof. Frank J. Cavaioli taught the successful television three-credit courses—the Adams Chronicles in 1976 and Roots in 1977.

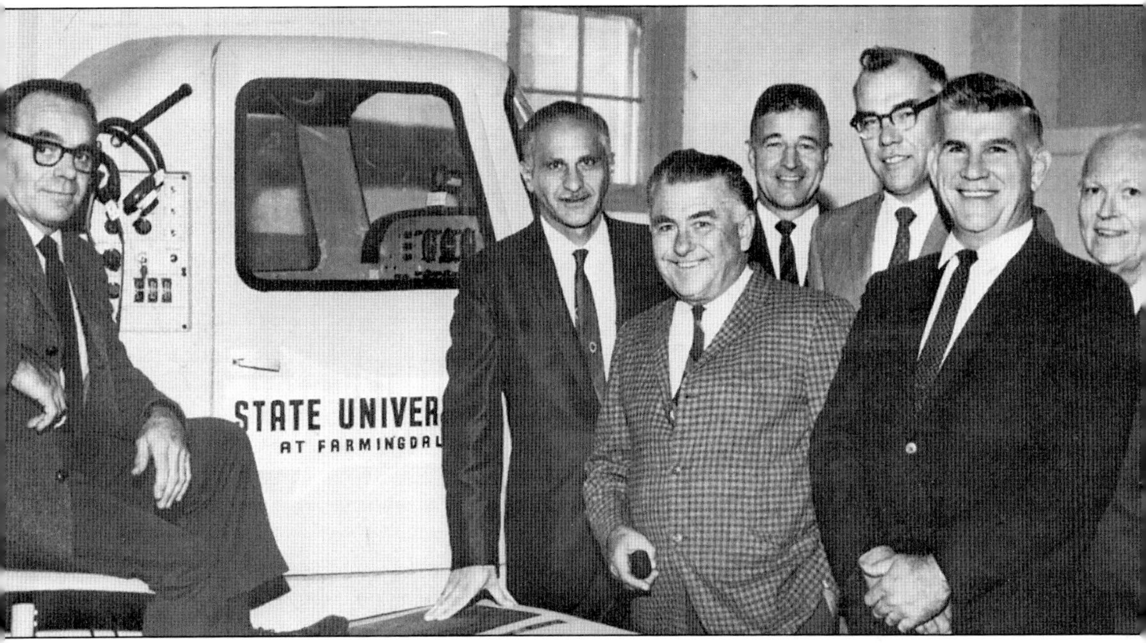

The members of the Aircraft Operations Department are enjoying a light moment in 1970. They have combined their skill and knowledge by bringing together practical experience with theory to produce graduates who will serve as dispatchers, airport managers, or related positions. Pictured, from left to right, are A. Dodorico, P. Fuhr, A. Hraba, L. Howard, R. Klemfuss, J. Valla, and W. George.

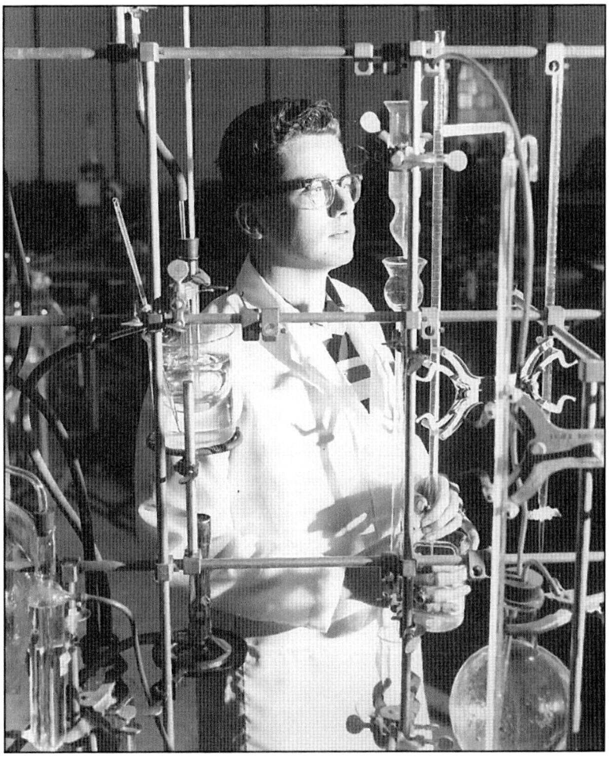

This student is conducting an experiment in the chemistry laboratory in 1968. He is majoring in chemistry, which is designed to be transferable to a baccalaureate program beyond Farmingdale that did not have four-year programs at this time. He will enter a profession that requires a foundation in science.

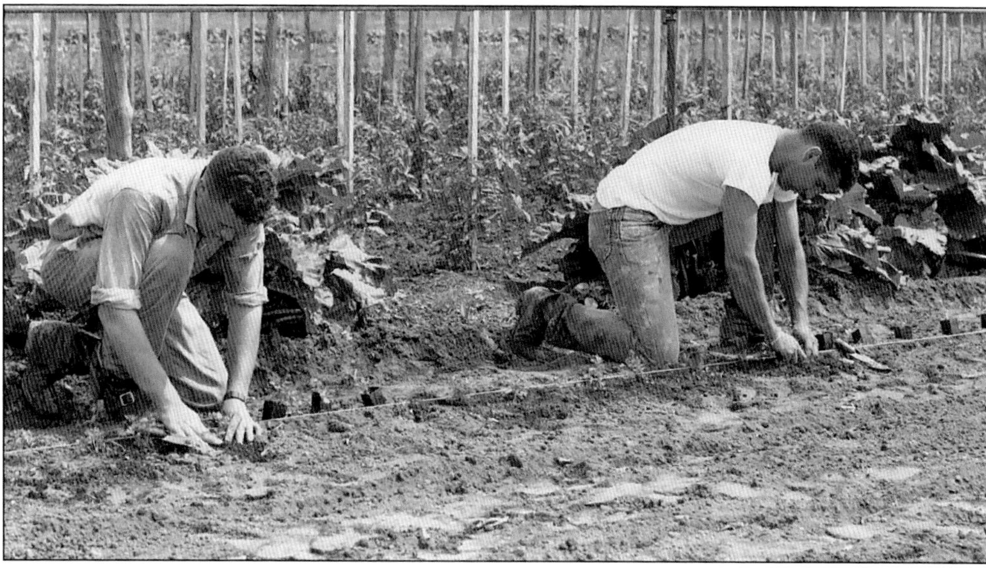

Two ornamental horticulture students are working on a project in their assigned garden in 1978. One of the oldest programs at the college, the curriculum focused on a current review of the horticulture industry's requirements in floriculture, horticulture management, and landscape development. Graduates in the program have been very successful in securing employment in the field of ornamental horticulture. As a result, Farmingdale has gained an outstanding reputation for its program and its graduates.

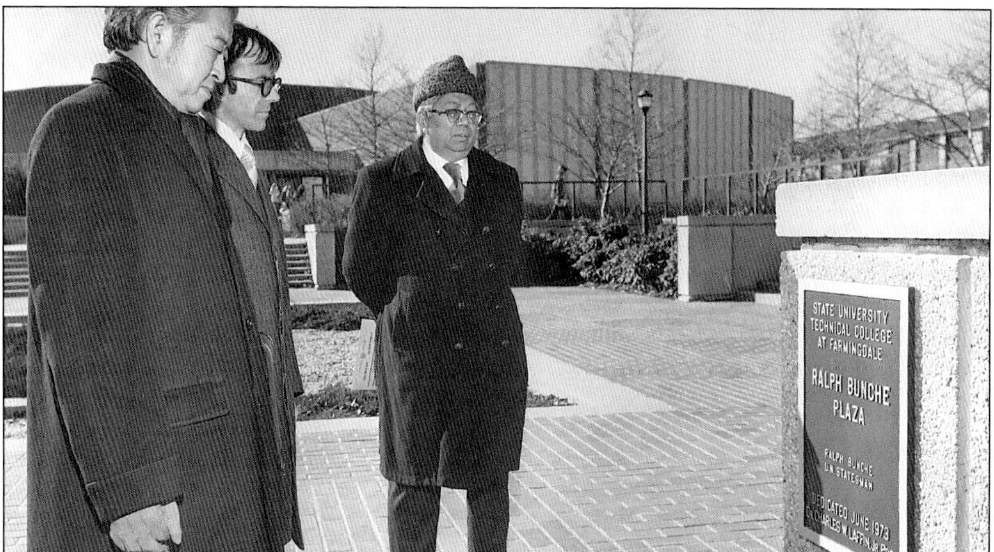

An unidentified United Nations representative, left, stands with Prof. Robert C. Blank, center, and Prof. Aung Thein (both of the History Department) as they fix their gaze on the plaque honoring Ralph Bunche (1904–1971) in June 1973. The plaza was named for Bunche for his achievements as a civil rights leader, scholar, and teacher; Bunche was the first person of color to win a Noble Peace Prize (1950). Professor Blank was advisor to Phi Theta Kappa, the two-year college honor society, and chair of the Department of History, Politics, and Economics. He retired in 1995. Roosevelt Hall is in the background. Today the SUNY Farmingdale Wall of Honor stands at the Ralph Bunche Plaza.

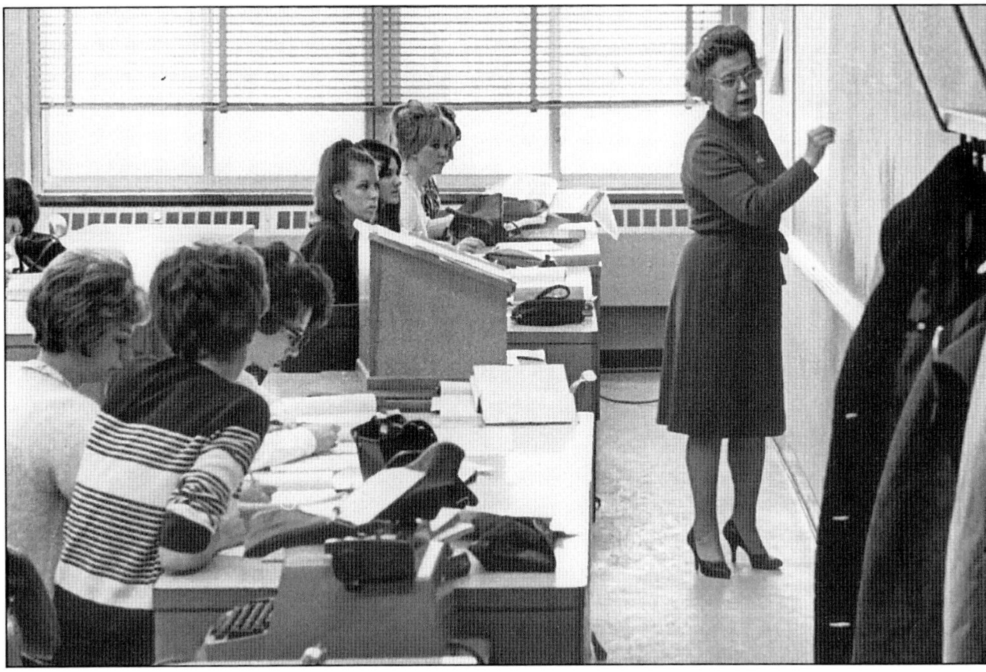

Prof. Elizabeth Roberts is shown teaching a secretarial science class in Whitman Hall in 1965. She has the students involved with the lesson as they concentrate on the material at hand. Professor Roberts's husband, Ed Roberts, was member of the Advertising Art and Design Department.

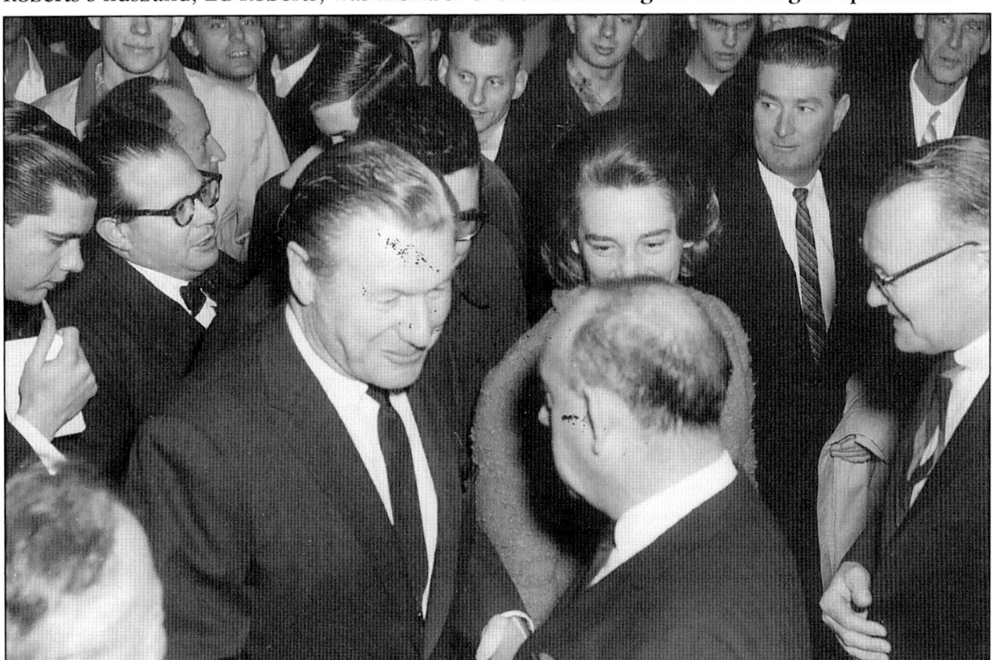

Governor of New York Nelson A. Rockefeller, left, is shaking hands with a faculty member during his visit to the college in 1965 as part of a series of visits to local communities. Mrs. Rockefeller is in the center, partially blocked from view. President Laffin, right, is looking on. During his tenure in office, Governor Rockefeller greatly expanded the State University of New York.

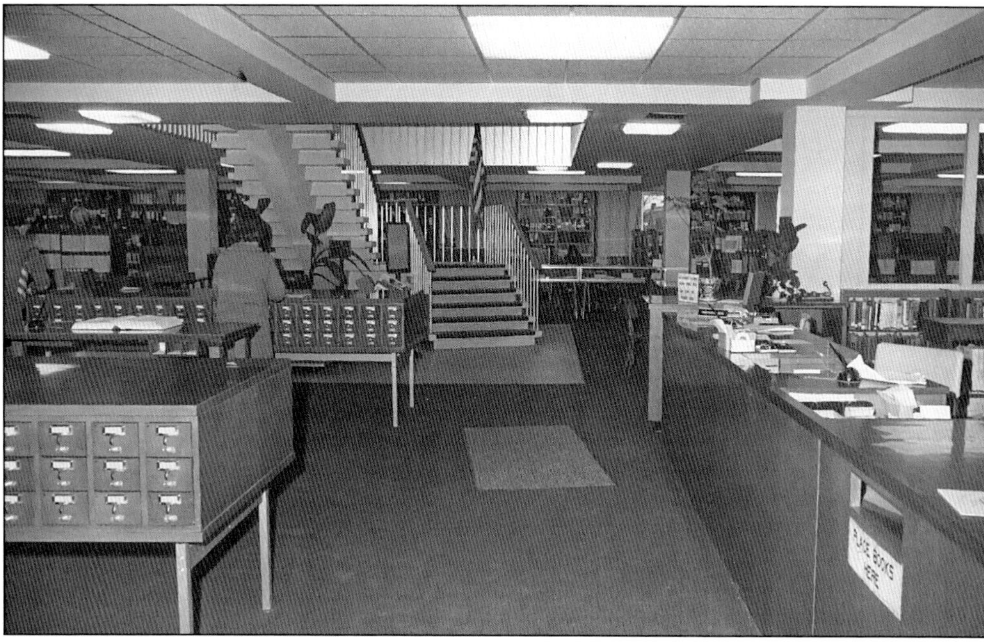

Before the present library in Greenley Hall was built, a two-floor wing of Whitman Hall was used for this purpose. These two photographs of the temporary Whitman Hall library, taken in December 1973, reveal an efficient facility for student reference and research. Nevertheless, its limited size soon made it inadequate. During its existence, this library was named in honor of Mary K. Peters, a longtime instructor who gave 21 years of dedicated service to the school. A graduate of the University of Michigan in 1896, Peters began work at Farmingdale in 1918 and retired in 1939. She taught botany, plant pathology, and entomology. In 1924, she assumed responsibility for the institute library.

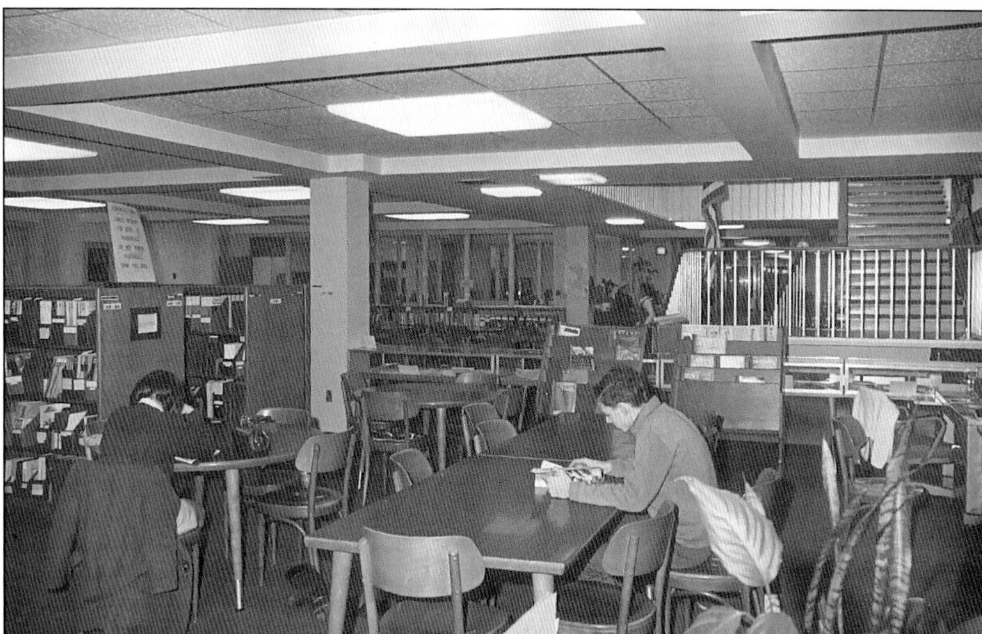

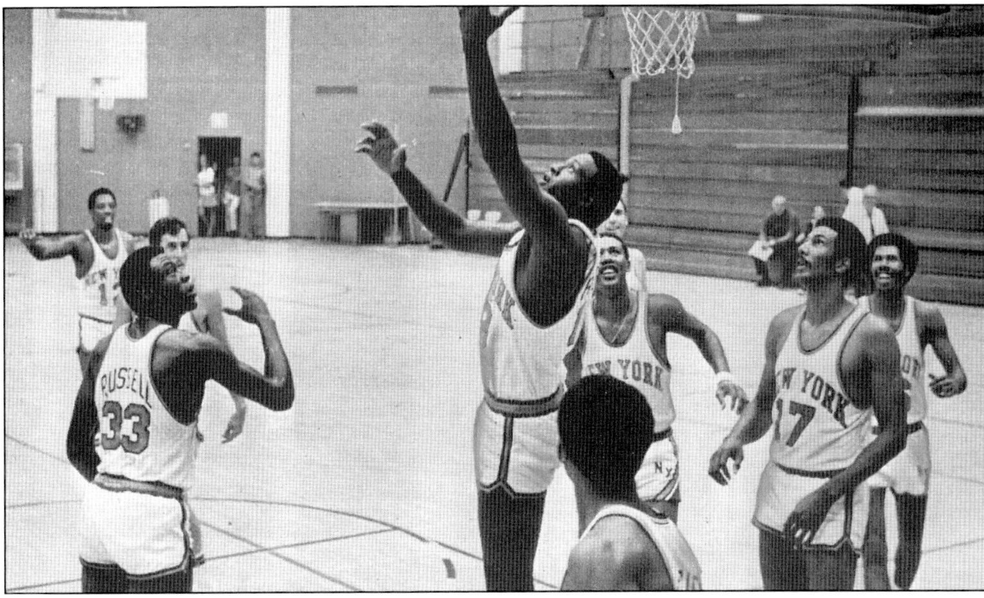

The National Basketball Association New York Knicks used the Roosevelt Hall gymnasium for their training and practice camp during the 1969–1970 season. Center Willis Reed is putting up a shot while Cazzie Russell and teammates look on. Coach Red Holzman is seated in the background with pad in hand.

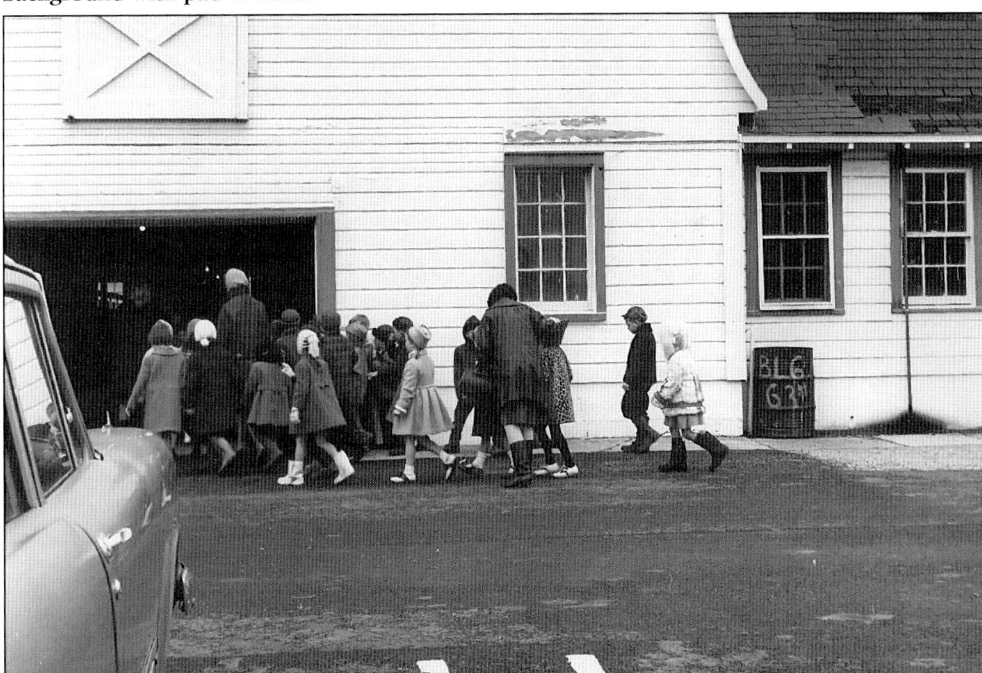
Young children from a local public school are accompanied by their teachers as they tour the campus in the late 1970s. They are visiting the barnyard area, where the children can see the farm animals. As Long Island became less of an agricultural area, children had little opportunity to see and appreciate animals, thereby limiting their total education. Many Long Islanders regretted the ending of the agricultural curriculum in 1987.

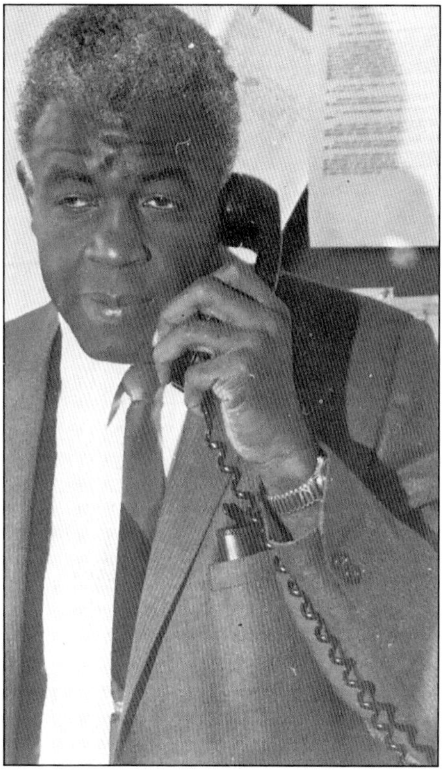

The Distinguished Speakers Series, sponsored by the College Union Board, has been held in the Roosevelt Hall auditorium. Leading personalities are invited to present their views on current issues and to engage them in challenging discussions. Jackie Robinson, left, and John Ciardi, below, were two guest speakers in the 1969 program. Robinson broke the color line in major league baseball in 1947 playing for the old Brooklyn Dodgers. His courage and talent led to an outstanding career and entrance into the Baseball Hall of Fame in Cooperstown, New York. Ciardi was a distinguished American poet, essayist, translator, editor, and teacher. He was poetry editor of the *Saturday Review* and was the author of more than 40 books.

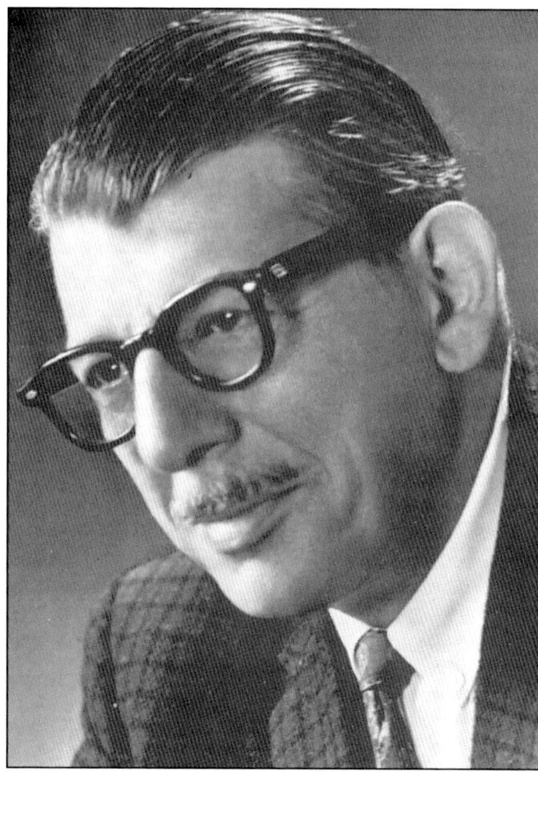

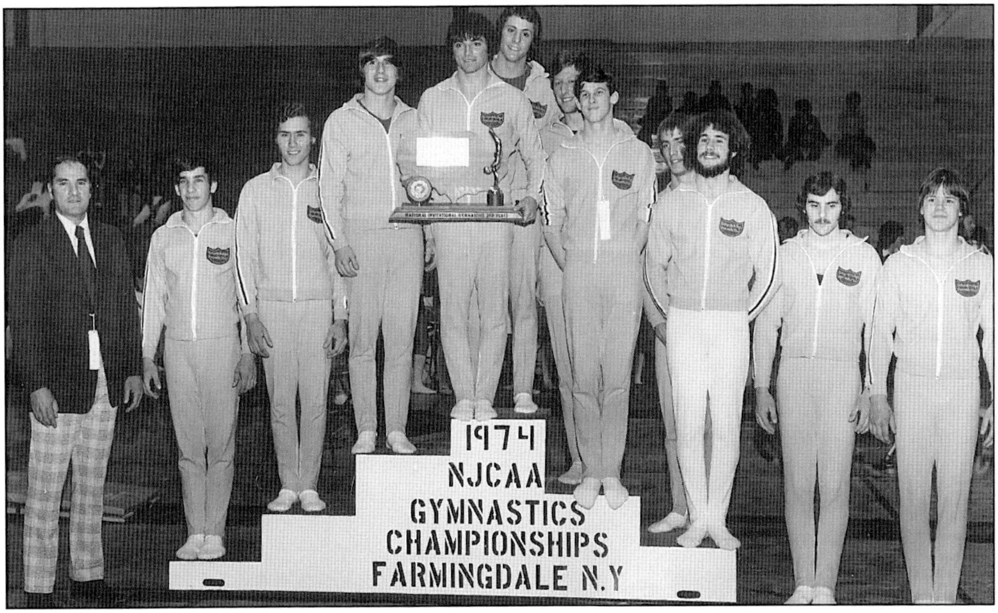

One of the most important developments in the college's athletic history was joining the National Junior College Athletic Association in the late 1960s. This move meant that all Farmingdale teams would compete within the same athletic association. In the early years, the school had only a few teams, there were no conferences, and only men competed. Until the WWII-era teams competed against high schools, colleges, and club teams. There were no teams from 1943 to 1945 because of the war. Shown is the 1974 Farmingdale NJCAA Gymnastics Championship team.

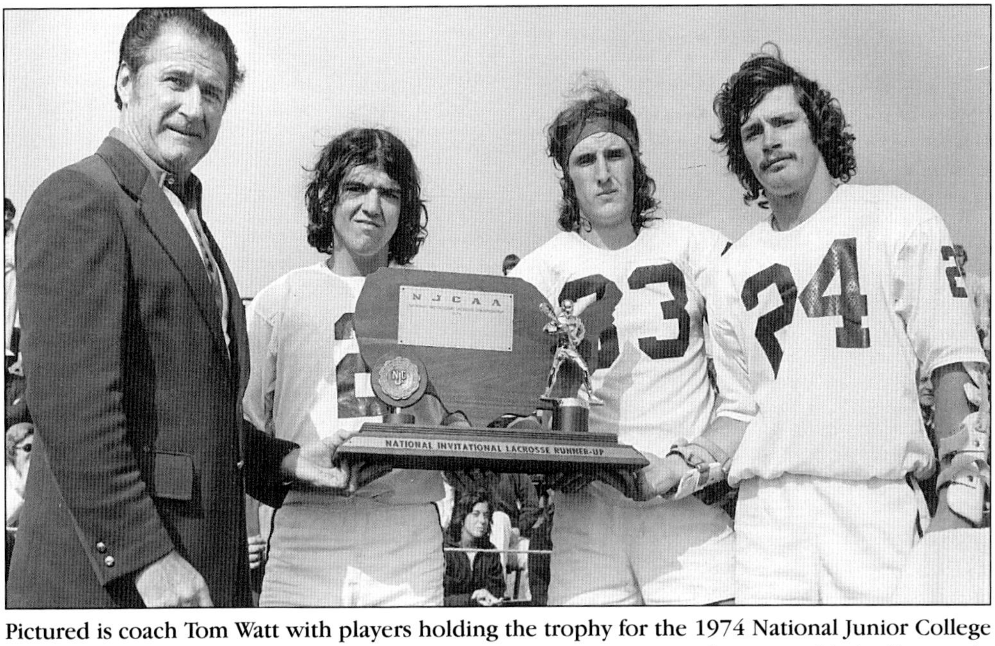

Pictured is coach Tom Watt with players holding the trophy for the 1974 National Junior College Athletic Association National Invitational Lacrosse runner-up. Watt became athletic director in 1964, replacing Gerald Allard (1929–1964). Bruce Robbins replaced Watt in 1980 and continued as athletic director until he retired in 2000.

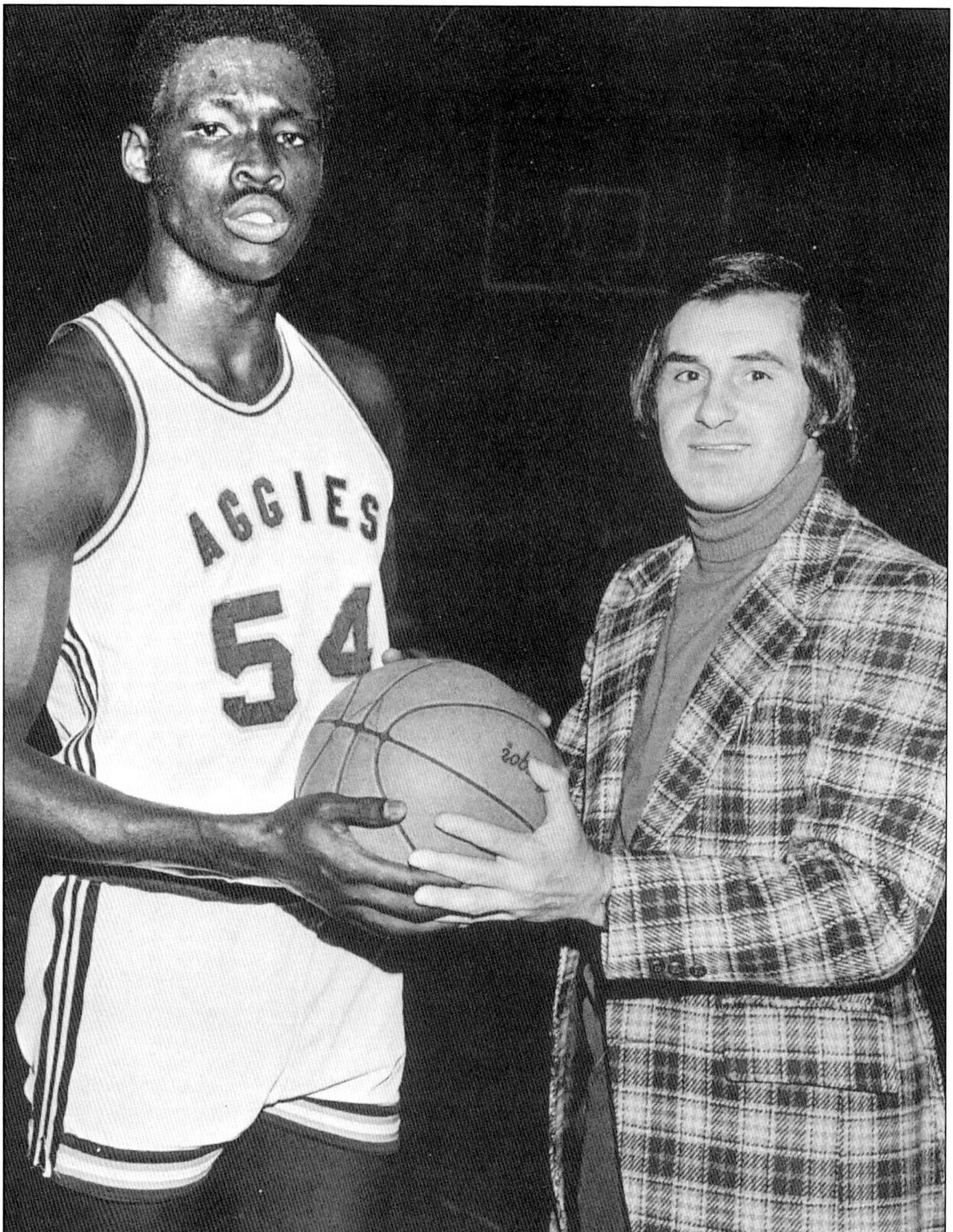

Basketball star Reed Addison poses with coach Tom Galeazzi after the 1975–1976 season, when Addison scored over 1,000 points. Addison was the first person to be inducted into the SUNY Farmingdale Athletics Hall of Fame for his outstanding contribution to the game. During his college career (1974–1976), he was selected for the Third Team All-American, First Team All-Long Island, and First Team All-Region. The SUNY Farmingdale Athletics Hall of Fame was established to honor the outstanding athletes and contributors to the college's intercollegiate athletic program. In 1990, Ray Rodriguez, the dean of students and chair of the Intercollegiate Athletic Board (IAB), suggested the idea of establishing a hall of fame. It became a reality in 1995.

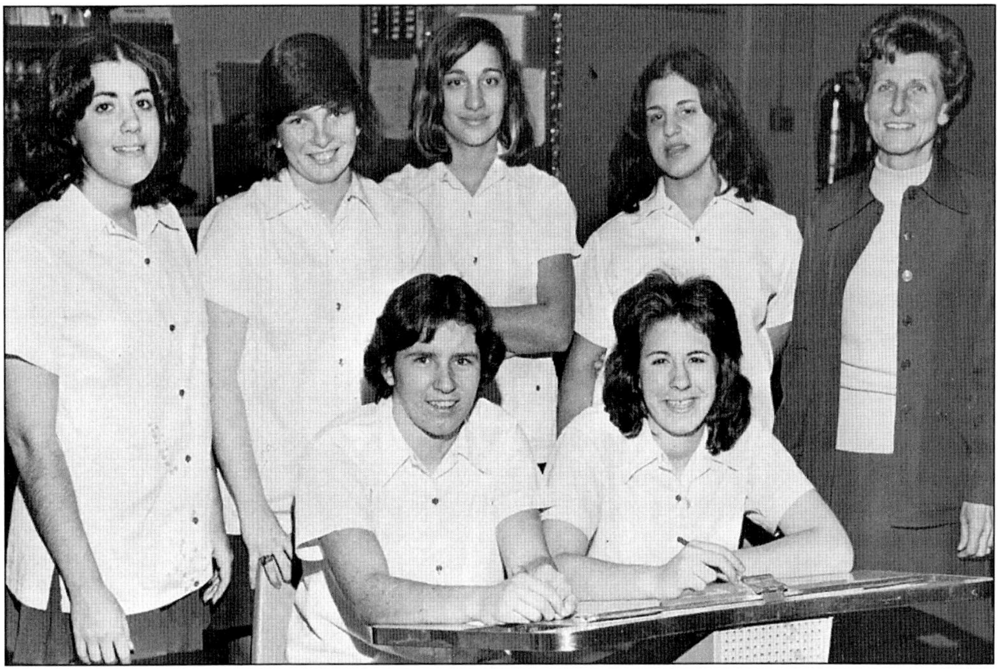

The year 1974 saw the first women's teams added to the intercollegiate program. Sofia Ellsworth (who became the first coordinator of women's athletics) and Christine Marasa (who became assistant athletic director for women's athletics) were instrumental in establishing the women's program. With the cooperation of Tom Watt, the athletic director, they proceeded to develop the women's athletic program. As a result, women's tennis, softball, and volleyball were added in 1974. By 2000, there were seven women's teams at the college. For their contributions, Sofia Ellsworth (1956–1977) and Christine Marasa (1966–1990) were inducted into the SUNY Farmingdale Athletics Hall of Fame. The top photograph shows Ellsworth, at right as coach of the women's bowling team. The bottom photograph shows Marasa, second from left, as coach of the women's tennis team in 1975.

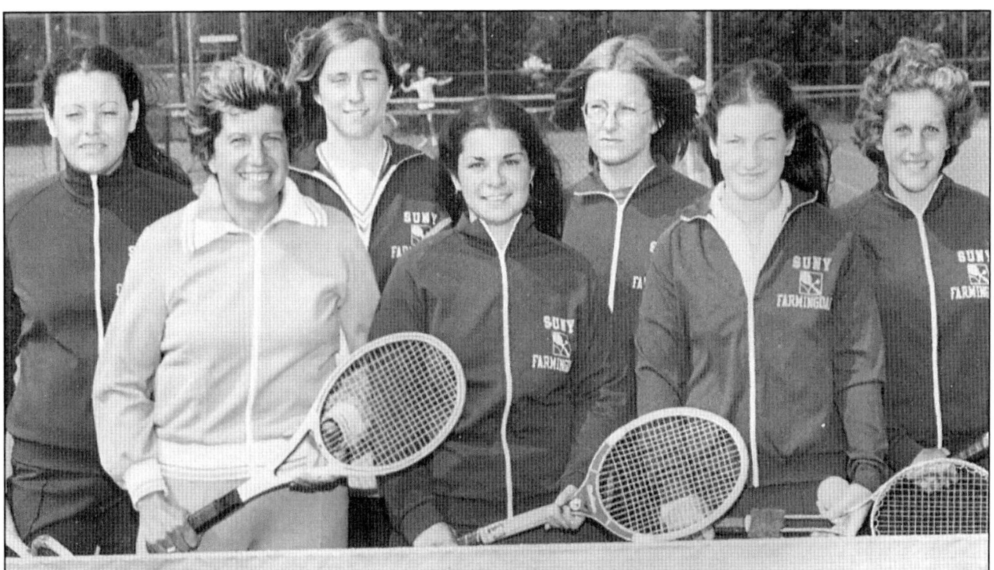

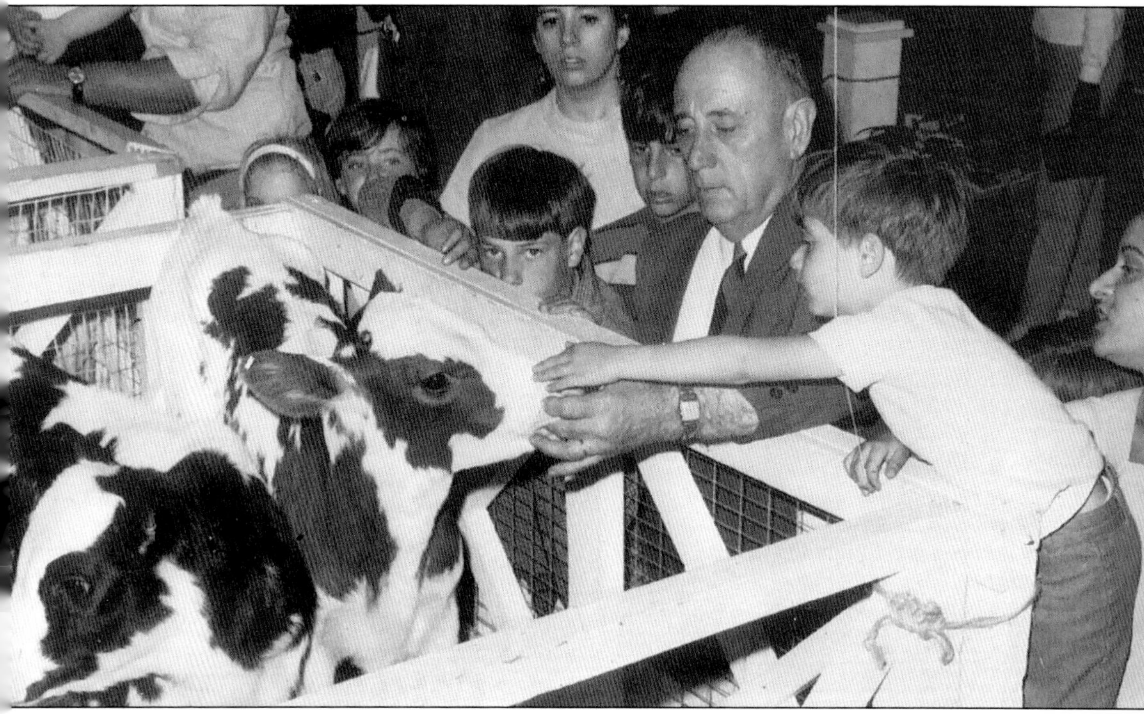

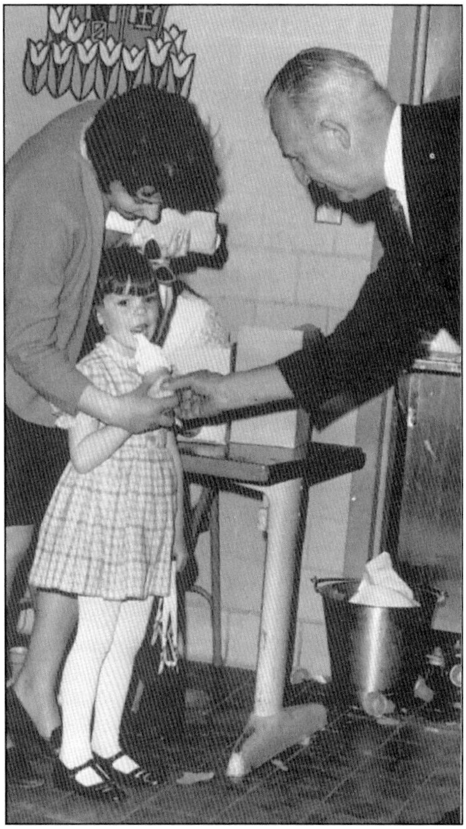

The 52nd Annual Open House was held for three days in the spring of 1971. It maintained a long tradition of opening the campus to the public. In order to display the latest educational and technical advances, each curriculum sponsored an exhibit. Guided tours were also conducted for the visitors. This important event provided an opportunity to stimulate interest in the college. In addition to the seriousness of the program, a joyous and sometimes carnival spirit took hold. In the top photograph, Prof. Robert Stockbridge, chair of the Agriculture Department, assists several young students as they pet the animals. In the lower photograph, Prof. George Cook, chair of the Food Processing Department, extends an ice-cream cone to a young visitor, accompanied by her mother, in Thompson Hall.

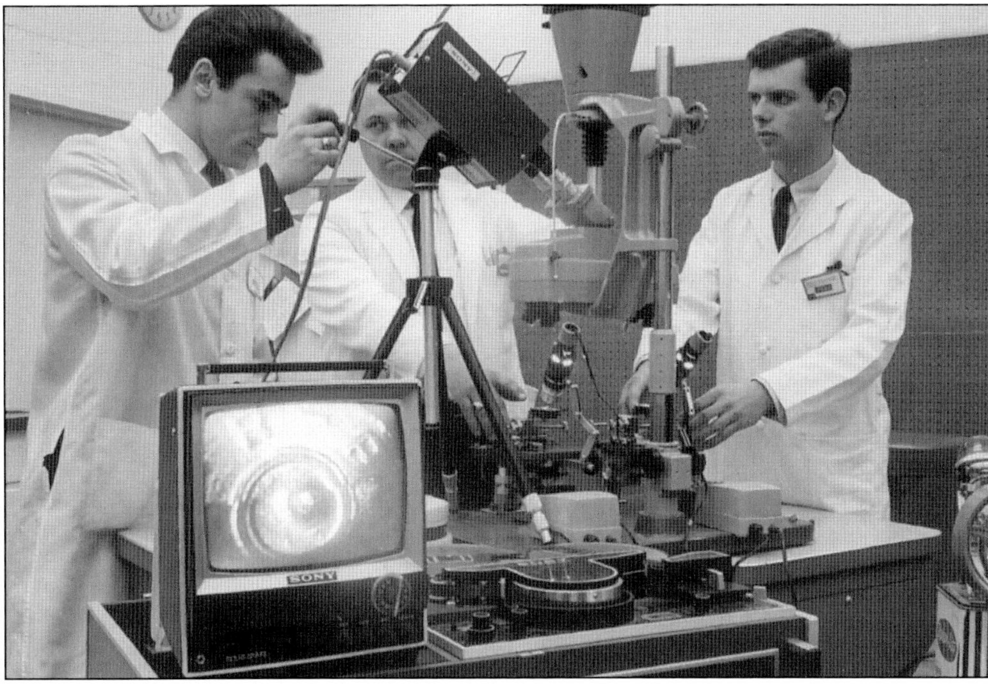

In the 1960s and 1970s, increasing numbers of students enrolled in police science courses in the college's day and evening programs. Public money was used to attract new students and to offer advanced education to those actively engaged in police work to make them sensitive to the needs of the communities, especially minorities. The college's Police Science Department, later renamed the Criminal Justice Department, expanded its curriculum. In this 1960 photograph, Prof. C.D. Kuhn, center, and his assistants are engaged in a scientific study in the police science laboratory.

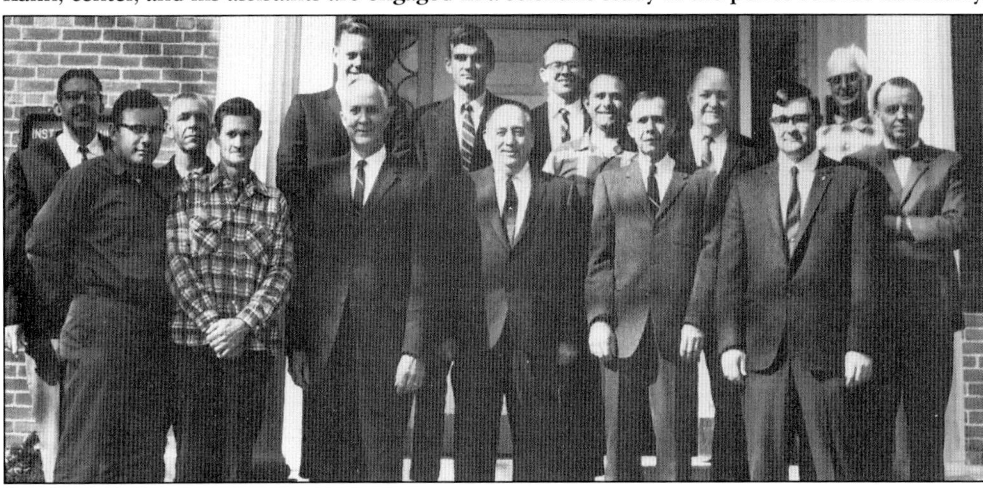

The members of the Agriculture Department pose for this group picture in 1970. Shown, from left to right, are the following: (front row) R. Reutlinger, E. Buck, G. Mowry, R. Stockbridge, E. Wallkam, and V. Bellard; (back row) W. Becker, S. Carubba, C. Struck, T. Bruetsch, D. Barney, J. Visco, K. Hilbert, E. Patterson, and J. Lawrence. Walter Becker was a graduate of the institute. He was hired as a technical assistant by Prof. D. Hart Horton, for whom Horton Hall is named. Becker lived in an apartment at the Campus Village from 1951 to 1955 with his wife and two children. He spent his entire professional career at Farmingdale, where he rose to the rank of professor.

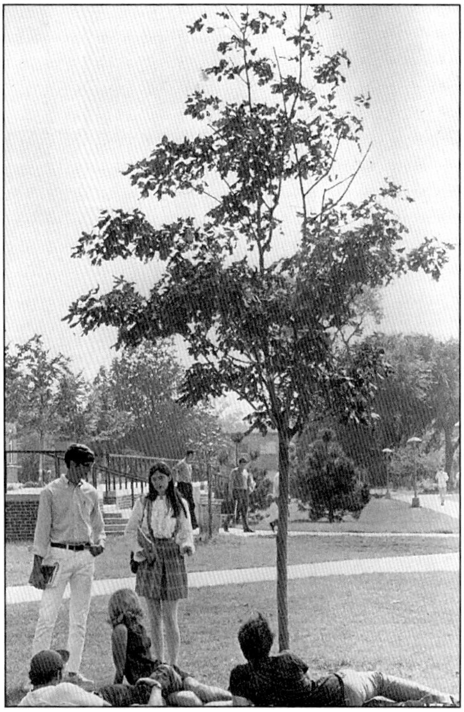

This campus scene during the spring semester of 1970 captures students relaxing between classes. Knapp Hall is to the left. The view looks south to Melville Road. Farmingdale, having been charted in 1912, was one of the six agricultural and technical colleges and is therefore older than the State University of New York, which was established in 1948.

Dental hygiene students strive to keep teeth in good shape through educating and treating patients. They go through a rigorous educational process at Farmingdale, gaining considerable practice as they learn. These students in 1961 are being tested to qualify for graduation. The first dental hygiene class graduated in June 1948, when seven students completed the program.

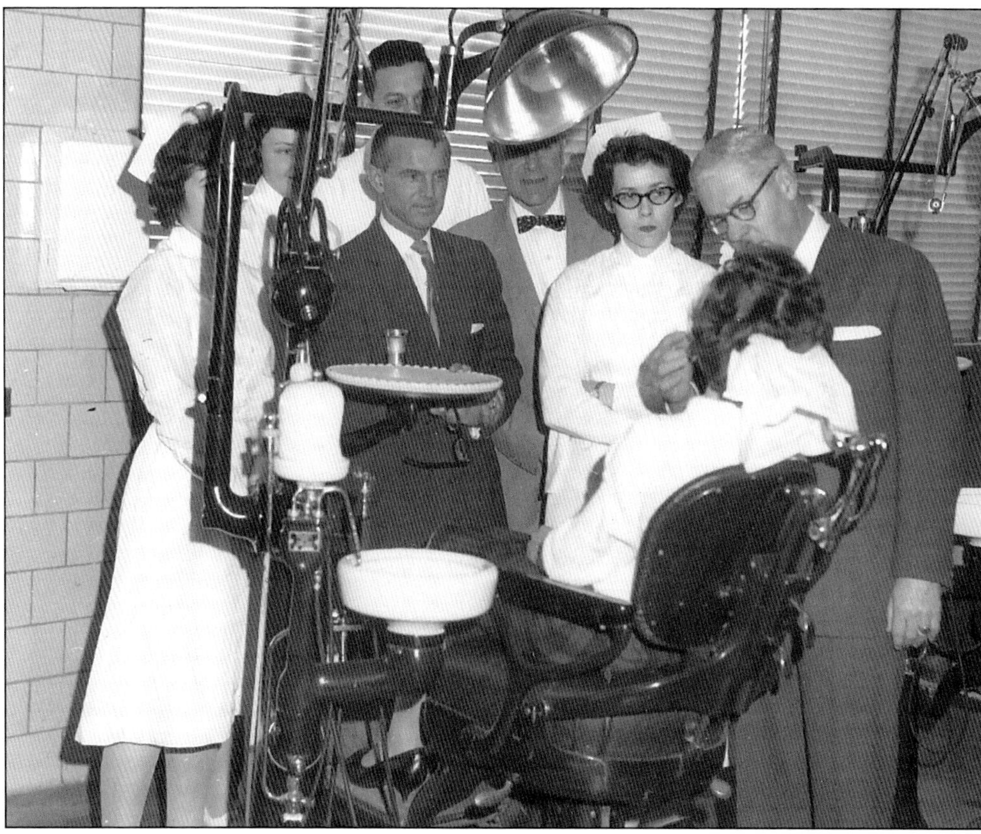

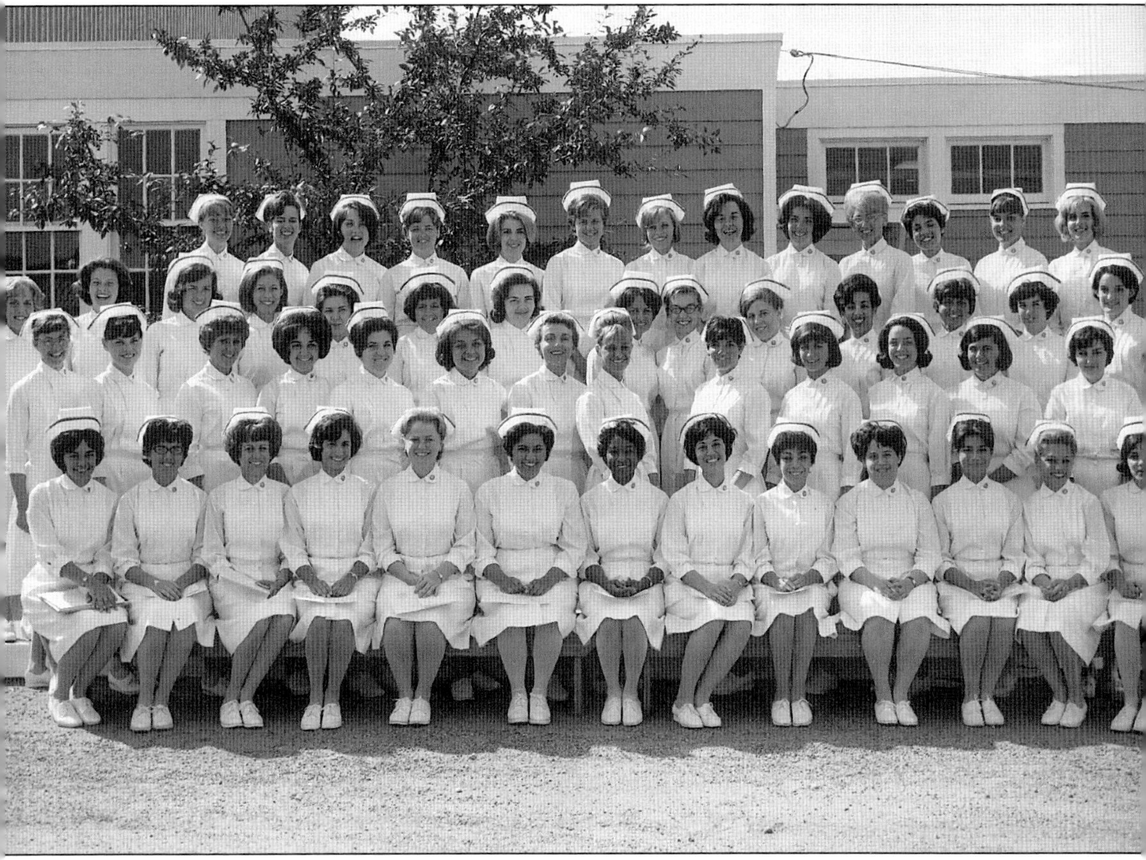

These young women are smiling because they are the 1965 dental hygiene graduating class. They have passed all tests for certification to practice in the field. At the inception of the dental hygiene program in 1946, facilities were limited. A clinic of five chairs had been set up in one of the classrooms. A Ritter x-ray machine was acquired and a darkroom was equipped. In the clinic, the students did their first prophylaxis on each other after completing mannequin training. They also did prophylaxis on other students at the college. A small amount of operative and dental work was performed on students by dentists on the faculty on a clinical basis. It provided an opportunity to give dental hygiene students practical experience in chair assisting, sterilization, and taking x-rays.

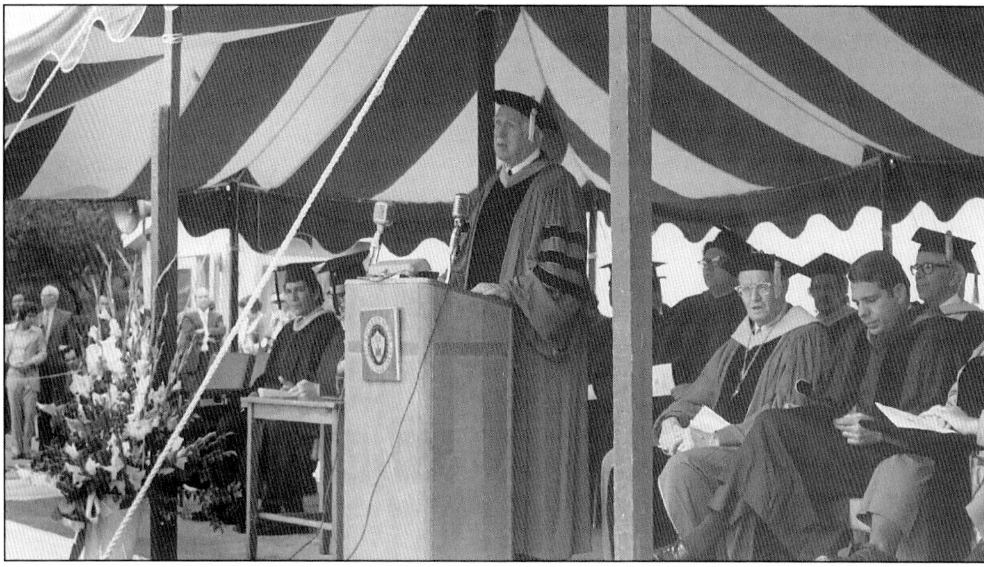

Mortimer J. Gleeson of Manhasset, the chairman of the College Council, addresses the 1972 graduating class. To his right, in back, is James Nihan, dean of the Evening College and later vice president. To Nihan's left, in front, is guest speaker and Chief Judge Sol Wachtler of the New York State Court of Appeals. To Wachtler's right is Pres. Charles W. Laffin. The members of the College Council are appointed by the governor and they set policy.

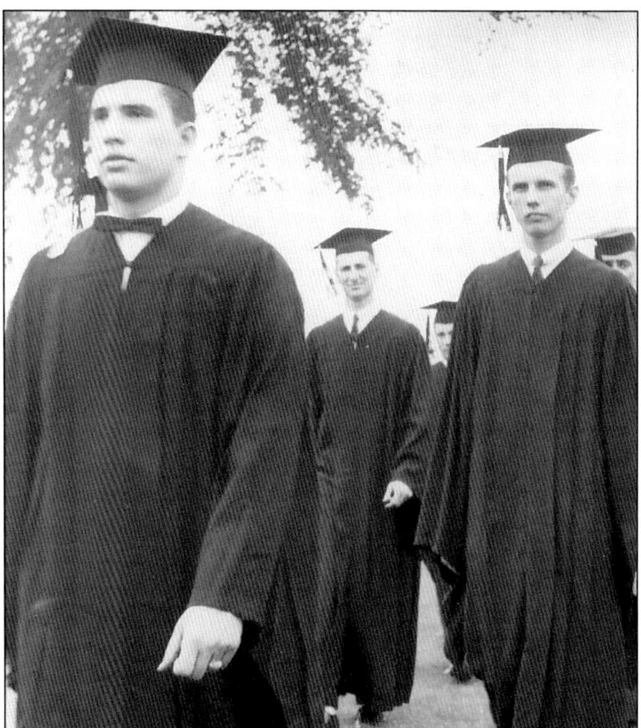

Students lead the way in the 1963 commencement processional to the Allard Field House. They have received associate degrees and will either continue their education for a four-year degree or seek employment. Graduates were very successful in securing jobs because of the special educational programs the college provided them.

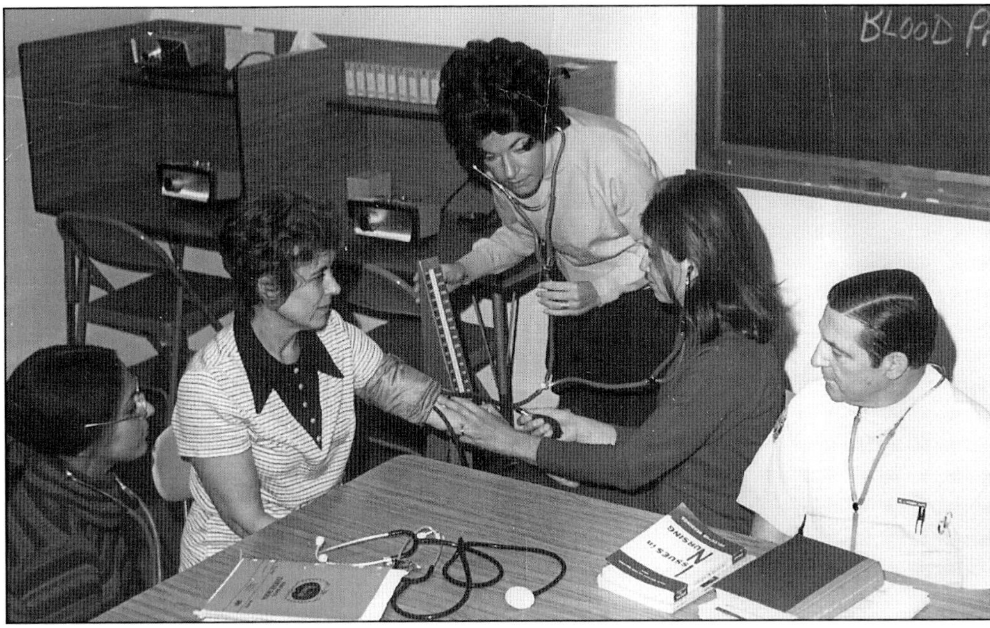

Prof. Barbara Steinbaum, center, chair of the Nursing Department, is instructing students on the technique of taking blood pressure in 1964. The nursing program, one of the most demanding and oversubscribed programs, prepared students for entry into this caring profession. Upon graduation, students received an associate in science degree and are eligible to take the New York State licensing examination for registered nurses.

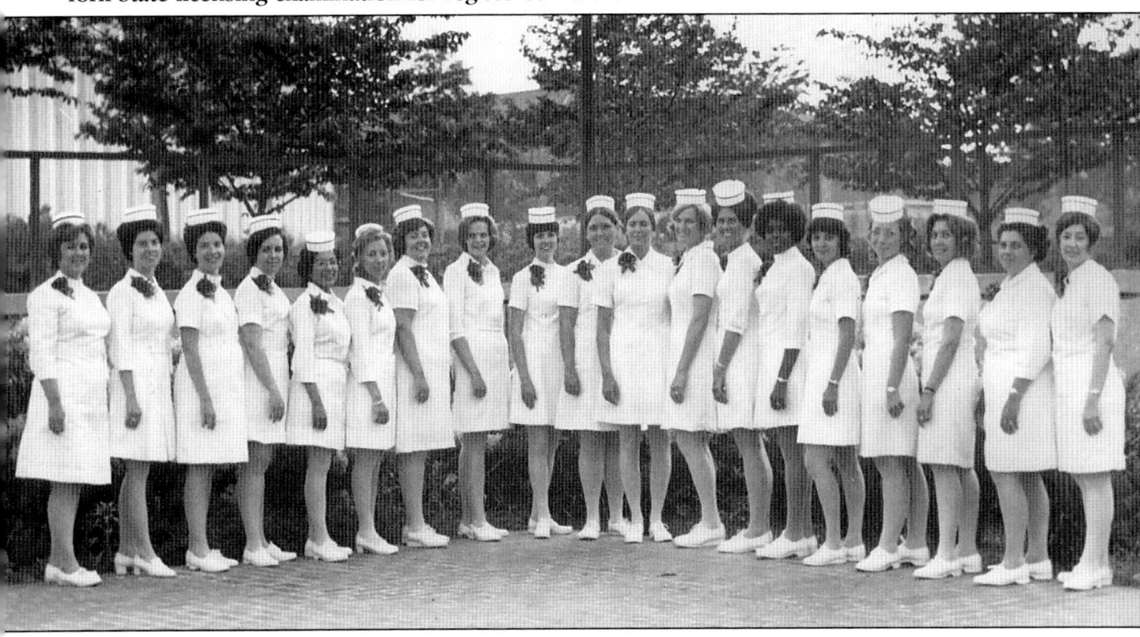

Pictured are the nursing graduates of the Evening College, Class of 1972. The curriculum was the same for these students as the Day College students. The curriculum included a balance of courses in the humanities and social sciences. It provided the theoretical knowledge on clinical practice needed to administer throughout the life cycle. The entire educational experience took place in the classroom, nursing laboratory, and in a variety of clinical settings.

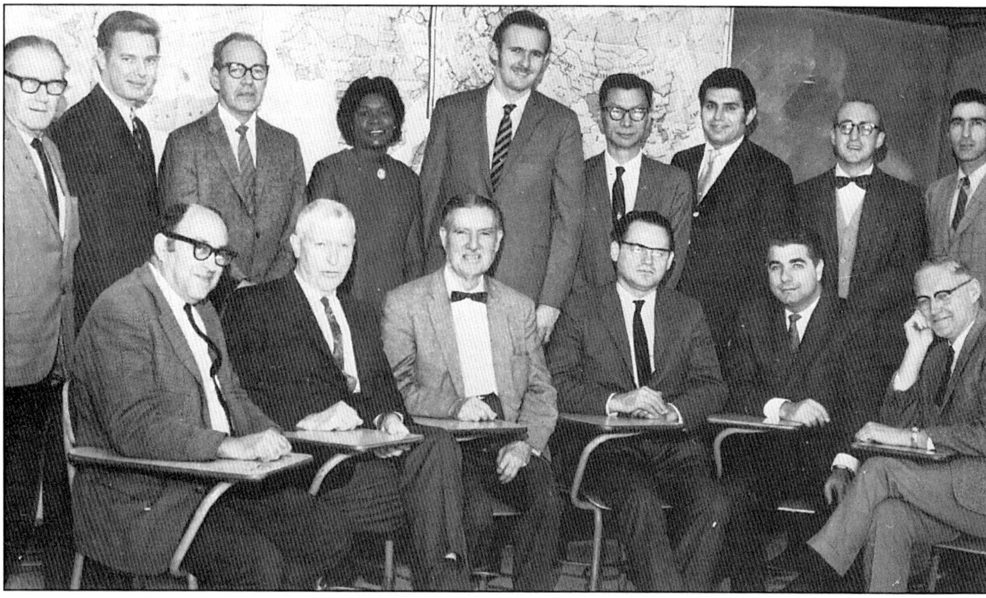

The Social Science Department, shown in 1970, was once part of the General Education Division and contributed to the enrichment of the students' education. In the early 1970s, the Liberal Arts and Sciences Department incorporated all of the social sciences to prepare students for a baccalaureate degree. Shown, from left to right, are the following: (front row) I. Levine, H. Amidon, L. Jones, S. Brozak, G. Roukis, and T. Ladonsky; (back row) W. Farrow, A. Scoufelis, G. Sweeney, E. Bryant, R. Hoffman, H. Lieu, P. Alimaris, J. Magee, and F.J. Cavaioli.

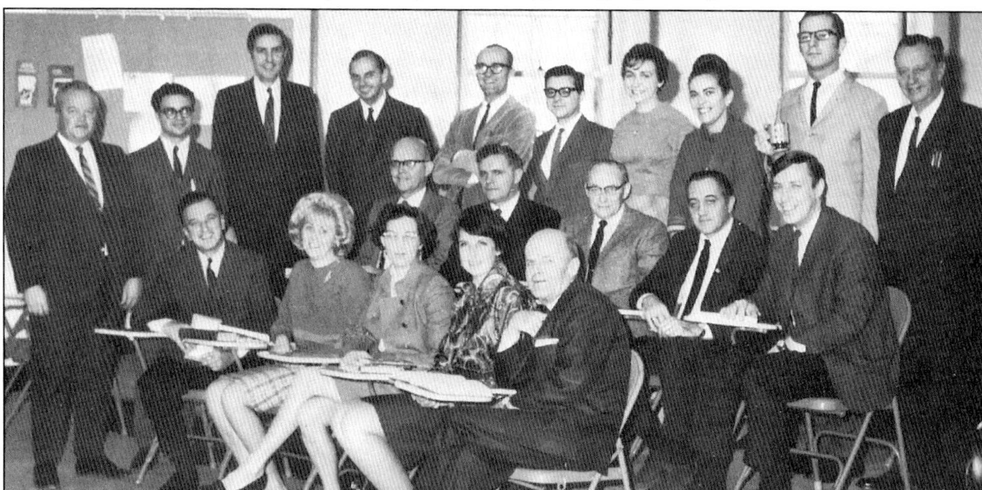

The English Department, shown in 1970, was also a part of the General Education Division and later joined the Liberal Arts and Sciences Department to continue its mission of providing a broad-based education to support students' technical education. Such a structural change of dropping the General Education Division and creating the Liberal Arts and Sciences Department kept pace with the demands of modern education. Shown, from left to right, are the following members: (seated, front row) J. Weiser, E. Wollett, J. Keller, E. Stwertka, and A. Hallock; (seated, middle row) R. Wallace, A. Blinderman, C.D. Thomson, P. Deland, and C. McAdorey; (standing, back row) H. Mikkelsen, C. Conford, W. Dennis, S. Fein, R. Kelly, H. Lieblich, B. Sherman, J. Carnesi, L. Taylor, and E. Ore.

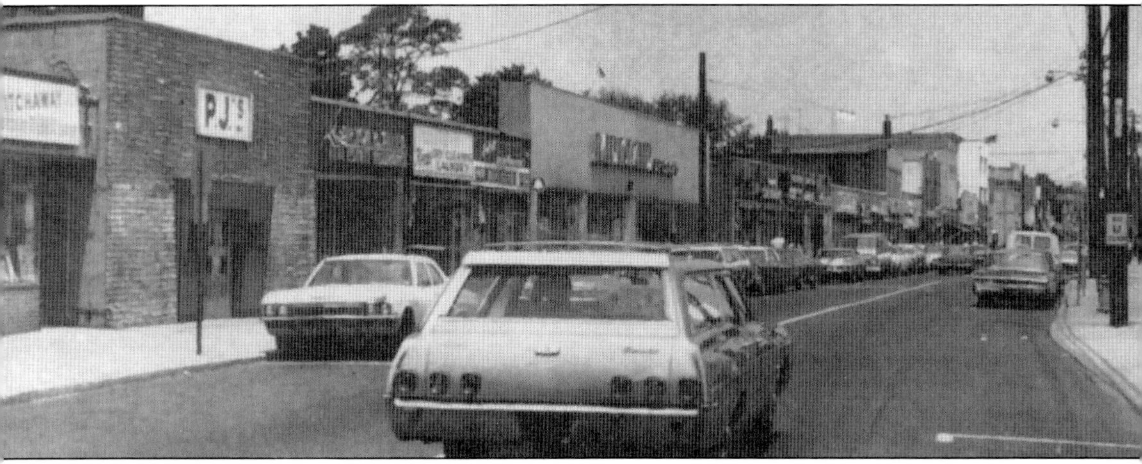

One and one-half miles from the campus is the village of Farmingdale, which offered the charm of a small college town and a proximity to New York City. The college encouraged students to visit the "Capital of the World." The village had a population of over 15,000 in 1970 and provided many conveniences of home. The Long Island Railroad was nearby. This photograph of Main Street will bring back many fond alumni memories.

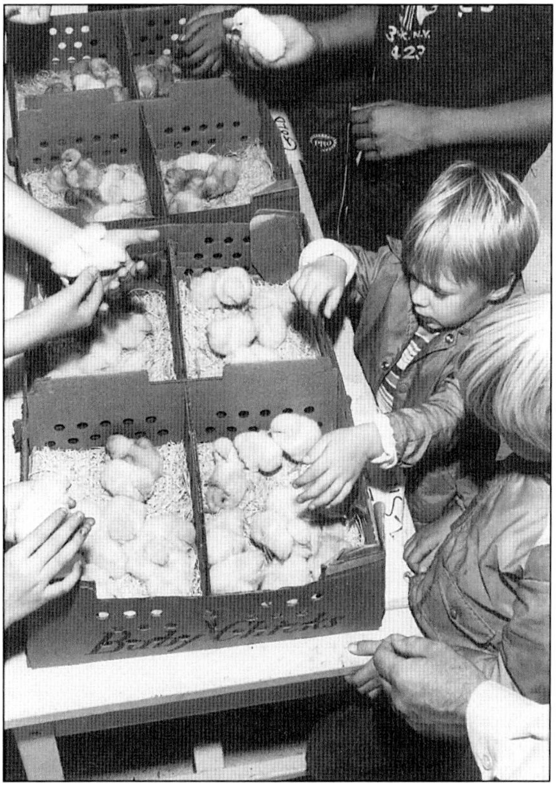

These children are part of a farm tour at the old farm complex during homecoming in 1983. They are having a delightful time playing with recently hatched chicks. With the passage of time and social progress, it was a rare opportunity for children to have direct contact with animals on Long Island.

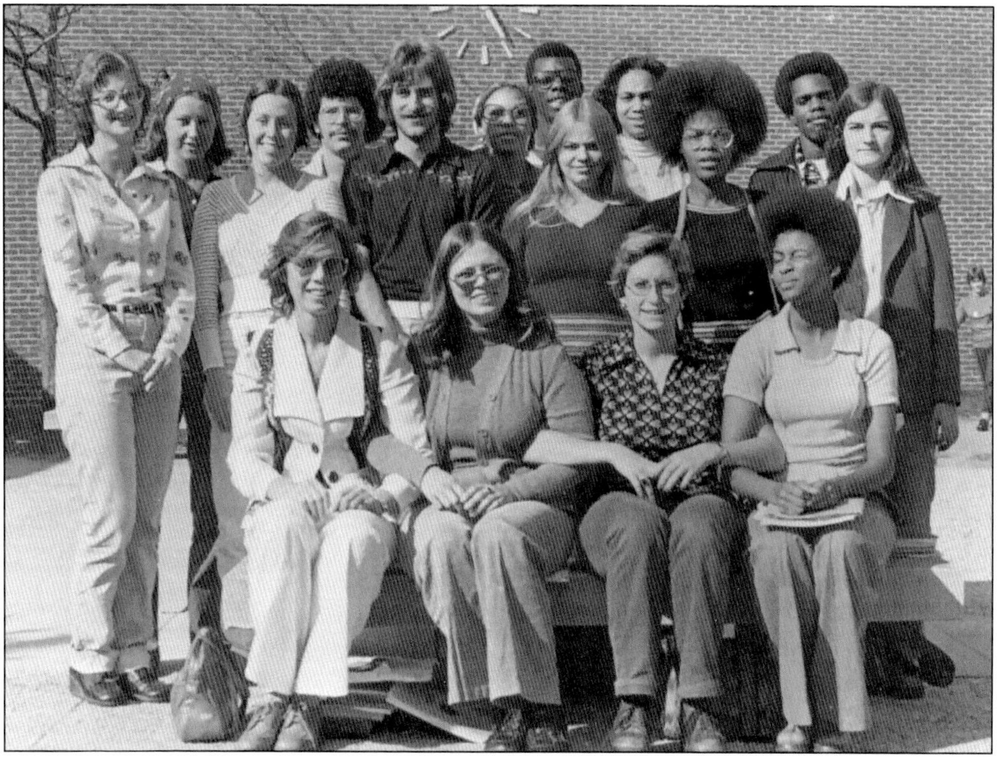

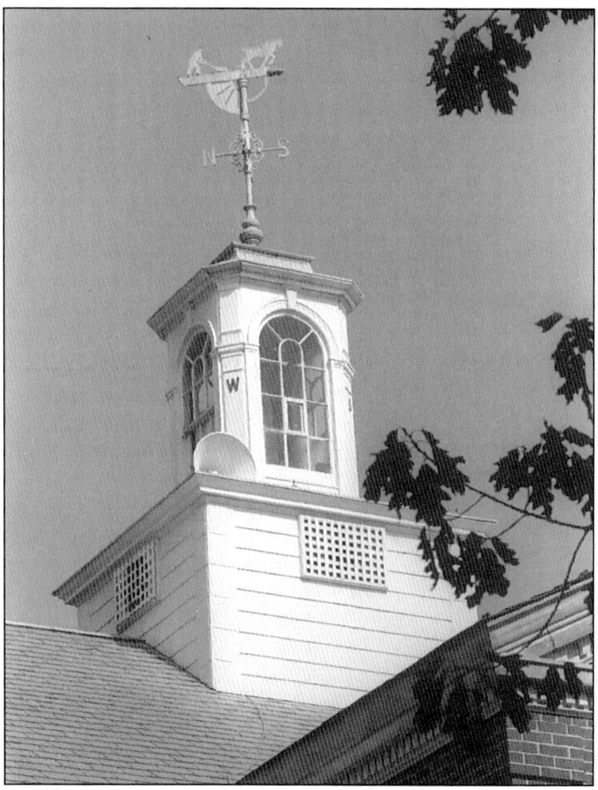

The College Union Board has provided the cultural and social programs in educating students outside the classroom. The CUB accomplished its task by sponsoring such cultural programs as lectures, film series, and nightclub nights. Pictured are the 1976 CUB members. The officers, from left to right, are as follows: (seated, front) Marcia McHugh, secretary; Nancy Shafer, president; Sandee Herlands, treasurer; Stella Lawrence, vice president.

The decorative weathervane and cupola stand atop Thompson Hall, complementing this stately building. It was designed and constructed in the 1930s, before the State University of New York was established in 1948. With its distinctive architectural elements in the Georgian style, Thompson Hall remains an attraction to campus visitors.

Five

The Frank A. Cipriani Era: Into the New Millennium

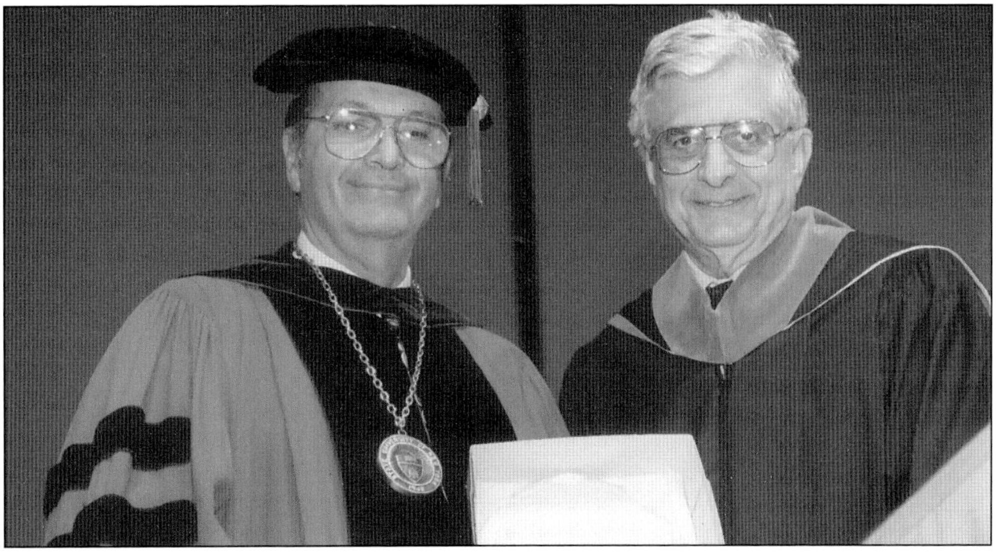

Pres. Frank A. Cipriani, left, is presenting an award to Anthony Mastroianni at the 1998 commencement for the latter's service on the College Council. Cipriani retired on January 1, 2000, after 35 years at the college, 22 of them as its president. He guided the transformation of SUNY Farmingdale from a two-year agricultural and technical college to a four-year baccalaureate degree institution. His final achievement was the establishment of the Broadhollow Bioscience Park, a joint venture with the world-renowned Cold Spring Harbor Laboratory. It opened in late 2000 and is located in the eastern section of the campus.

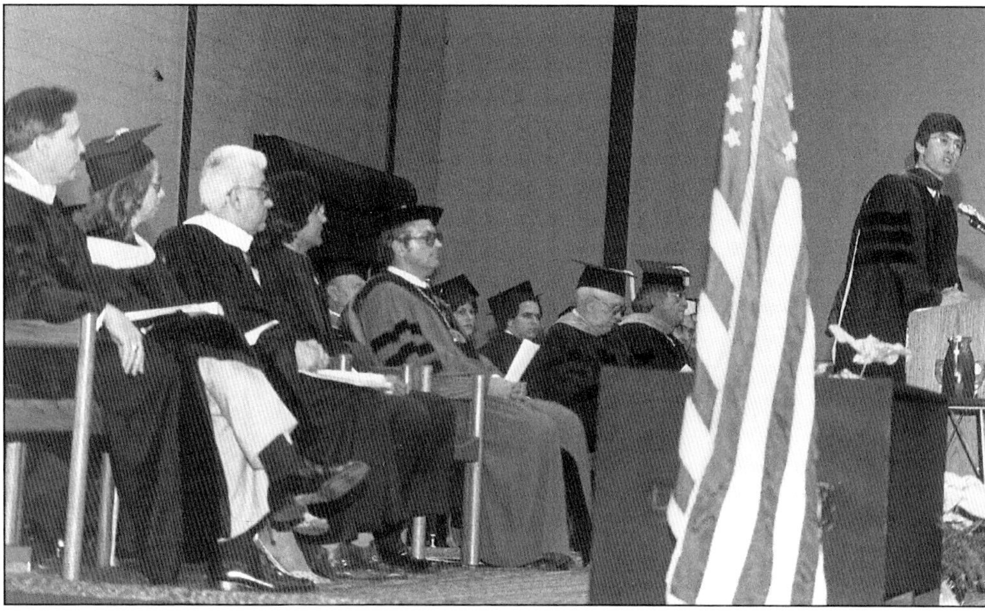

Congressman Thomas Downey, right, of Suffolk County addresses the graduates at the spring 1982 commencement ceremonies. He urged the graduates to be proud of their alma mater and to use their knowledge and skills wisely and productively.

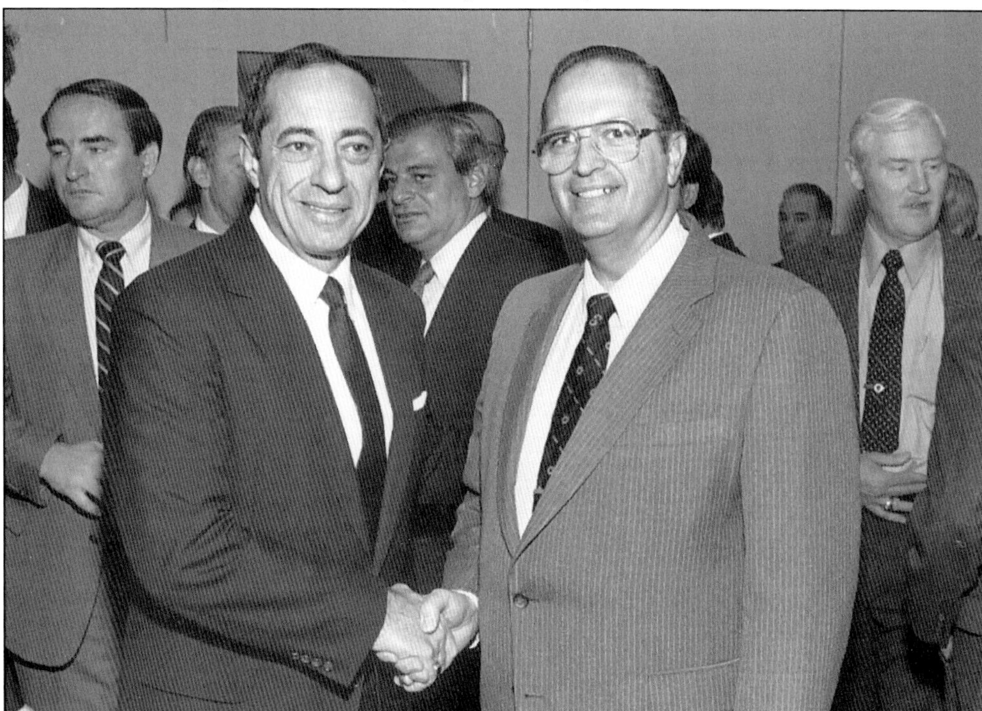

President Cipriani (right center) greets Gov. Mario Cuomo (left center) in 1990 during a campus visit. In the background, between Cipriani and Cuomo, is Nassau County executive Thomas Gullotta. To the right is Sen. Owen Johnson of Suffolk County. Local and state political leaders often visited the campus .

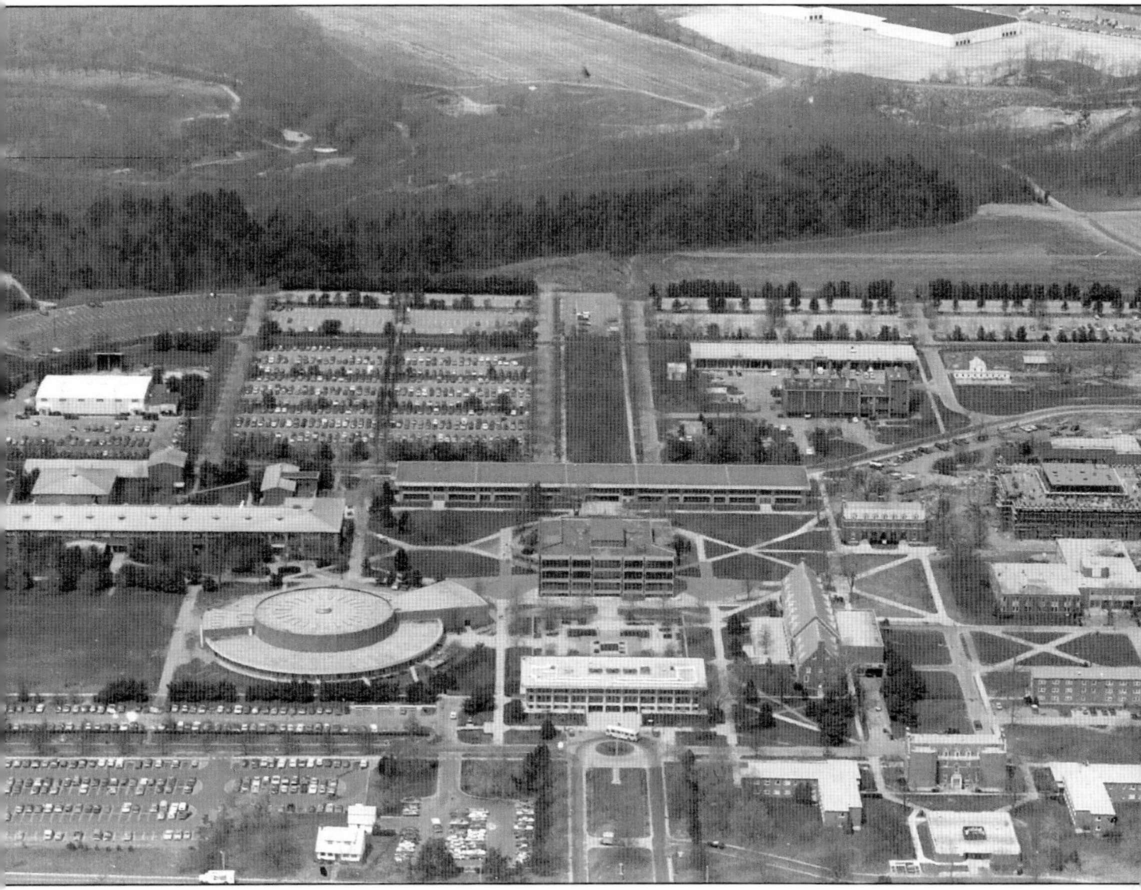

This 1990 aerial view, looking north from Melville Road, reveals the campus at an advanced stage. The large circular building in the left foreground is Roosevelt Hall, home of the Student Government Association and student activities. The long building at left center is Lupton Hall. At the lower center, by the Melville Road flagpole entrance, is Laffin Hall, the former administration building. Above Laffin Hall is Ralph Bunche Plaza; above it is Greenley Hall (Library); and above it, extending left to right, is Hale Hall. To the right of Ralph Bunche Plaza is Knapp Hall, and below it is Memorial Hall. Hooper Hall (the tall building) is to the right of Memorial Hall. Below Hooper Hall is Cohen Infirmary, and across the quadrangle going north is Ward Hall. Farther north is the Heating Plant, and beyond it is the Service Building. At the extreme lower right, going north, are the following buildings: the Alumni Residence Hall, the Nassau Residence Hall, Whitman Hall, and Gleeson Hall. Thompson Hall, Hicks Hall, Cutler Hall, and Horton Hall are not in the picture.

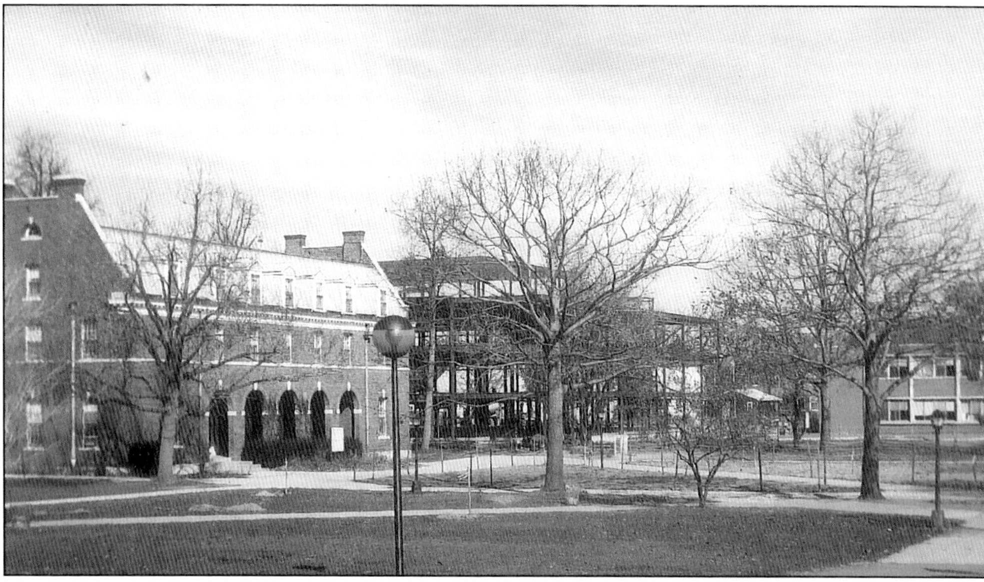

As the college grew rapidly in the 1970s, there was a need for more classroom space. In the center of this view, Gleeson Hall is being constructed on November 13, 1981. Gleeson Hall, named for the former chairman of the College Council, provided the necessary classroom space. Ward Hall is at the left, and Whitman Hall is at the right.

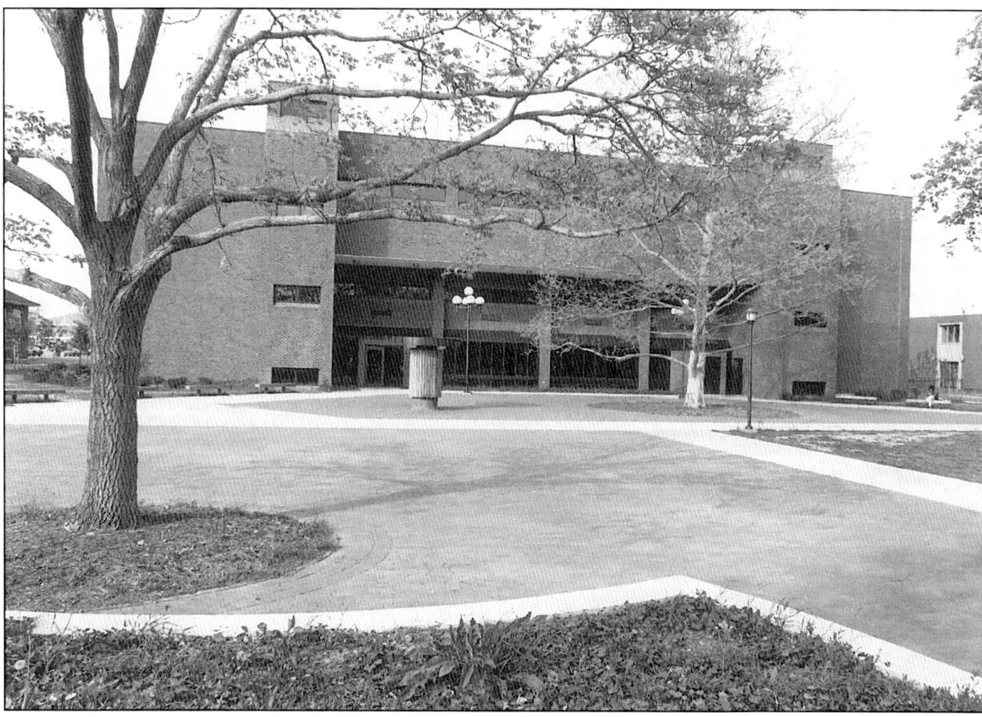

Gleeson Hall makes an impressive view as it fills this campus space. A much-needed facility, it houses the Departments of Nursing, Dental Hygiene, and Criminal Justice, as well as the Registration and Conference Center and the Institute for Learning in Retirement. Conklin Hall is at the extreme left. Whitman Hall is at the extreme right.

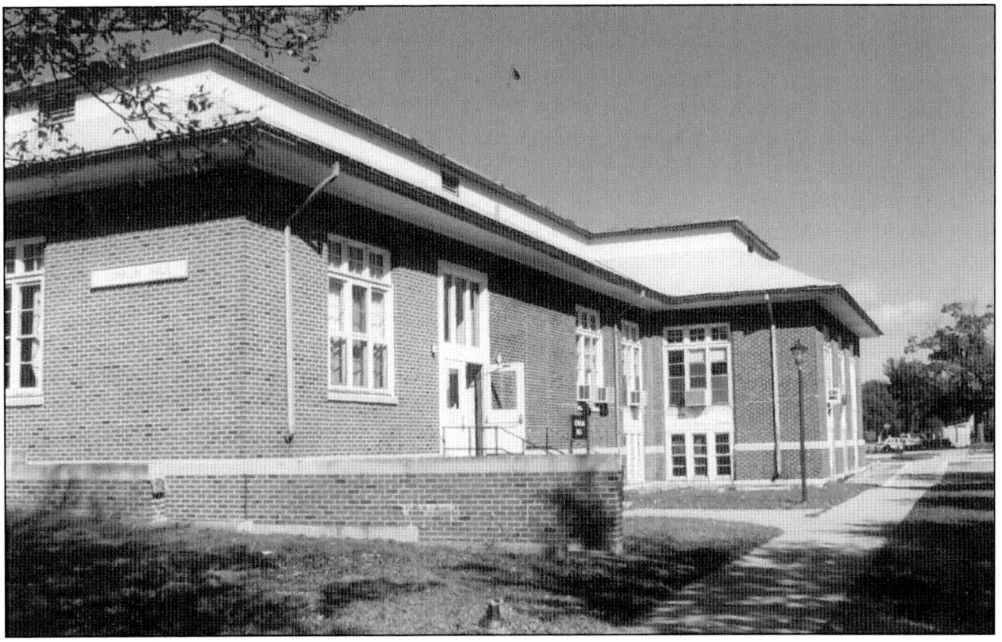

Conklin Hall, one of the original buildings on the campus, is shown as it appears today. Its name is derived from 520 Conklin Street, Farmingdale, where the Technical Industrial Division started. It was constructed at a cost of $190,000 in 1914 to serve as the power plant. The Evening College Association and the Advanced Manufacturing Technology Incubator are now housed there.

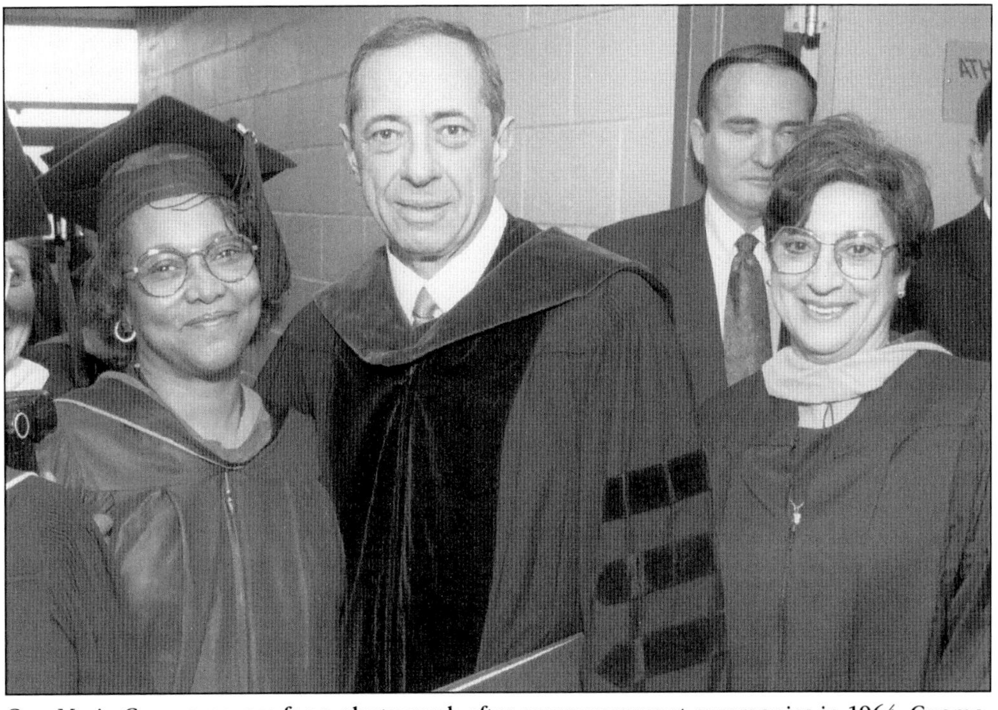

Gov. Mario Cuomo pauses for a photograph after commencement ceremonies in 1964. Cuomo, a graduate of St. John's College and St. John's University Law School, was a frequent visitor to SUNY Farmingdale during his 12 years as governor.

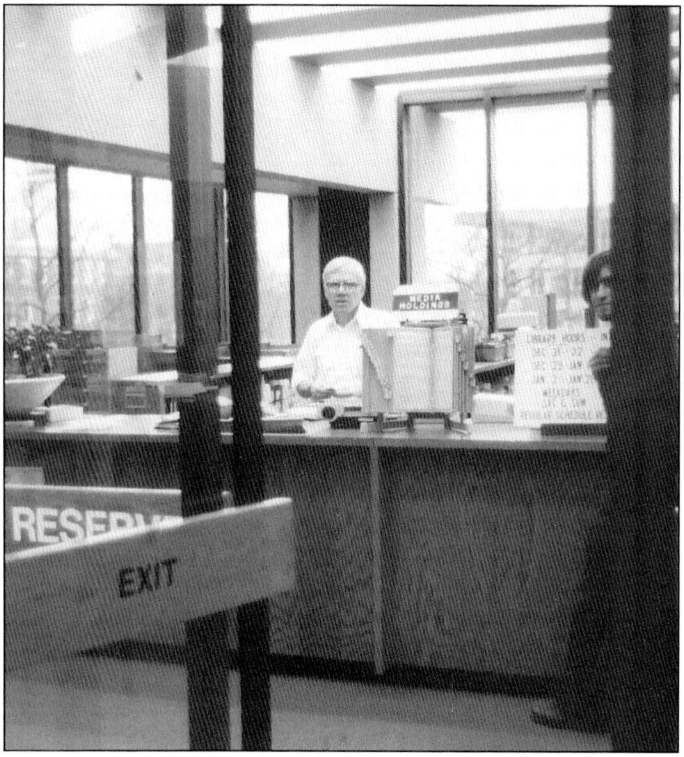

Librarian Parker Van Hoogenstyn looks out from the Media Reserve Room of Greeley Hall in 1982. In the background, right, is Laffin Hall, which housed the administration. The library was always a special place to meet friends, to study, to do research, and to solve the William Shakespeare riddle: "We know what we are, but not what we may be."

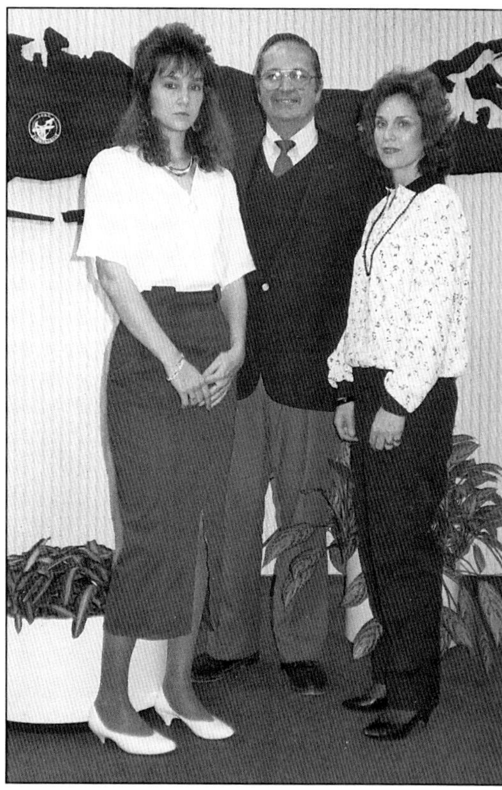

Pictured in 1988, from left to right, are the following: Michele M. Balacich, a resident of Hicksville and the Day College valedictorian, with a 4.0 grade average in the college's Veterinary Science Technology program; Pres. Frank A. Cipriani; and Diane Leone, a resident of North Babylon and the Evening College valedictorian with a 3.93 grade average in the area of business administration.

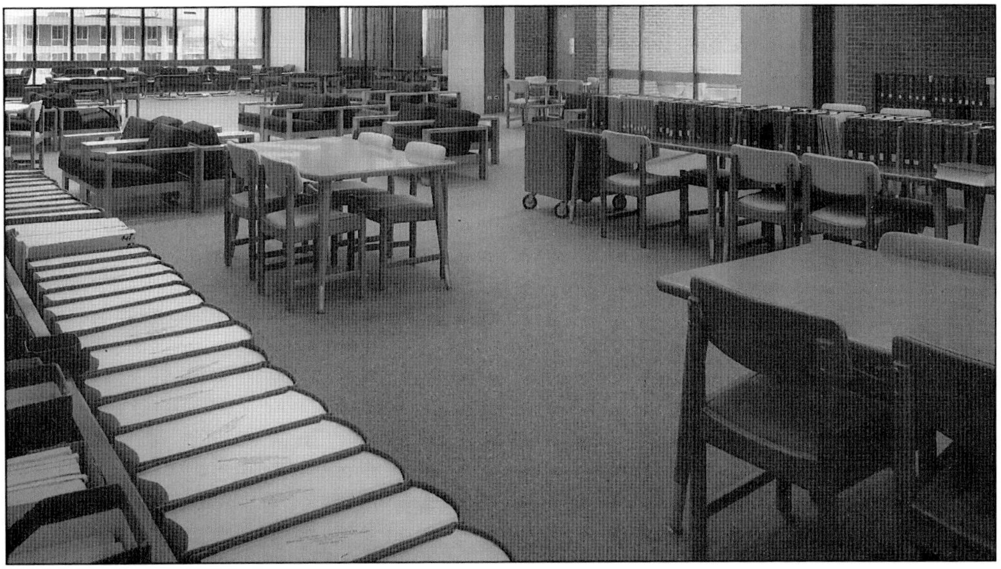

A rare scene of the reference section of Greenley Hall (Library) captures a placid moment with not a person in sight. Through the window at the left, Laffin Hall is visible. The library is named for Thomas D. Greenley, a professor who played a strong role in developing the Advertising Art and Design Department. He came to Farmingdale in 1947. He died in 1971 soon after hem retired.

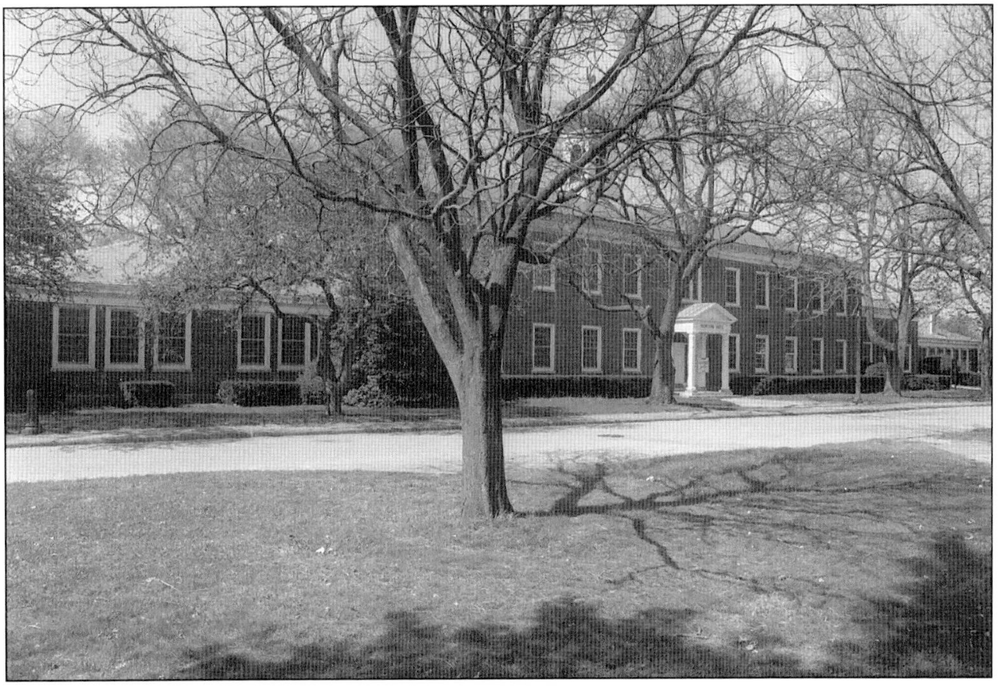

Horton Hall has been converted into the new administration building. It is named for D. Hart Horton, a longtime teacher and supervisor of the Poultry Science Department. Horton's contributions to the school from the 1920s to the 1940s led to the construction of modern brooder houses, laying pens, incubators, a killing room, and the inauguration of the Egg Laying Contest. Pens of birds were represented from all over the country at the school.

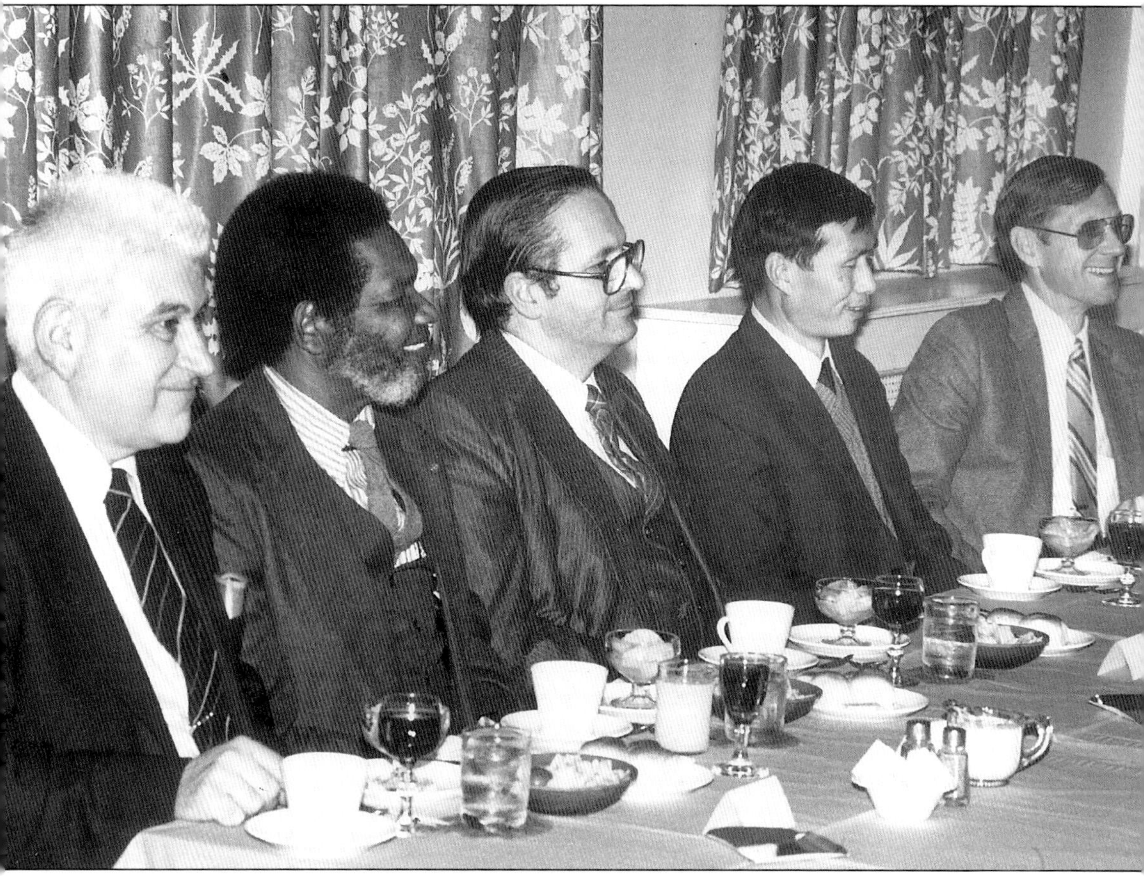

Shown, from left to right, are Provost Mauro Zulli, Vice Pres. Noel Palmer, Pres. Frank A. Cipriani, Professor Pei, and Prof. Herb Zipper at a farewell luncheon for Professor Pei, December 1982. Pei was a visiting professor from mainland China from September 1981 to December 1982, teaching in the Electrical Technology Department. He was sponsored by Professor Zipper. Others who participated in the cultural exchange in the 1980s were Professor Tang, Professor Lee, and Professor Chow. Farmingdale professors Hal Brennen and Dash Petrela went to teach in China at the University of Xian in 1988. Prof. Leon Taub and Prof. Herb Zipper went the following year.

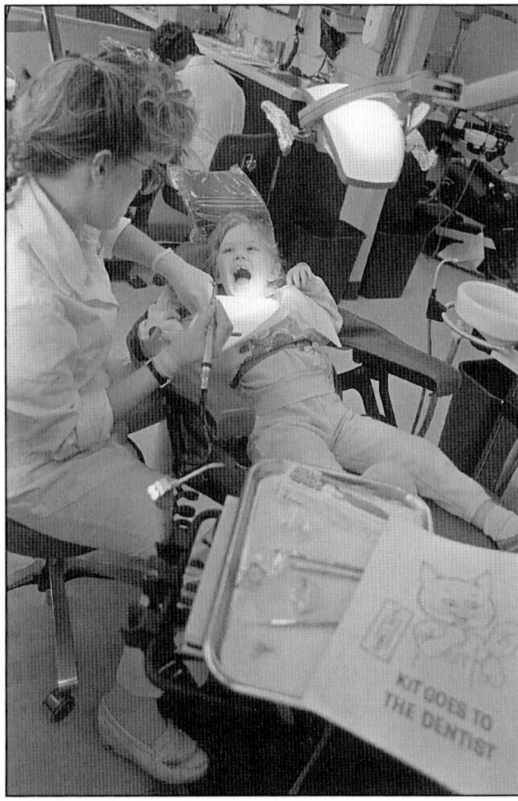

One of the extraordinary services offered by the college is the provision of dental prophylaxis for schoolchildren. Time and effort are spent on acquainting children with the dental office procedure and environment, so that they will be comfortable and unafraid. This dental hygiene student is treating her young patient in the Gleeson Hall clinic in 1990.

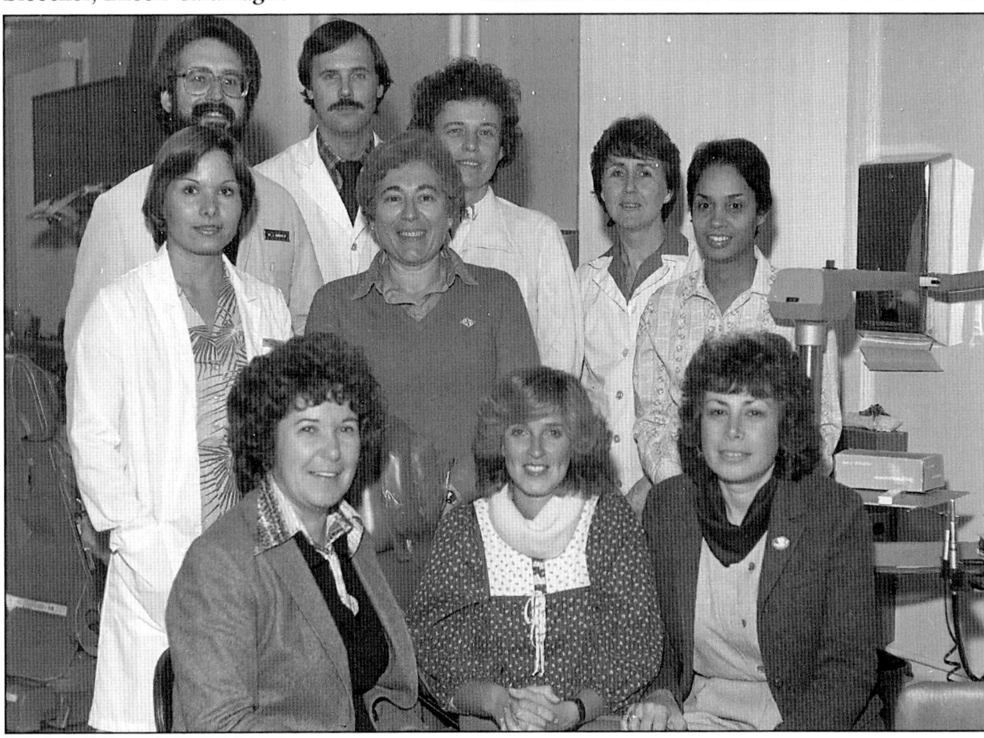

The members of the Dental Hygiene Department take time out to pose for this group picture in 1981. Shown, from left to right, are the following: (front row) Marie Peterson, Judy McCauley, and Judy Friedman; (middle row) Georgette Pergola, Beth Goldberg, and Margaret Ayala; (back row) Jeffrey Margolin, Ray Thomas, Charlotte Bleecker, Eileen Caramagno.

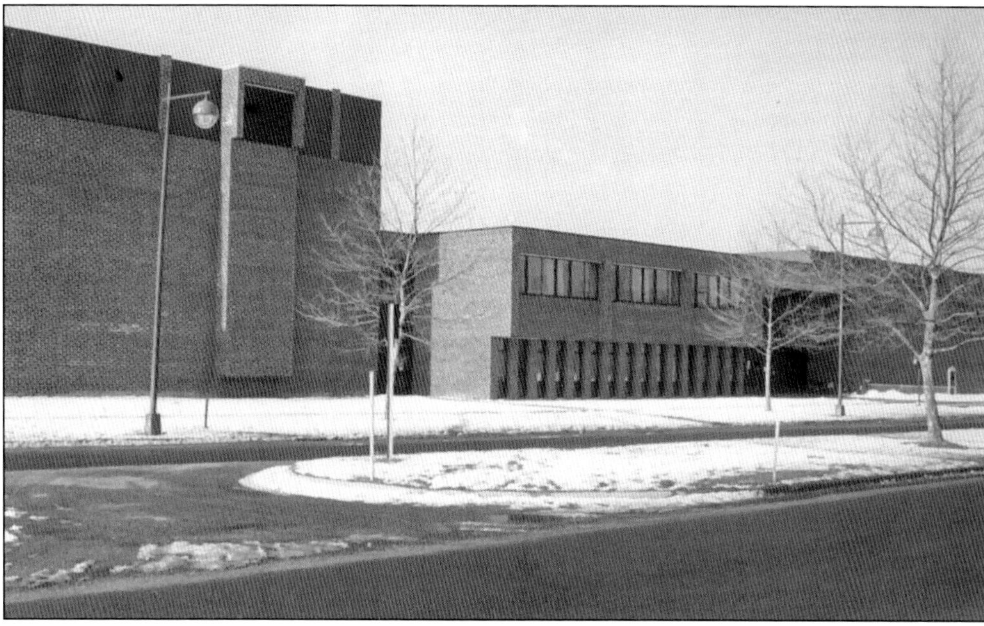

In 1972, a state-of-the-art athletic facility was built on campus—George E. Nold Hall, shown here. In the early days of its existence, the school used gymnasiums in downtown Farmingdale, the present bookstore, the Allard Field House, and Roosevelt Hall. Not only was Nold Hall a completely new facility, but it was also the first centrally located indoor-outdoor complex that the Farmingdale athletic program could call home.

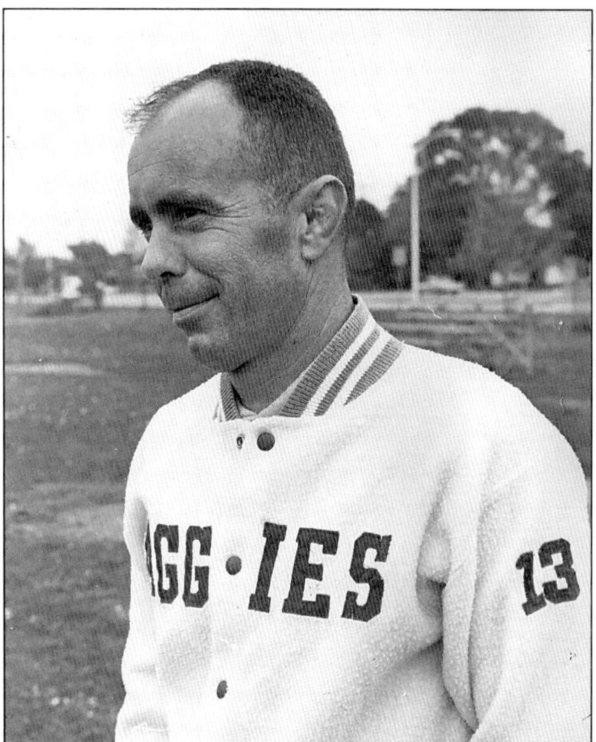

Robert Hartman joined the Farmingdale faculty in 1957 and retired in 1978. During those years, he coached cross-country, golf, and wrestling. A popular sports innovator, his 1972 wrestling team won the National Championship title. For his display of high standards of character, decency, and principles, representative of the college, he was inducted into the SUNY Farmingdale Athletic Hall of Fame in 1997.

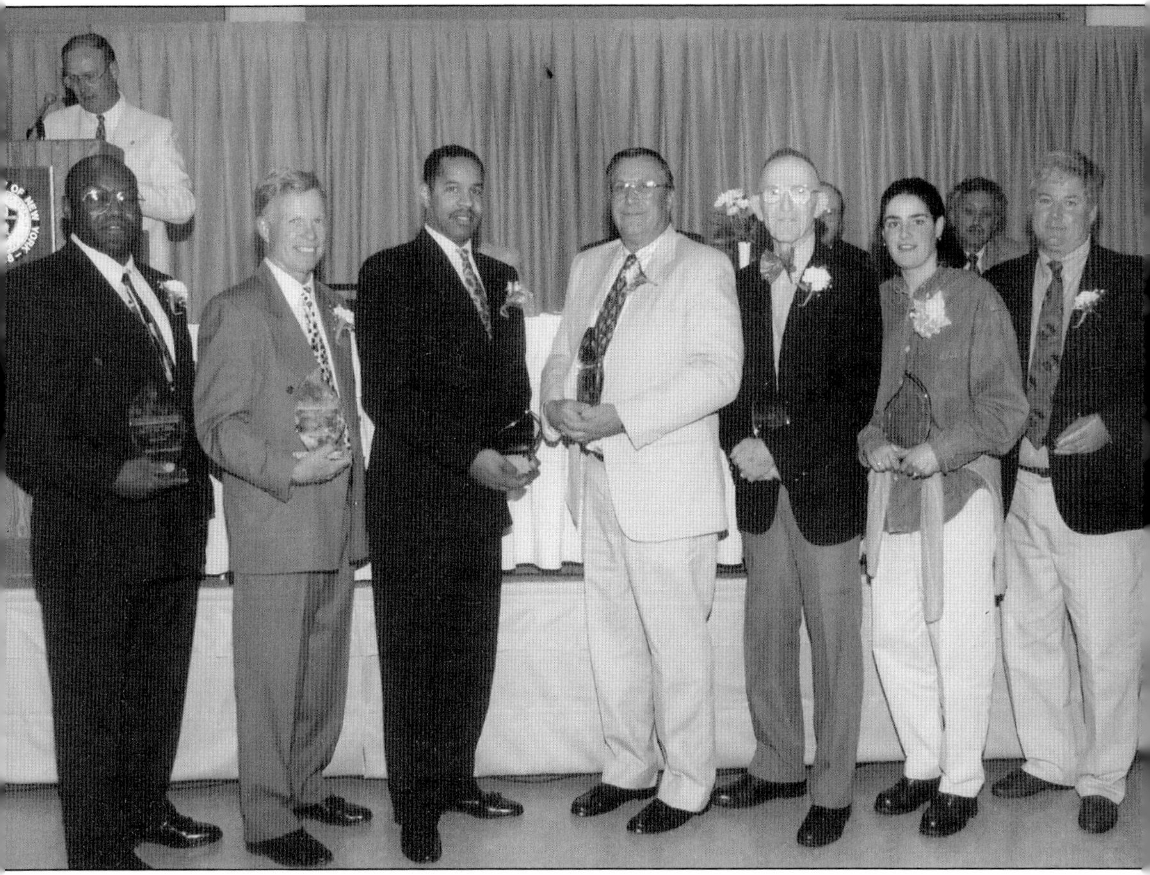

In 1990, Ray Rodriquez, the dean of students and chair of the Intercollegiate Athletic Board, suggested the creation of a SUNY Farmingdale Hall of Fame. After much planning and fundraising, it became a reality in 1995. For his contribution, Rodriguez was among the inductees in 2000. The first group of inductees of 1995 consisted of 23 individuals who were major contributors to the history of the college athletic program. The seven persons in this photograph were 1997 inductees to the SUNY Farmingdale Hall of Fame. They are, from left to right, Charles Gadson, Bob Hess, Norman Luckett, Bill DeCollibus, Manny Rolnick, Shannon Sepe, John Thearle. Athletic director Bruce Robbins, upper left, presides over the proceedings.

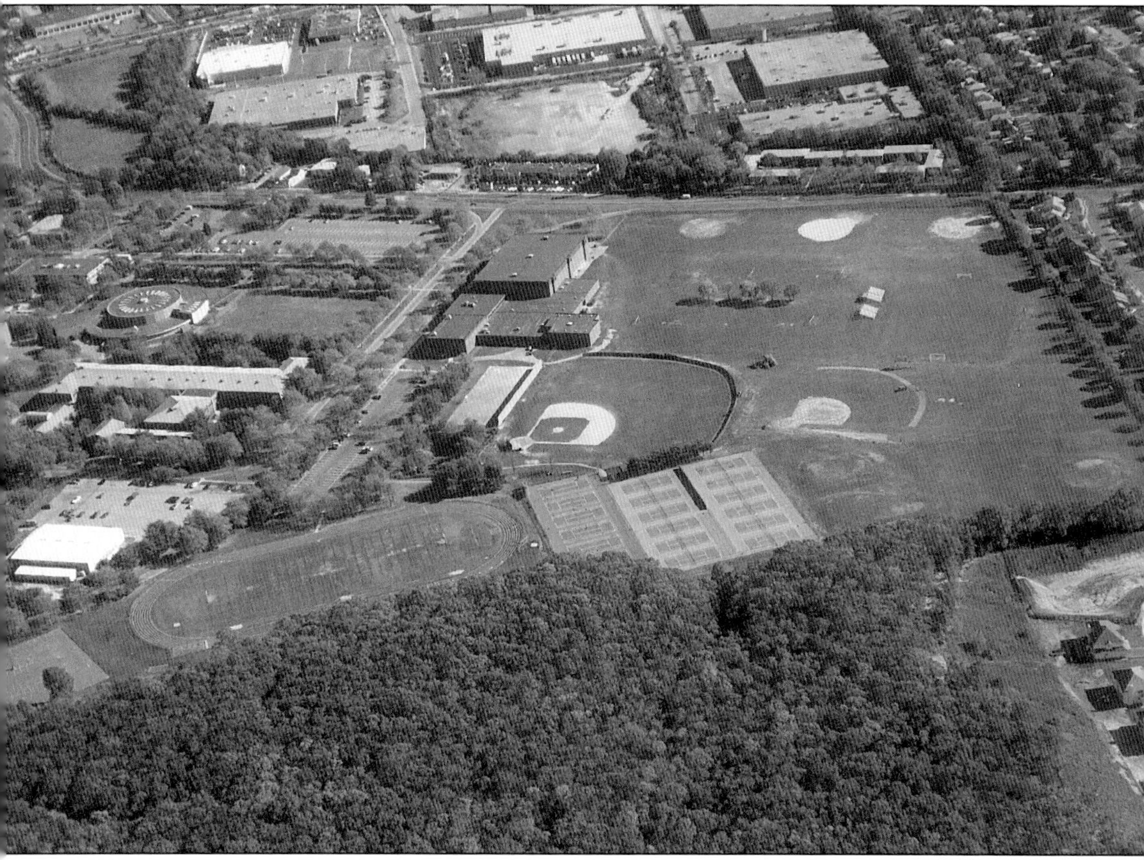

This impressive view of the western end of the campus features the athletic complex in 1990. The track and athletic field are at left, while the tennis courts are at the center. Above the tennis courts are the baseball field and Nold Hall. At left, the circular building is Roosevelt Hall; below it is Lupton Hall, and below Lupton Hall at left is the Allard Field House. Melville Road is at the top of the photograph flowing into Route 110, at the extreme top left corner. The centerpiece of the athletic complex is Nold Hall, which encompasses 94,000 square feet, with a seating capacity of over 4,000 in the Walter A. Lynch Sports Center. Also included in the complex are a deck swimming pool, a gymnasium with three basketball courts, eight badminton courts, four volleyball courts, four tennis courts, a ten-lap-to-the mile track, a weight-training room, and a wrestling room.

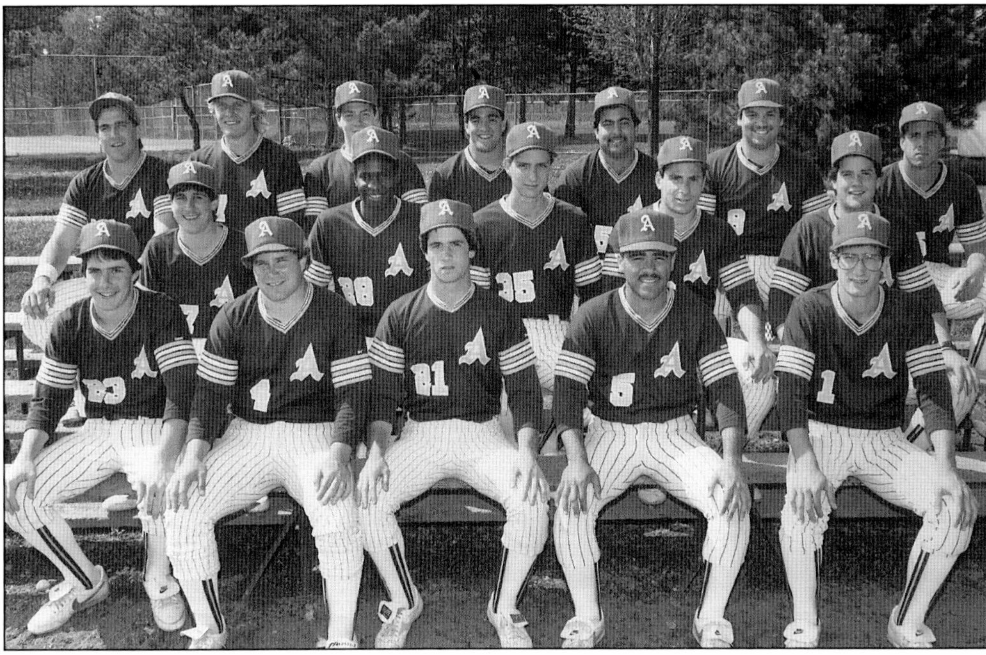

The members of the 1986 baseball team smile for this group photograph. Longtime successful coach Ken Rocco is not present. When the first students entered the school in March 1916, the first sport they organized was baseball, followed by football. Basketball was inaugurated the following year. The baseball team of 1916 recorded nine wins and two losses. Two of the wins were against the faculty. The team also made the baseball field, which is still in use today.

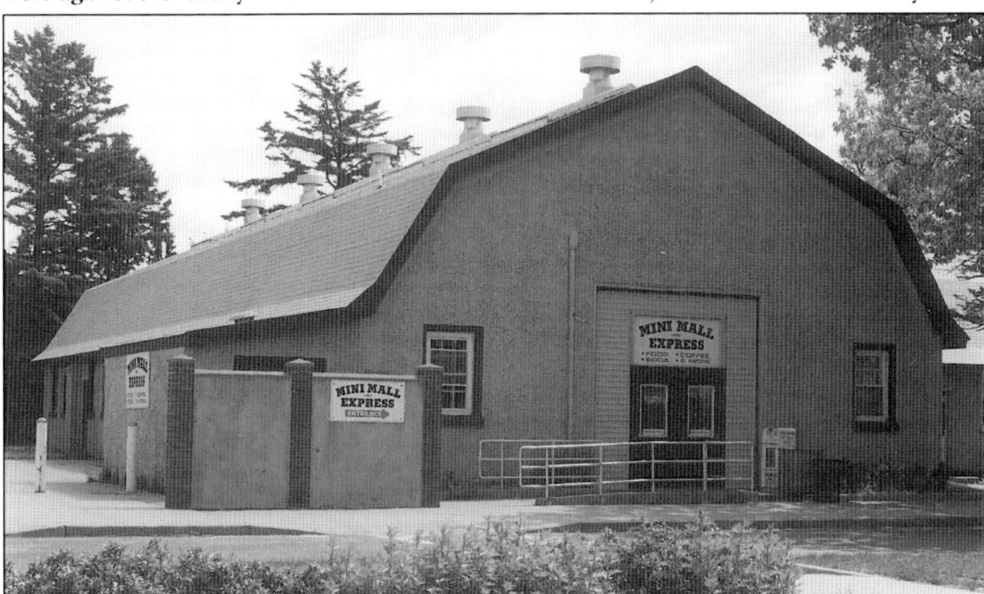

The Mini Mall, shown as it looks today on the Campus Commons, was originally the Agricultural Equipment Building. Standing near Thompson Hall and the bookstore, it serves as a convenient place for students and faculty to have a light snack, a beverage, or to meet with friends and colleagues in a relaxed environment.

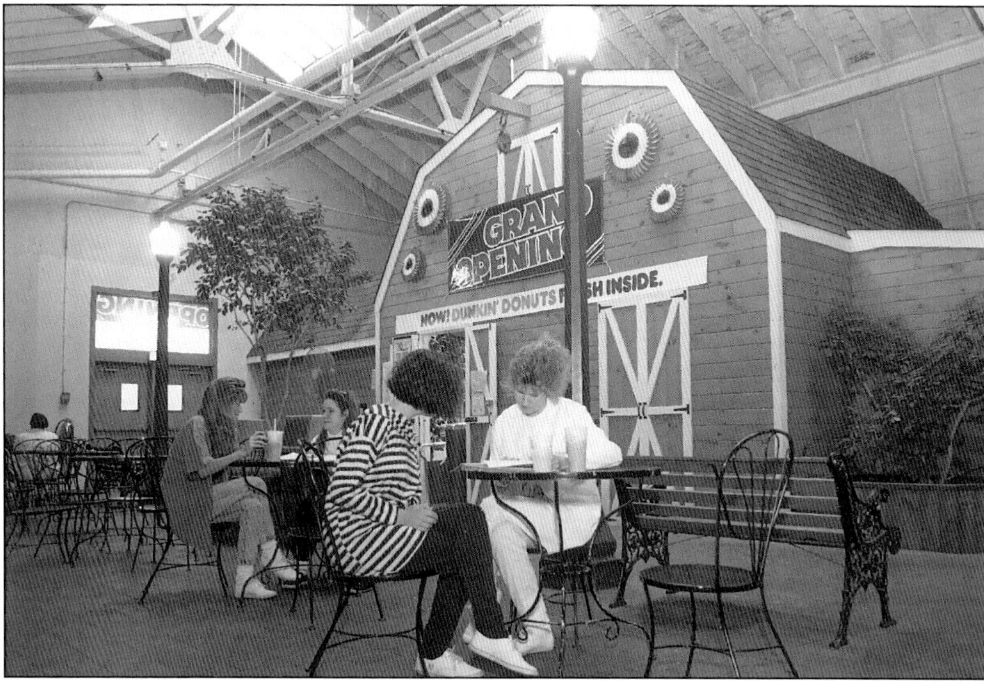

These students are having a light beverage inside the Mini Mall, chatting and preparing for their next class. The interior of the Mini Mall conveys a rustic appearance, which is consistent with the campus environment. Since it is centrally located, with lots of available nearby parking, special attractions are held here, such as Christmas Open House, conducted by the ornamental horticulture floral design classes.

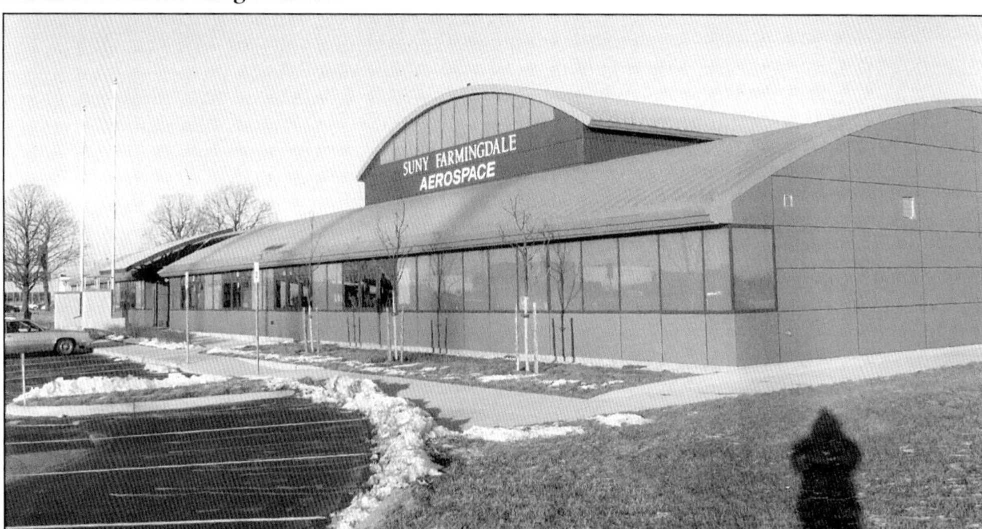

The SUNY Farmingdale Aerospace facility and aircraft are located south of the campus on Route 110. Bachelor degree programs are offered in aeronautical science–professional pilot and aviation administration. The first program is structured to enable students to attain at least the FAA commercial pilot license with instrument rating and a certificate flight instructor rating. The second program, aviation administration, prepares graduates for entry-level administrative positions in three major segments of aviation manufacturing, airlines, and general aviation.

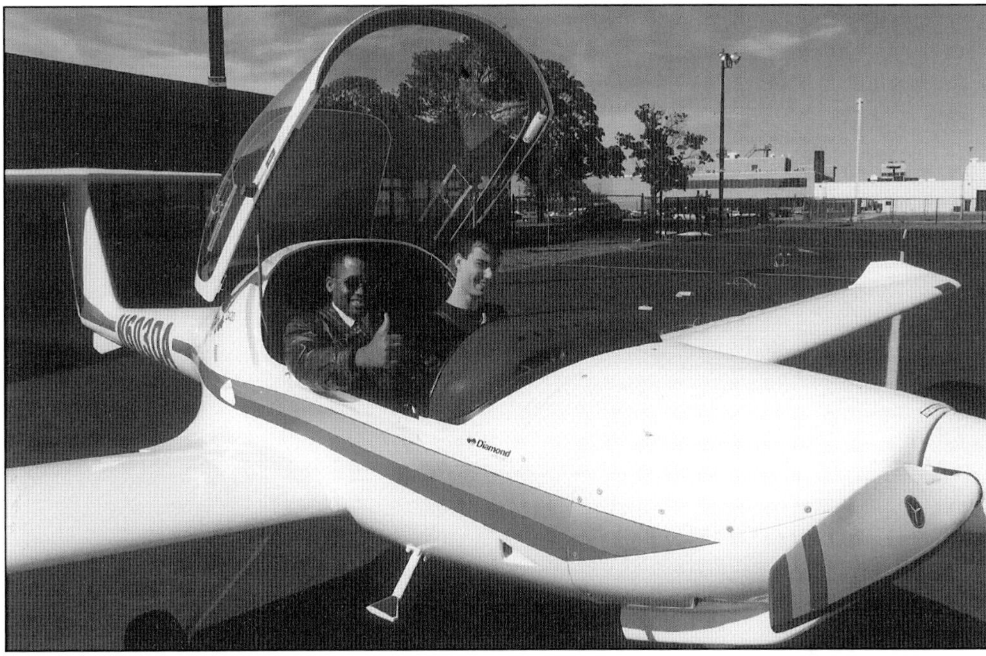

An instructor and student occupy a trainer aircraft at the college's aerospace facility in 1997. Ever since SUNY Farmingdale was founded, it has responded to the challenges in technology by developing programs to prepare its graduates for the modern workplace. The aerospace technology curriculum, which offers an associate in applied science degree, has produced skilled technicians for positions in flight control, air carrier operations, airport management, and related governmental activities.

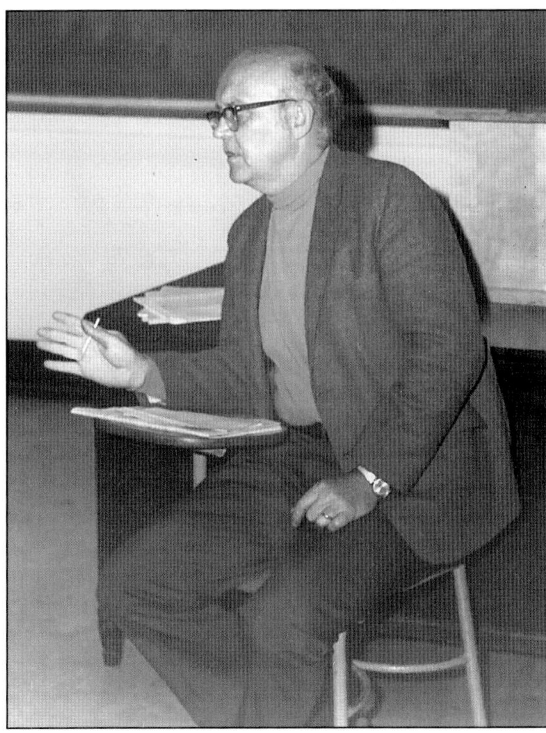

Alumni will remember Prof. Raynor Wallace of the English Department. While he held several administrative positions, it was his teaching prowess and professional demeanor that appealed to students. He was also known for his human interest stories of campus life. A dynamic teacher, his classes filled quickly during registration. In this 1985 photograph, he directs a class discussion.

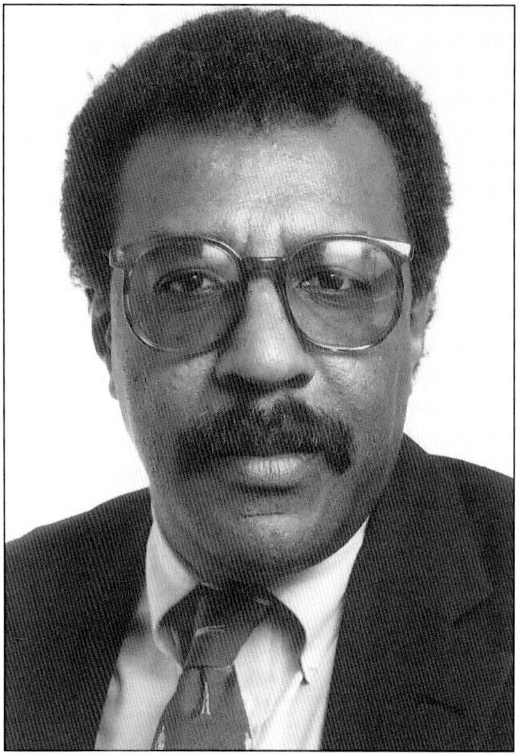

Reginald "Tye" Marshall, shown in 1989, had a distinguished career as a caring educator-administrator. A recipient of the SUNY Chancellor's Award for Excellence in Professional Service in 1989 and the NYS–United University Professions Excellence Award in 1990, he served in several college positions: director of the Learning Center and dean of the Long Island Educational Opportunity Center.

SUNY Farmingdale has been known for its small classes taught by dedicated instructors. One such person was Dr. John A. Fiorillo, who was always available for student consultation. He is shown below in 1996, importuning his electrical engineering technology class to grasp an intricate concept. A recipient of the SUNY Chancellor's Award for Excellence in Teaching, his credentials and contributions have led to the success of the new bachelor of technology program in EET.

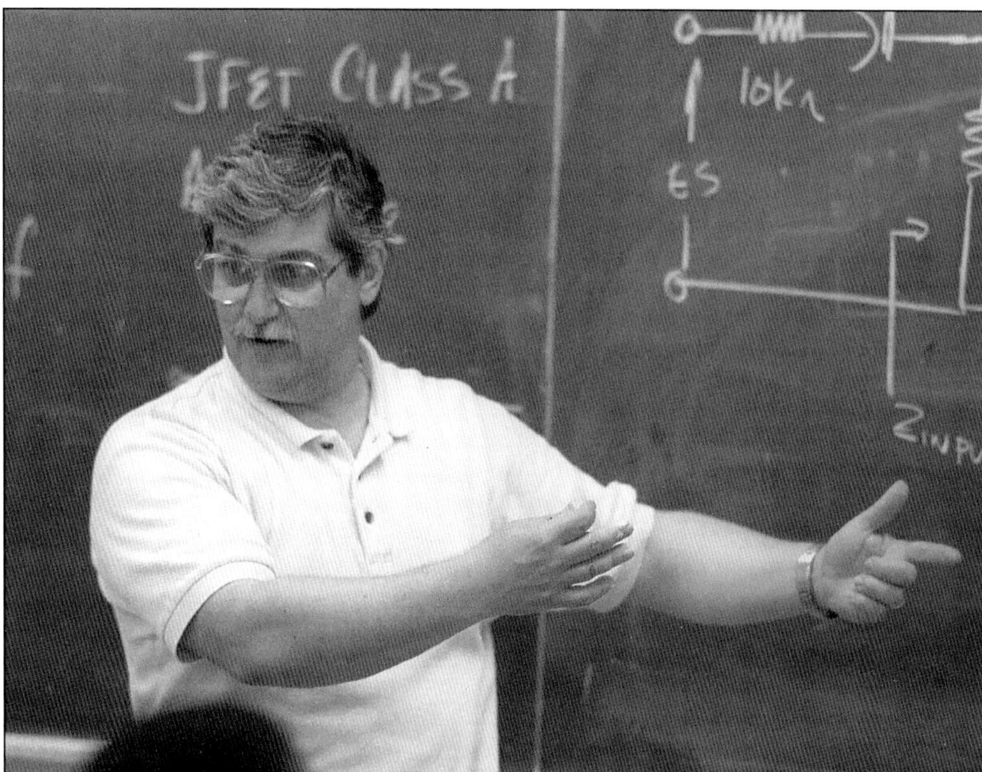

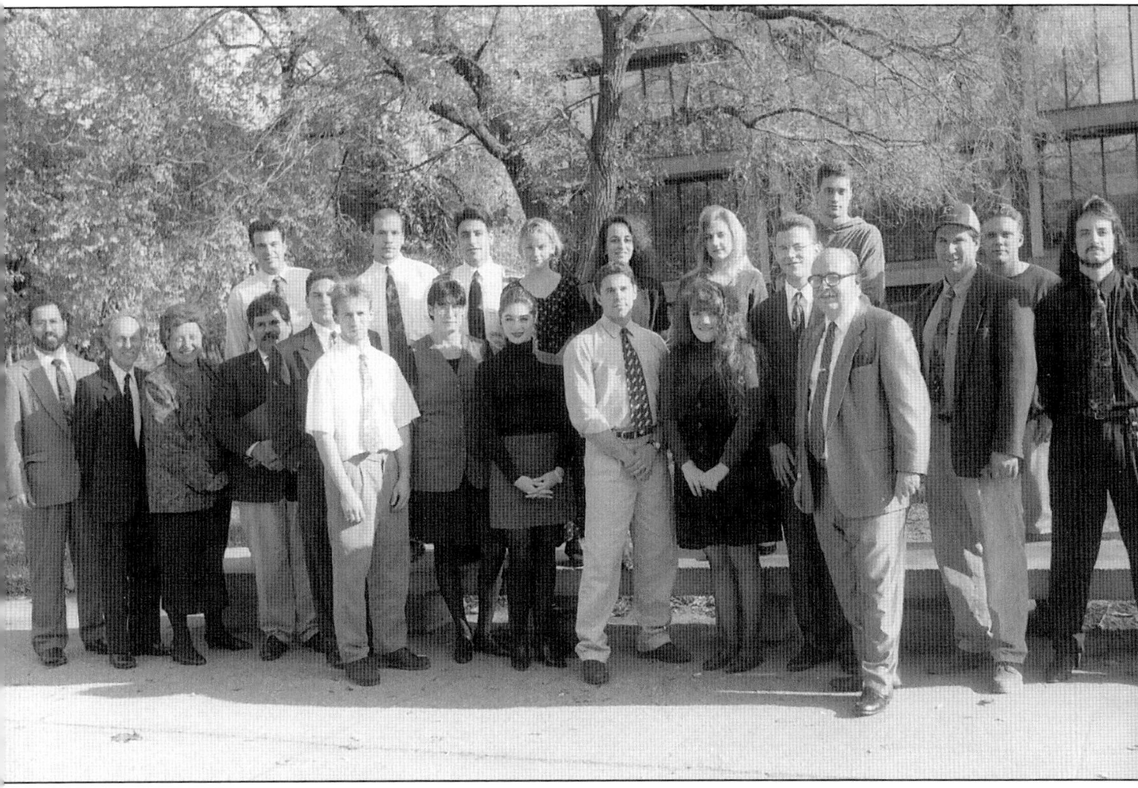

The first graduating class of the Visual Communications Department poses in 1995 with those faculty and administrators who made it possible. These successful graduates have received the bachelor of technology degree and will enter the commercial world with artistic skills and a proficiency in computer literacy. At the far left in the front row are the following: Prof. William J. Steedle, the department chair; Michael J. Vinciguerra, provost; and Nancy C. Thomson, vice president for academic affairs. Fourth from the right (with glasses) is the dean of the School of Business, Frank Del Bene.

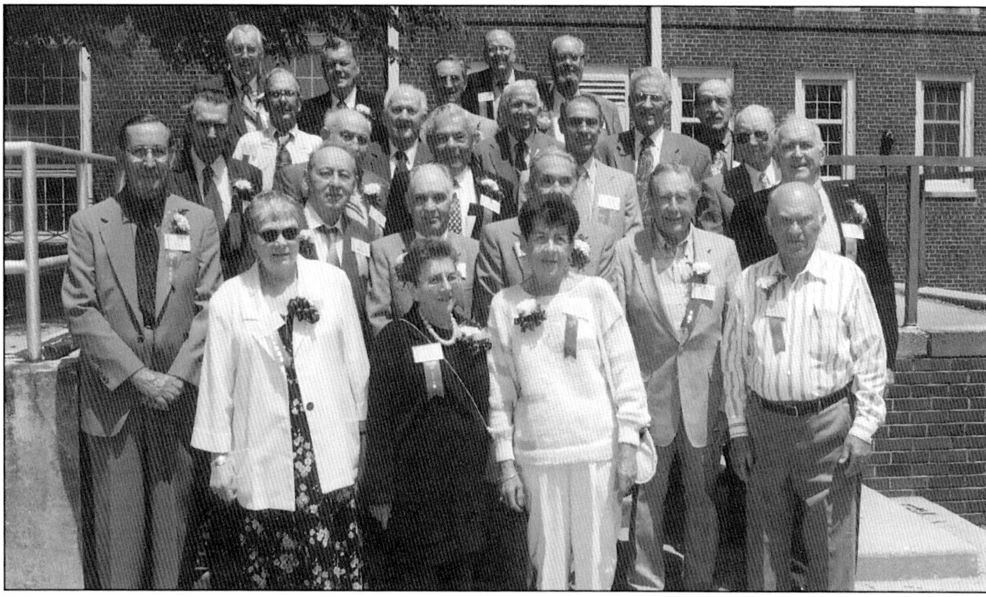

Each year, the college invites its 50th anniversary graduates back to celebrate with the new graduates at commencement time. Shown is the Class of 1948 at a reunion in front of Knapp Hall in May 1998. It was also the occasion of the establishment of the State University of New York in 1948 when Farmingdale joined the newly created system.

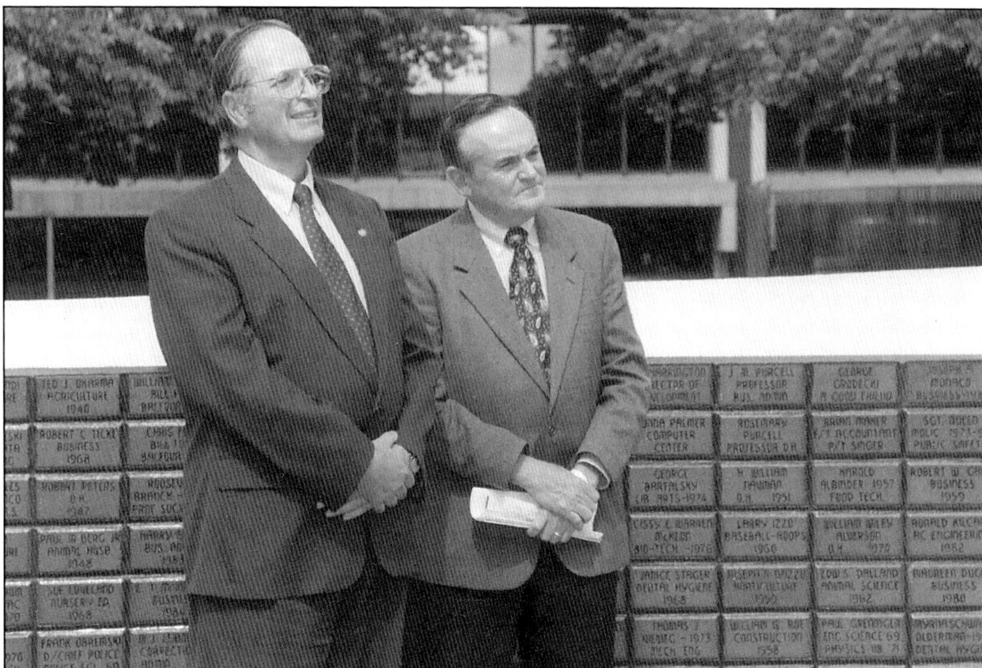

Pres. Frank A. Cipriani and College Council member Robert Ench view events during the dedication ceremonies of the SUNY Farmingdale Wall of Honor at the Ralph Bunche Plaza, September 6, 1997. Welcoming remarks on the occasion were made by Deputy Pres. Joseph A. Monaco, College Council Pres. Anthony Mastroianni, and Alumni Association Pres. Christopher Rutkowski. Behind the Wall of Honor is Greenley Hall.

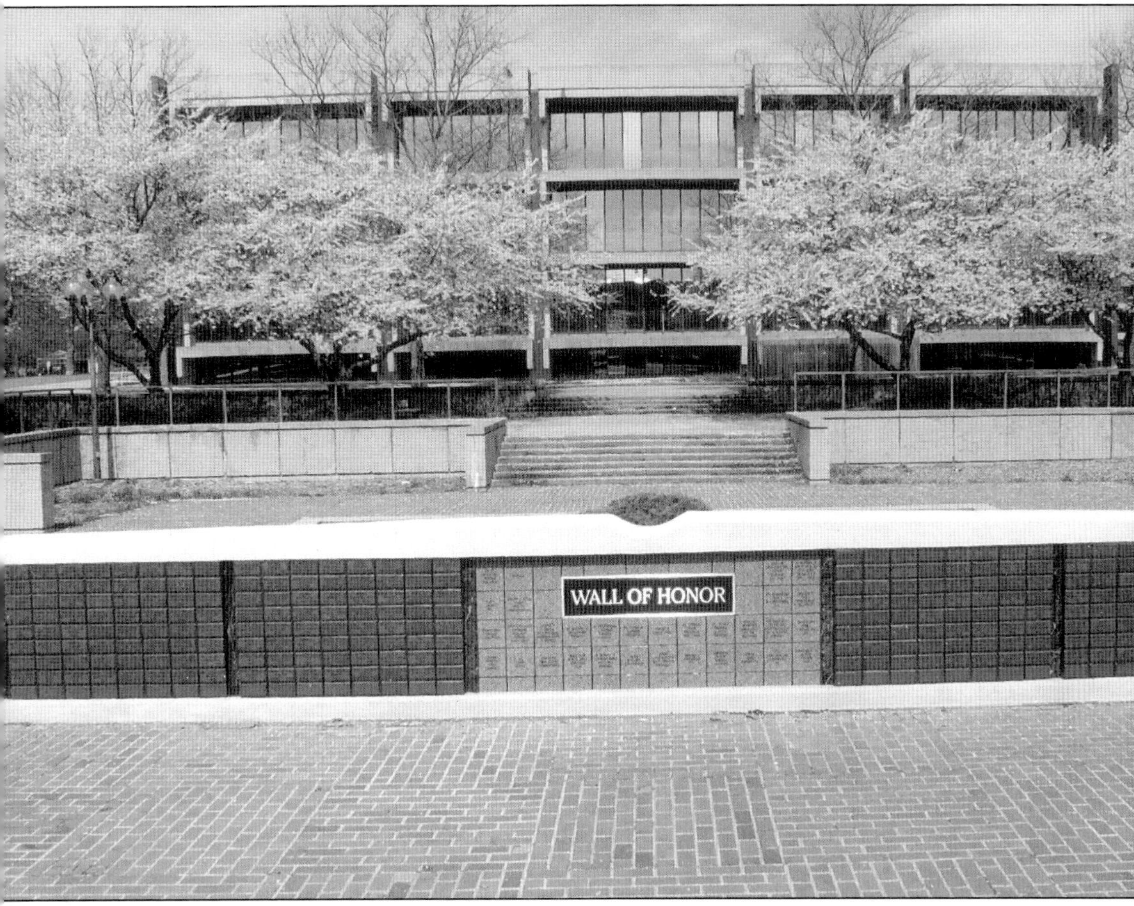

The Wall of Honor, shown here in 1998, was established to recognize graduates and other friends of SUNY Farmingdale. The cost of a brick for the wall is $100. Bricks for alumni are inscribed with the name, curriculum, and year of graduation. Faculty, retirees, and staff could also purchase a brick with their names inscribed. A larger granite brick is available for a $300 donation. This remembrance will identify graduates and friends of the college and perpetuate their legacy by placing their names on the Wall of Honor. The funds generated from this project will be used for student scholarships.

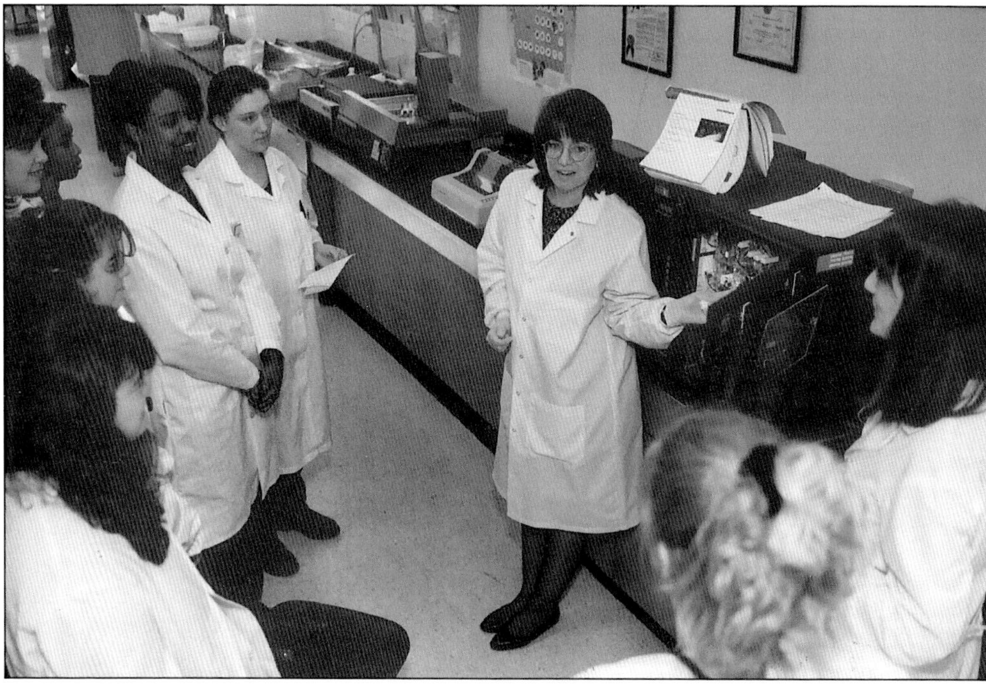

Prof. Karen Escolas, center, of the Medical Laboratory Technology Department, is presenting a lecture-demonstration to a class in 1995. It is this type of small-class instruction for which Farmingdale is famous. Professor Escolas has served in the position of chair of the department and was appointed acting dean of the School of Health Sciences and Human Services.

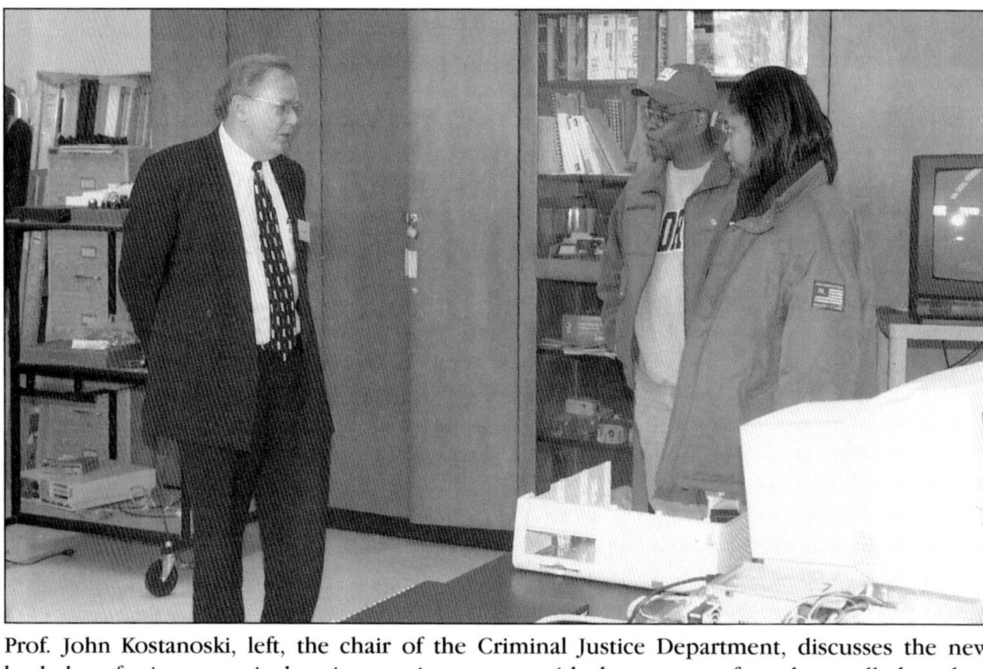

Prof. John Kostanoski, left, the chair of the Criminal Justice Department, discusses the new bachelor of science curriculum in security systems with the parents of newly enrolled student in the fall of 1999. Such conferences, formal and informal, exemplify the personal attention so necessary in a successful educational enterprise such as SUNY Farmingdale.

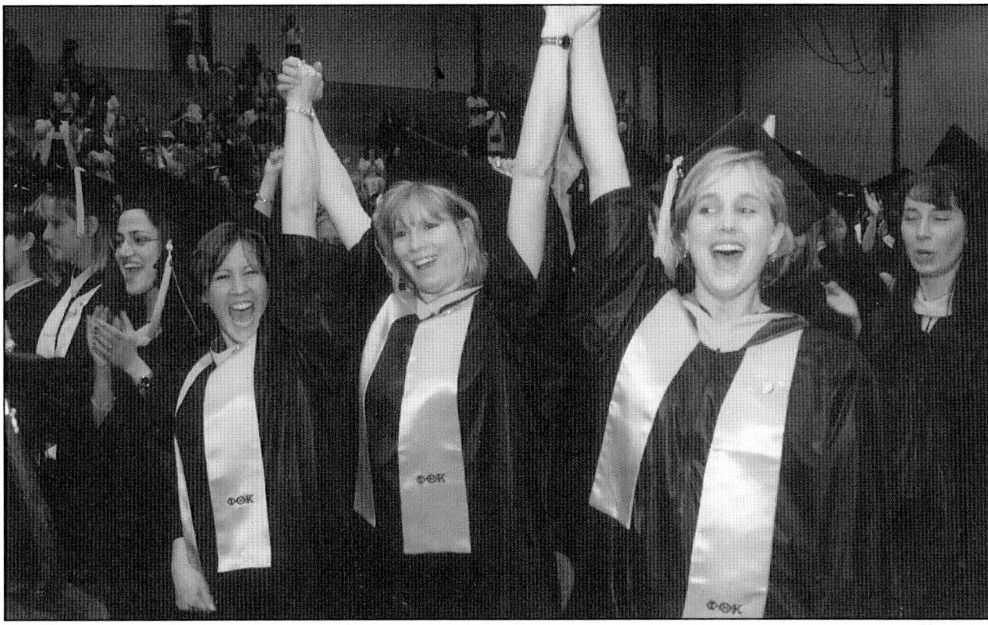

The day has finally arrived. These joyous honor students are celebrating the occasion of their graduation in May 1998. The years of study have paid off. They will enter the world of work and become productive citizens, or they will continue their education by studying for a baccalaureate degree at Farmingdale or elsewhere.

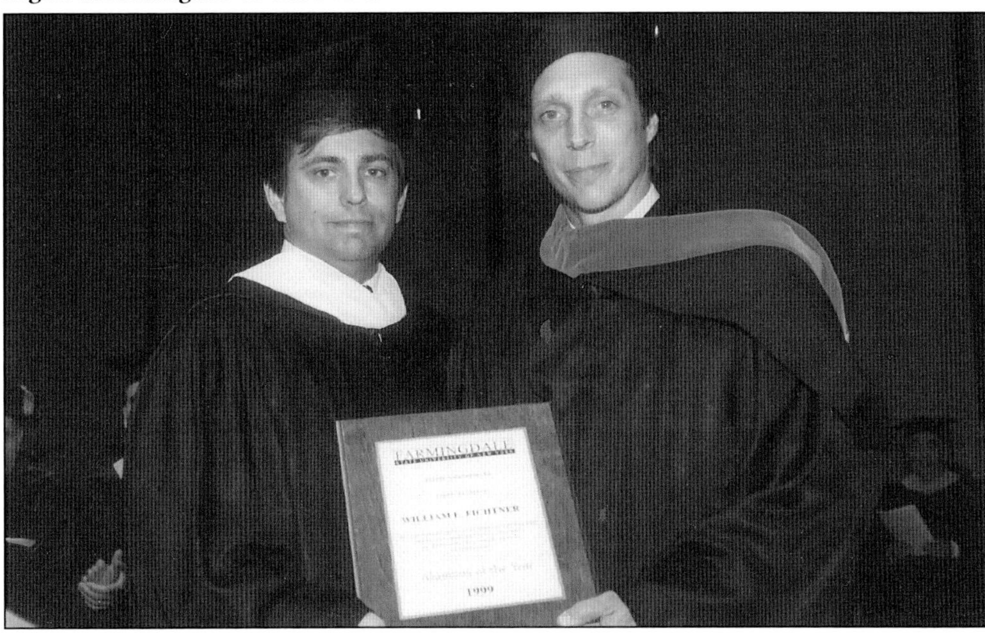

Alumni Association Pres. Richard Rapp presents the 1998 Alumnus of the Year Award to William Fichtner, graduate of the criminal justice class of 1976. Fichtner is a world-famous actor of stage, screen, and television. A native of Cheektowaga (near Buffalo), he came to the college through the recruitment efforts of a former Farmingdale administrator, Don Harvey. Coming from a small town, a whole new world opened for him at SUNY Farmingdale—explosive and precious in terms of his own personal and professional growth.

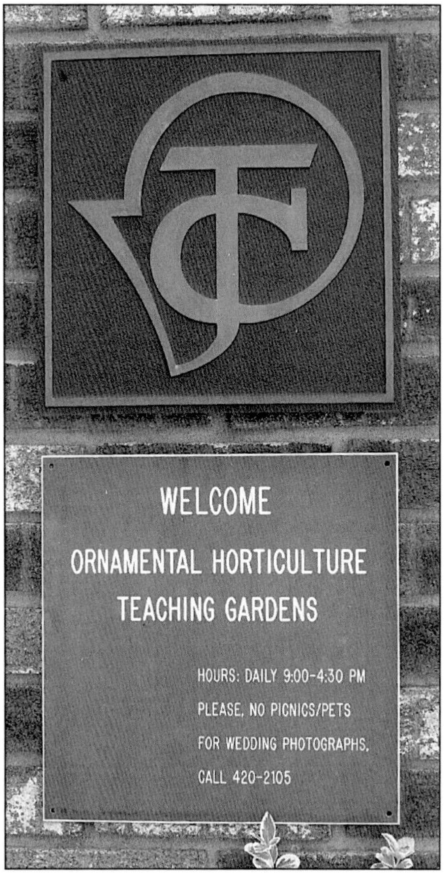

Plaques welcome visitors to the Ornamental Horticulture Teaching Gardens, left, near the eastern campus entrance at Route 110. The beautiful gardens, shown below, are located behind Thompson Hall and Hicks Hall. The ornamental horticulture curriculum is one of the oldest and most successful at the college. For more than eight decades, it has prepared graduates to become leaders in floriculture, horticulture management, and landscape development. Upon the completion of study, graduates receive an associate in applied science degree. The students in the program plan and maintain the gardens.

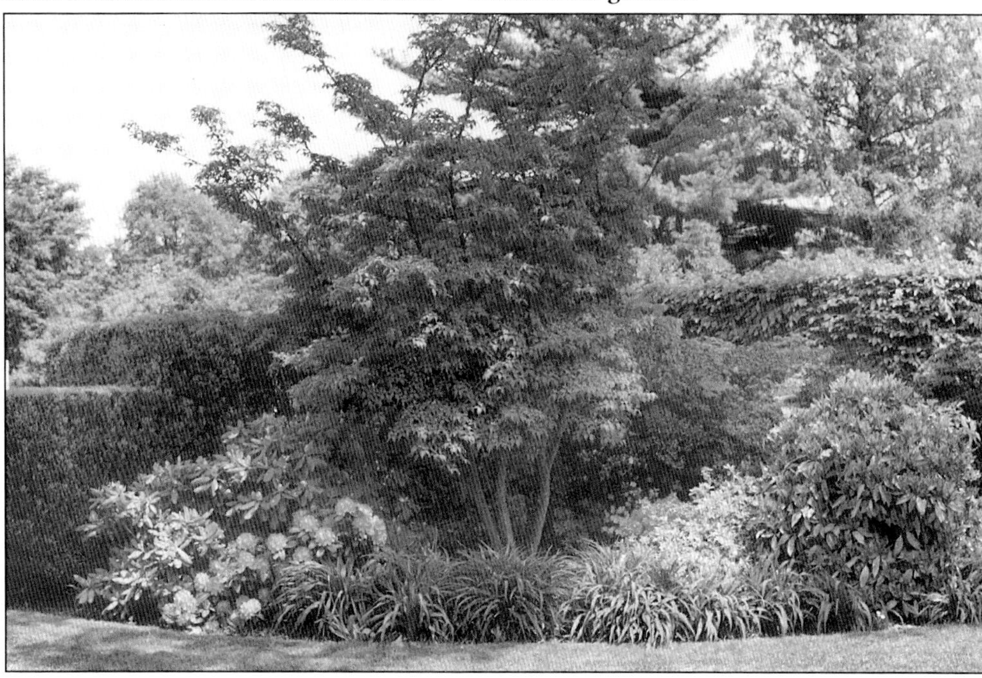

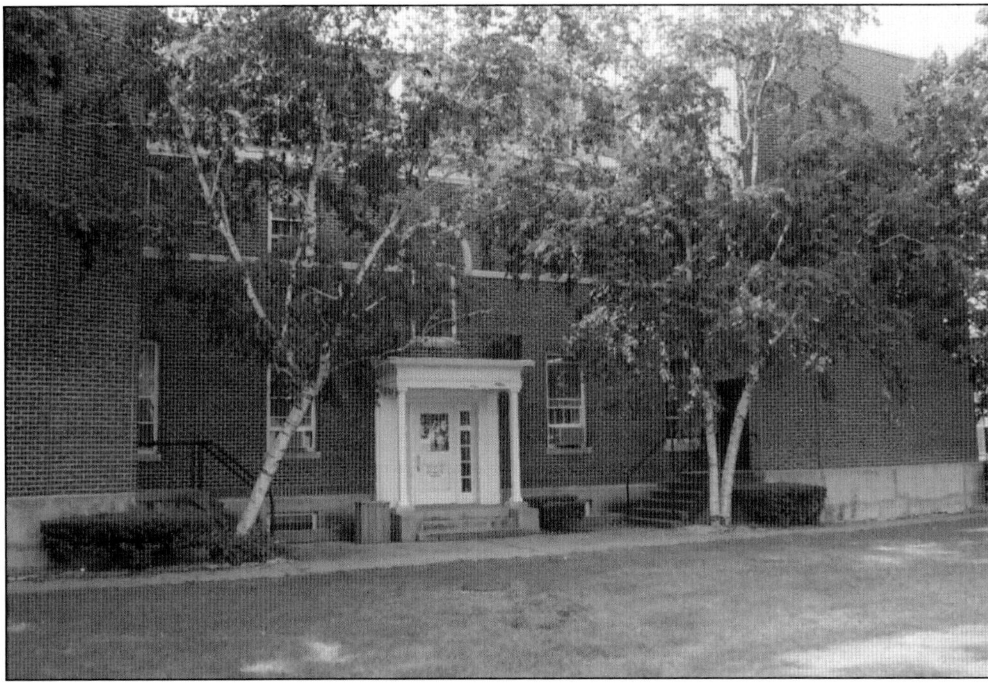

Hooper Hall was constructed in 1917. It stands today flanked by graceful birch trees and is an architectural relic and a reminder of the past. Franklin W. Hooper, for whom the building is named, fought successfully to establish an agricultural school on Long Island. He was born in New Hampshire, graduated from Harvard, and accepted a professorship in natural science at Adelphi Academy in Brooklyn. In 1889, Hooper became director of the Brooklyn Academy of Arts and Sciences.

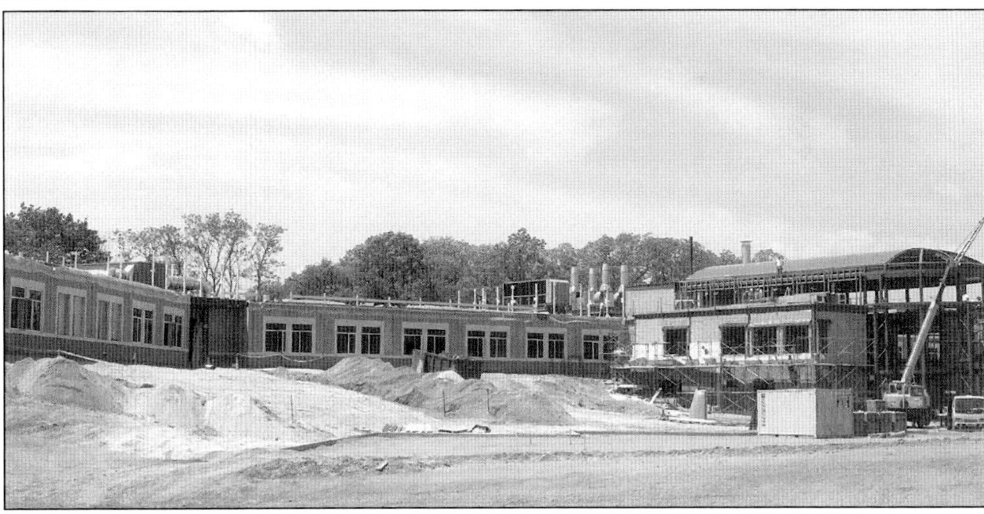

On May 11, 2000, construction of the Broad Hollow Bioscience (Biotechnology) Park is nearing completion. Located at the northeastern area of the campus in full view of the passing traffic on Route 110 (Broadhollow Road), it is an economic development collaboration of New York State, Cold Spring Harbor, and SUNY Farmingdale. As an academic-industrial park, it established incubators in biotechnology, software, and other emerging technologies on Long Island. The Cold Spring Harbor Laboratory is known for its leading research scientists from around the world.

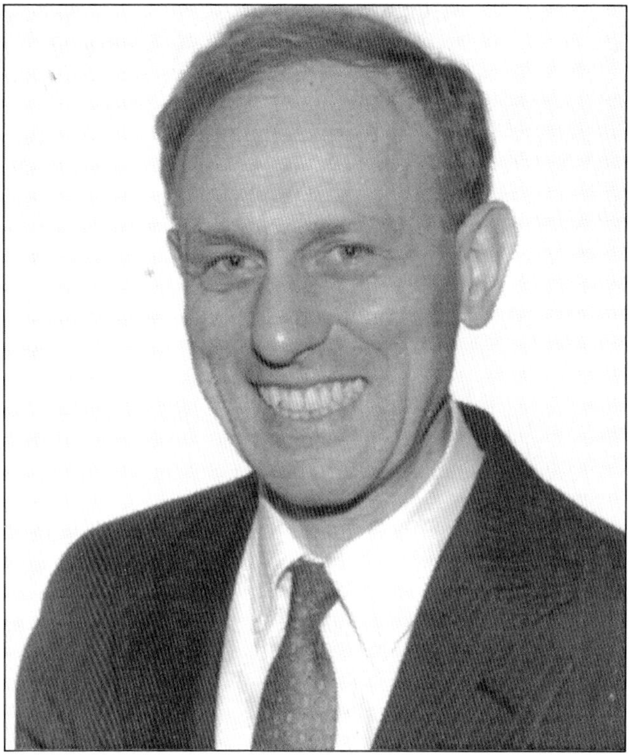

Upon the retirement of Frank A. Cipriani on January 1, 2000, Michael J. Vinciguerra, shown here, was appointed acting president. A professor of chemistry, Vinciguerra also has served in positions of vice president and provost, and was an indispensable member on President Cipriani's staff. He received a bachelor's degree from Iona College and a master's degree and doctorate from Adelphi University. Vinciguerra is widely respected by the faculty.

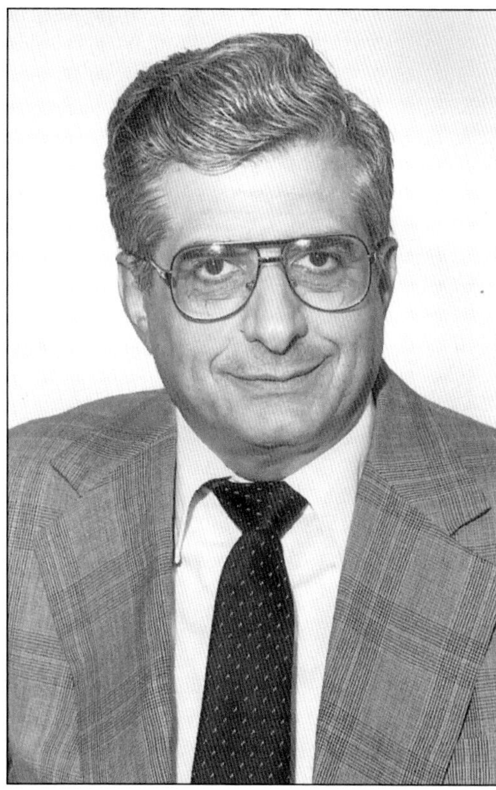

Anthony Mastroianni, a resident of Huntington Station, has had a very long association with the college. In 1950, he received the associate in applied science degree at Farmingdale. He went on to receive BS and MPA degrees. He has served on the College Council as vice chair and chair. Each year, the college invites its 50th anniversary class back to celebrate with its new graduates. Since the State University of New York was created in 1948, the Class of 1950 was the first class to graduate as a member of the SUNY system. On May 21, 2000, Mastroianni and his Class of 1950 were honored.

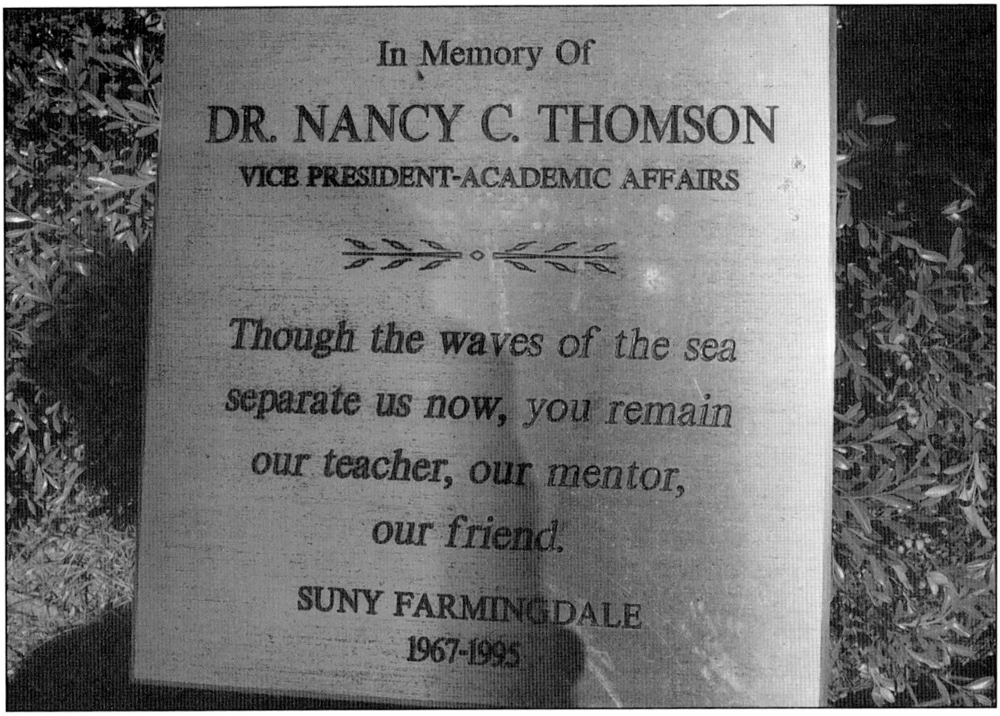

This memorial plaque has been placed in the Ornamental Horticulture Teaching Gardens in honor of Dr. Nancy C. Thomson, whose dedicated service to the college from 1967 to 1995 will always be remembered. She began as an instructor in the Mathematics Department and rose to vice president of academic affairs. Colleagues and students remembered her as a caring person whose devotion to her work helped to make Farmingdale the special place it is. Thomson died of cancer in 1995.

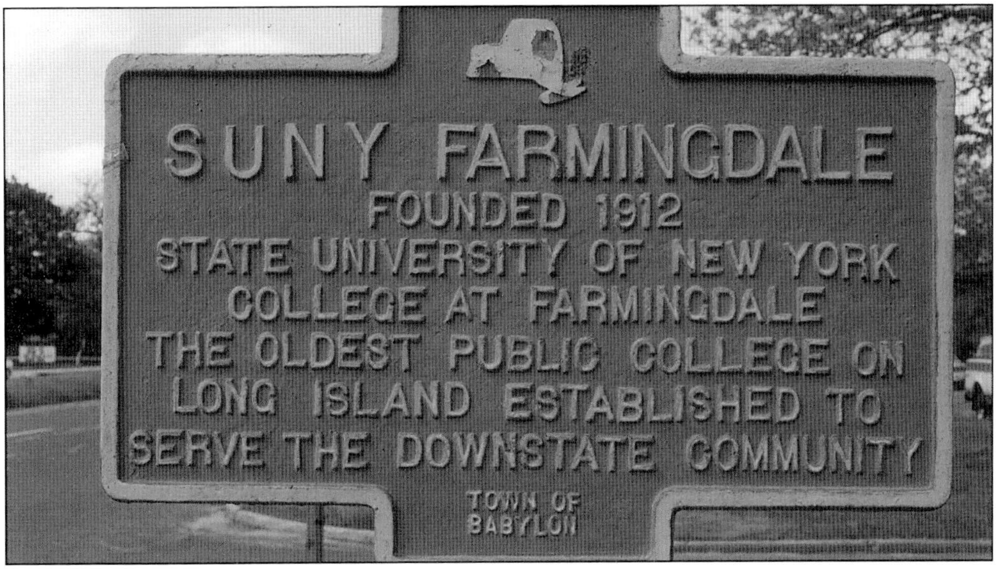

This distinctive historical marker stands on Melville Road. It announces that SUNY Farmingdale, having been established in 1912, is the oldest public college on Long Island. It conveys a sense of time and place in the historical development of Long Island.

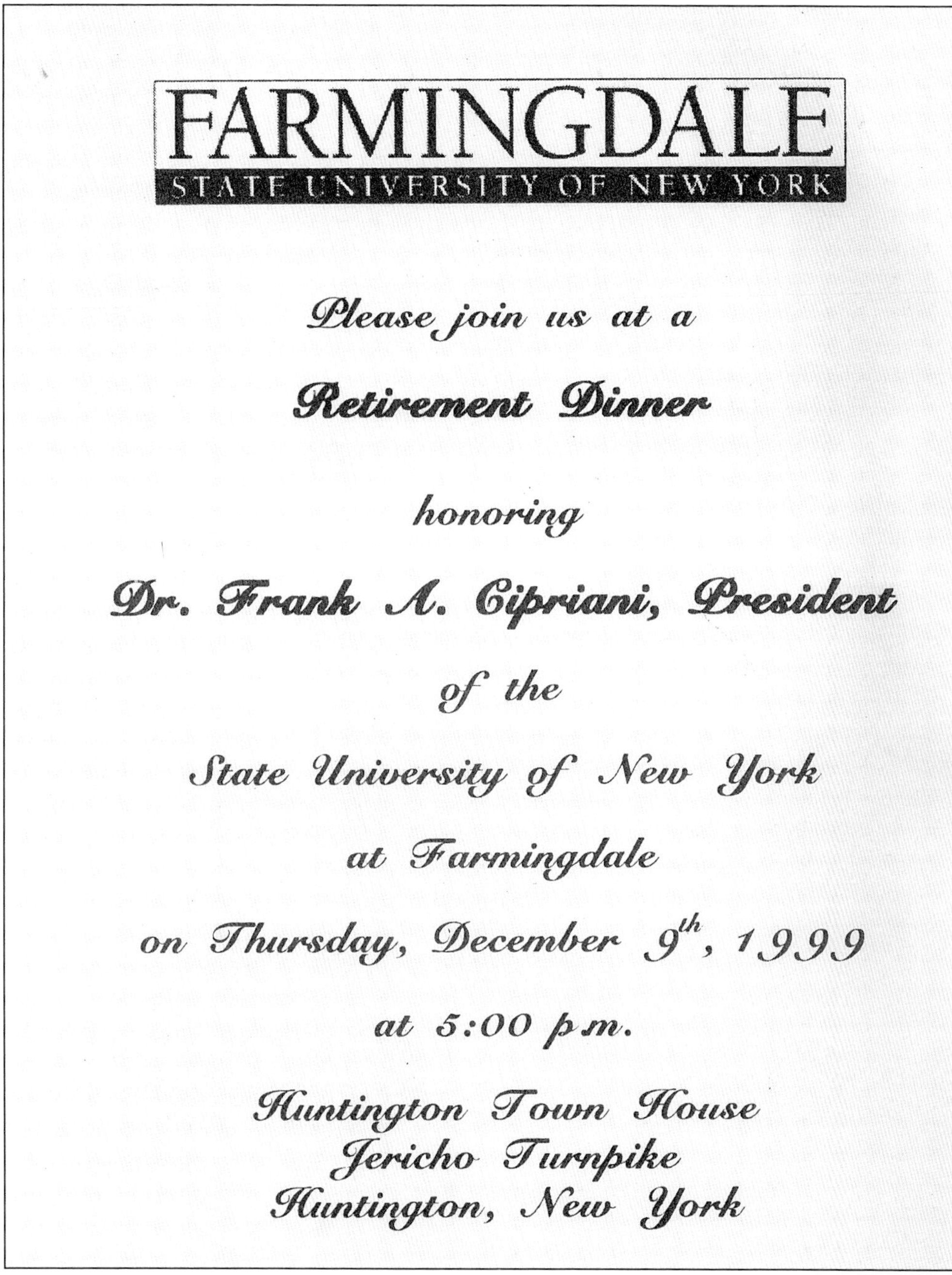

FARMINGDALE

STATE UNIVERSITY OF NEW YORK

Please join us at a

Retirement Dinner

honoring

Dr. Frank A. Cipriani, President

of the

State University of New York

at Farmingdale

on Thursday, December 9th, 1999

at 5:00 p.m.

Huntington Town House
Jericho Turnpike
Huntington, New York

After spending more than 35 years at SUNY Farmingdale with the rank of professor of history, Frank A. Cipriani retired on January 1, 2000, having been the dean, vice president, and president. Nearly all of his adult life was spent in higher education. He remembered well the "Aggie" traditions as he led the college into the new age of high technology and four-year baccalaureate degrees. He was born in Corona, Queens, received a BA from Queens College, and an MA and a Ph.D. from New York University. For his contributions to the college, Cipriani was honored by faculty, family, friends, and staff at the Huntington Town House, December 9, 1999, at a retirement dinner, as indicated by this invitation.

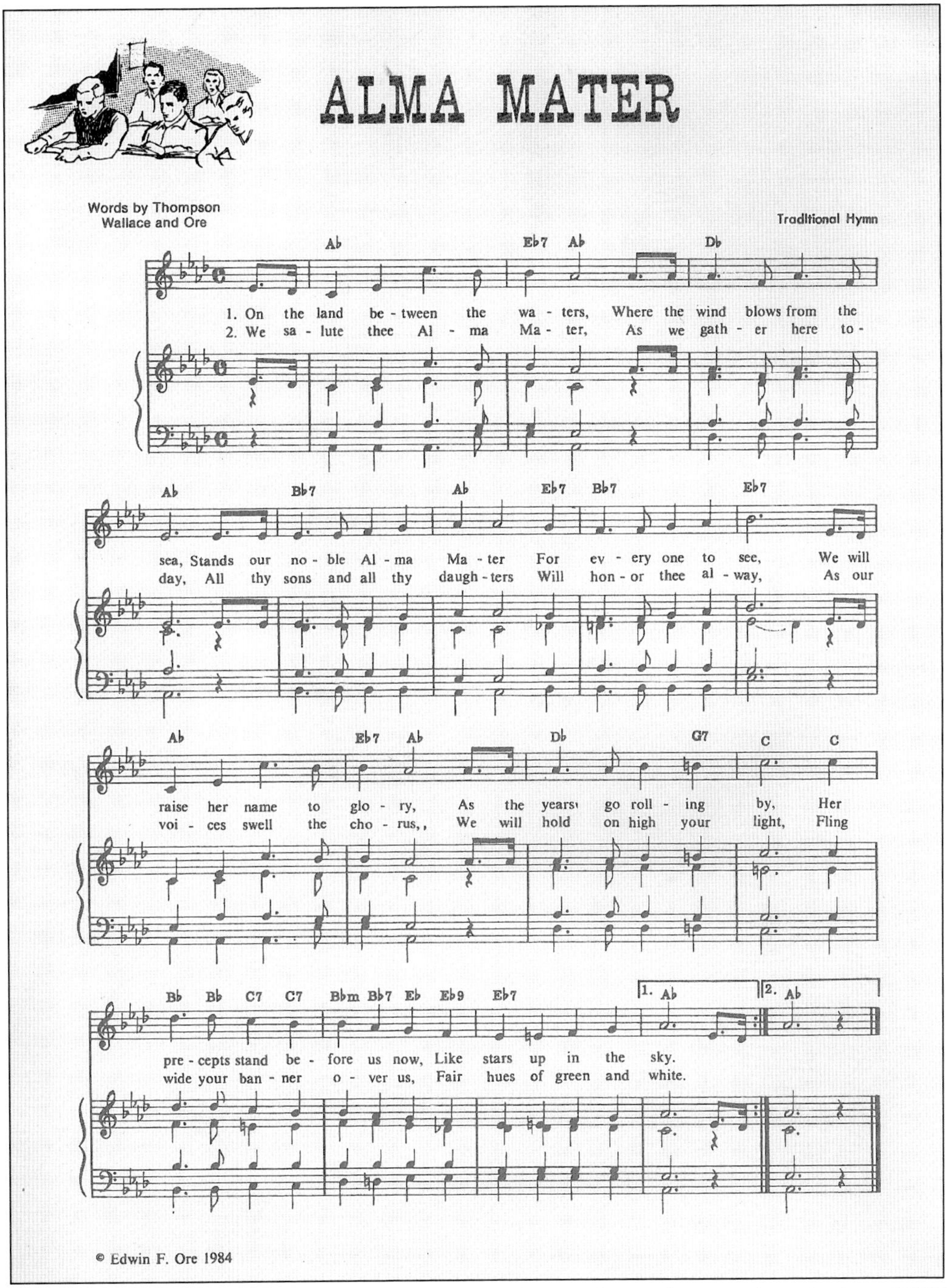

All colleges have an alma mater for students to honor their educational institution. SUNY Farmingdale's alma mater was written by Edwin F. Ore, C.D. Thomson, and Raynor Wallace in 1984. The words and music are displayed here in the original form. Professors Ore, Thomson, and Wallace were all members of the English Department.

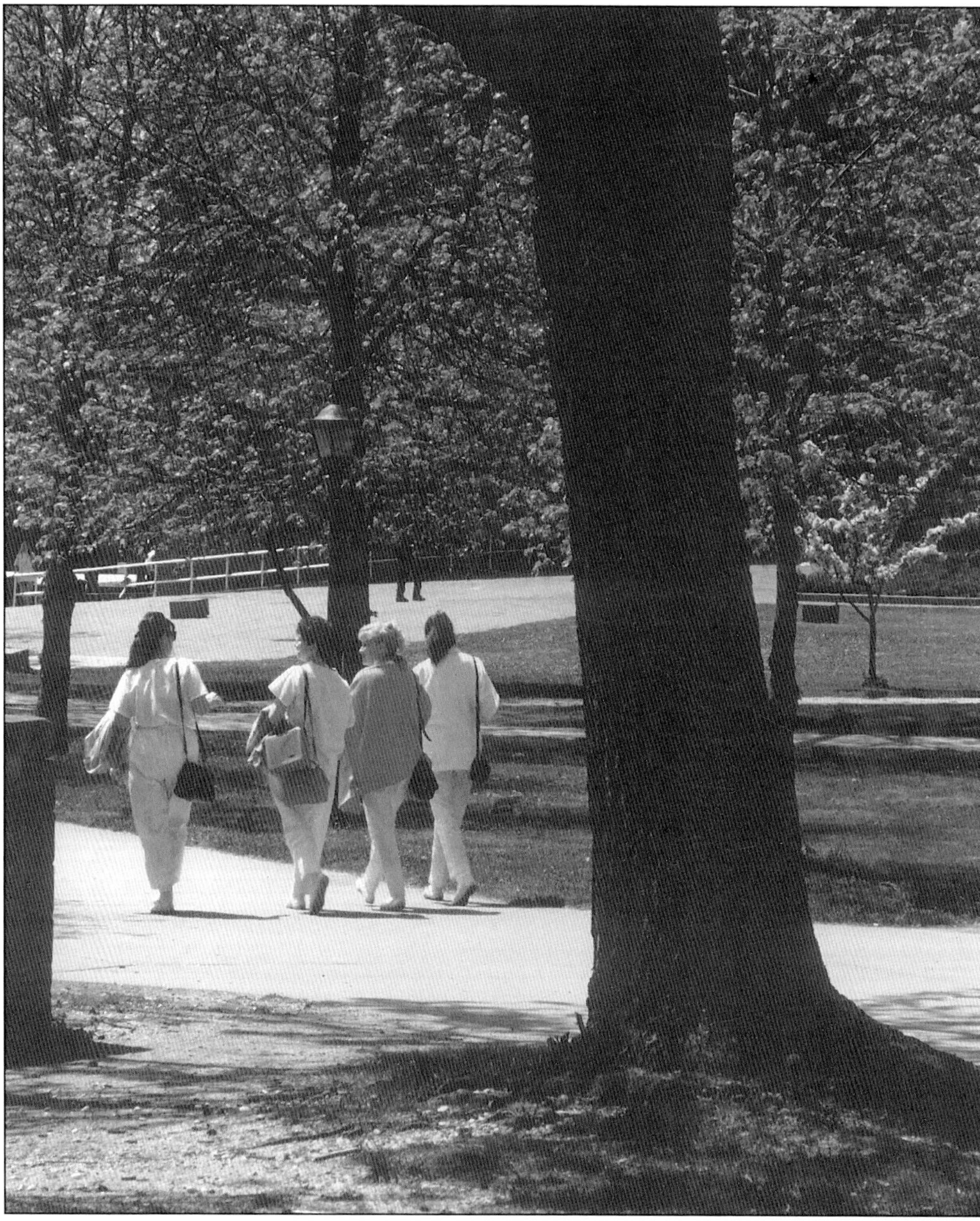

Four nursing students have completed classes on this tranquil afternoon in springtime, 1999, and are on their way home. In spite of nearly nine decades of growth, the college has striven to maintain its pristine appearance, as this photograph attests. Since it is the oldest public college on Long Island, growth has come gradually without the pressure of attempting to achieve instantaneous institutional success. Thus, the State University of New York at Farmingdale remains a treasured public resource amid a suburban-commercial environment. Its historical development has mirrored Long Island's growth and progress.